Big Data Analytics in Fog-Enabled IoT Networks

The integration of fog computing with the resource-limited Internet of Things (IoT) network formulates the concept of the fog-enabled IoT system. Due to a large number of IoT devices, the IoT is a main source of Big Data. A large volume of sensing data is generated by IoT systems such as smart cities and smart-grid applications. A fundamental research issue is how to provide a fast and efficient data analytics solution for fog-enabled IoT systems. *Big Data Analytics in Fog-Enabled IoT Networks: Towards a Privacy and Security Perspective* focuses on Big Data analytics in a fog-enabled-IoT system and provides a comprehensive collection of chapters that touch on different issues related to healthcare systems, cyber-threat detection, malware detection, and the security and privacy of IoT Big Data and IoT networks.

This book also emphasizes and facilitates a greater understanding of various security and privacy approaches using advanced artificial intelligence and Big Data technologies such as machine and deep learning, federated learning, blockchain, and edge computing, as well as the countermeasures to overcome the vulnerabilities of the fog-enabled IoT system.

Big Data Analytics in Fog-Enabled IoT Networks

Towards a Privacy and Security Perspective

Edited By:
Govind P. Gupta, Rakesh Tripathi,
Brij B. Gupta, and Kwok Tai Chui

CRC Press
Taylor & Francis Group
Boca Raton London New York

CRC Press is an imprint of the
Taylor & Francis Group, an **informa** business

First edition published 2023
by CRC Press
6000 Broken Sound Parkway NW, Suite 300, Boca Raton, FL 33487–2742

and by CRC Press

4 Park Square, Milton Park, Abingdon, Oxon, OX14 4RN

Library of Congress Cataloging-in-Publication Data

Names: Gupta, Govind P., 1979- editor. | Tripathi, Rakesh, editor. | Gupta, Brij, 1982- editor. | Chui, Kwok Tai, editor.
Title: Big data analytics in fog-enabled IoT networks : towards a privacy and security perspective / edited by Govind P. Gupta, Rakesh Tripathi, Brij B. Gupta and Kwok Tai Chui.
Description: First edition. | Boca Raton : CRC Press, 2023. | Includes bibliographical references.
Identifiers: LCCN 2022049027 (print) | LCCN 2022049028 (ebook) | ISBN 9781032206448 (hardback) | ISBN 9781032206455 (paperback) | ISBN 9781003264545 (ebook)
Subjects: LCSH: Internet of things--Security measures. | Cloud computing--Security measures. | Big data. | Deep learning (Machine learning)
Classification: LCC TK5105.8857 .B54 2023 (print) | LCC TK5105.8857 (ebook) | DDC 005.8--dc23/eng/20230103
LC record available at https://lccn.loc.gov/2022049027
LC ebook record available at https://lccn.loc.gov/2022049028]

ISBN: 9781032206448 (hbk)
ISBN: 9781032206455 (pbk)
ISBN: 9781003264545 (ebk)

DOI: 10.1201/9781003264545

Typeset in Adobe Caslon Pro
by KnowledgeWorks Global Ltd.

Contents

Preface

The rapid growth in the IoT technologies enables the large-scale deployment and connectivity of smart IoT devices such as sensors, smartphones, smart meters, smart vehicles, and so forth for different applications such as smart cities, smart grids, smart homes, smart healthcare systems, smart video surveillance, e-healthcare, etc. Due to the limited resources of the IoT devices, both in terms of computation capabilities and energy resources, a fog computing infrastructure is required to offload computation and storage from resource-limited IoT devices to resource-rich fog nodes. Thus, the integration of fog computing with the resource-limited IoT network formulates the concept of a fog-enabled IoT system. Due to large number of deployments of IoT devices, the IoT is a main source of Big Data. A large volume of sensing data are generated by IoT systems such as smart cities and smart-grid applications. To provide a fast and efficient data analytics solution for fog-enabled IoT systems is a fundamental research issue. For the deployment of the fog-enabled IoT system in different applications such as healthcare systems, smart cities, and smart-grid systems, the security and privacy of IoT Big Data and IoT networks are key issues. The current centralized IoT architecture is heavily restricted with various challenges such as a single point of failure, data privacy, security, robustness, etc. Thus, this book emphasizes and facilitate a greater understanding of various security and privacy approaches using advanced artificial intelligence and Big Data technologies like machine and deep learning, federated learning, blockchain, edge computing as well as the countermeasures to overcome these vulnerabilities.

Dr. Govind P. Gupta
Dr. Rakesh Tripathi
Dr. Brij B. Gupta
Dr. Kwok Tai Chui

About the Editors

Dr. Govind P. Gupta received his Ph.D. in Computer Science & Engineering from the Indian Institute of Technology, Roorkee, India. He is currently working as an assistant professor in the Department of Information Technology, National Institute of Technology, Raipur, India. He has made practical and theoretical contributions in the Big Data processing and analytics, Wireless Sensor Network, Internet of Things (IoT), and cyber-security domains and his research has a significant impact on Big Data analytics, *WSN*, IoT, information, and network security against cyber-attacks. He has published more than 50 research papers in reputed peer-reviewed journals and conferences including IEEE, Elsevier, ACM, Springer, Wiley, Inderscience, etc. He is an active reviewer of various journals such as *IEEE Internet of Things*, *IEEE Sensors Journal*, *IEEE Transactions on Green Communications*, *Elsevier Computer Networks*, *Ad-Hoc Networks*, *Computer Communications*, *Springer Wireless Networks*, etc. His current research interests include IoT, IoT security, software-defined networking, network security, Big IoT Data analytics, blockchain-based application development for IoT, and enterprise blockchain. He is a professional member of the IEEE and ACM.

Dr. Rakesh Tripathi received his Ph.D. in Computer Science and Engineering from the Indian Institute of Technology Guwahati, India. He is an associate professor in the Department of Information Technology, National Institute of Technology, Raipur, India. He has more than sixteen years of experience in academia. He has published more than 52 referred articles and served as a reviewer of several journals. His research interests include mobile-ad hoc networks, sensor networks, data center networks, distributed systems, network security, blockchain, and game theory in networks. He is a senior member of the IEEE.

Prof. Brij B. Gupta is working as director of International Center for AI and Cyber Security Research, Incubation and Innovations, and full professor with the Department of Computer Science and Information Engineering (CSIE), Asia University, Taiwan. In more than 17 years of his professional experience, he published over 500 papers in journals/conferences including 30 books and 10 Patents with over 18000 citations. He has received numerous national and international awards including Canadian Commonwealth Scholarship (2009), Faculty Research Fellowship Award (2017), MeitY, GoI, IEEE GCCE outstanding and WIE paper awards and Best Faculty Award (2018 & 2019), NIT KKR, respectively. Prof. Gupta was recently selected for 2022 Clarivate Web of Science Highly Cited Researchers (0.1% Researchers in the world) in Computer Science. He was also selected in the 2022, 2021 and 2020 Stanford University's ranking of the world's top 2% scientists. He is also a visiting and adjunct professor with several universities worldwide. He is also an IEEE senior member (2017) and also selected as 2021 Distinguished Lecturer in IEEE CTSoc. Prof. Gupta is also serving as Member-in-Large, Board of Governors, IEEE Consumer Technology Society (2022-2024). Prof. Gupta is also leading IJSWIS, IJSSCI, STE and IJCAC as editor-in-chief. Moreover, he is also serving as lead-editor of a book series with Taylor & Francis Group and IET Press. He also served as TPC members in more than 150 international conferences also serving as associate and guest editor of various journals and transactions. His research interests include information security, Cyber physical systems, cloud computing, blockchain technologies, intrusion detection, AI, social media and networking.

Dr. Kwok Tai Chui received the Bachelor's degree in electronic and communication engineering with a business intelligence minor, and Ph.D. in electronic engineering from City University of Hong Kong. He had industry experience as a senior data scientist in an Internet of Things (IoT) company. He is with the Department of Technology, School of Science and Technology, at Hong Kong Metropolitan University as an assistant professor. He has more than 90 research publications including edited books, book chapters, journal papers, and conference papers. He has served in various editorial positions in ESCI/SCIE-listed journals including managing editor of *International Journal on Semantic Web and Information Systems*, topic editor of *Sensors*, and associate editor of *International Journal of Energy Optimization and Engineering*. His research interests include computational intelligence, data science, energy monitoring and management, intelligent transportation, smart metering, healthcare, machine learning algorithms, and optimization.

Contributors

K. Balaji
School of Mechanical
  Engineering
Vellore Institute of Technology
  (VIT) University
Vellore, Tamil Nadu, India

Shuchi Bhadula
Department of Computer
  Science & Engineering
Graphic Era (Deemed to be
  University)
Dehradun, Uttarakhand, India

Sakshi Bhagwat
Department of Information
  Technology
National Institute of Technology
Raipur, Chhattisgarh, India

Govind P. Gupta
Department of Information
  Technology
National Institute of Technology
Raipur, Chhattisgarh, India

Chandrashekar Jatoth
Department of Information
  Technology
National Institute of Technology
Raipur, Chhattisgarh, India

C. K. Jha
Department of Computer
  Science
Banasthali Vidyapith
Banasthali, Rajasthan

Tejaswini Kar
School of Electronics
   Engineering
KIIT Deemed to be University
Bhubaneswar, Odisha, India

Prabhat Kumar
Department of Information
   Technology
National Institute of Technology
Raipur, Chhattisgarh, India

Sanjay Kumar
Department of Information
   Technology
National Institute of
   Technology
Raipur, Chhattisgarh, India

Indrashis Mitra
School of Electronics
   Engineering
KIIT Deemed to be University
Bhubaneswar, Odisha, India

Potu Narayana
Department of Computer
   Science and Engineering
Osmania University Hyderabad
Hyderabad, Telangana, India

Kirti Pandey
Department of Computer
   Science
Banasthali Vidyapith
Banasthali, Rajasthan, India

Premchand Paravataneni
Department of Computer
   Science and Engineering
Osmania University Hyderabad
Hyderabad, Telangana, India

R. K. Pareriya
Maulana Azad National
   Institute of Technology
Bhopal, Madhya Pradesh, India

C. Rakesh
School of Mechanical
   Engineering
Vellore Institute of Technology
   (VIT) University
Vellore, Tamil Nadu, India

Kananbala Ray
School of Electronics Engineering
KIIT Deemed to be University
Bhubaneswar, Odisha, India

G. Rekha
Department of Computer
   Science and Engineering
Koneru Lakshmaiah Education
   Foundation
Vijayawada, Andhra Pradesh,
   India

Monika Saxena
Department of Computer
   Science
Banasthali Vidyapith
Banasthali, Rajasthan, India

Sachin Sharma
Department of Computer
    Science & Engineering
Graphic Era (Deemed to be
    University)
Dehradun, Uttarakhand, India

Sourav Singh
Department of Computer
    Science & Engineering
Graphic Era (Deemed to be
    University)
Dehradun, Uttarakhand, India

Santosh K. Smmarwar
Department of Information
    Technology
National Institute of Technology
Raipur, Chhattisgarh, India

Yashi Srivastava
School of Electronics Engineering
KIIT Deemed to be University
Bhubaneswar, Odisha, India

Pathan Suhana
Maulana Azad National
    Institute of Technology
Bhopal, Madhya Pradesh, India

Rakesh Tripathi
Department of Information
    Technology
National Institute of Technology
Raipur, Chhattisgarh, India

Priyanka Verma
Maulana Azad National
    Institute of Technology
Bhopal, Madhya Pradesh, India

T. Vivek
School of Mechanical
    Engineering
Vellore Institute of Technology
    (VIT) University
Vellore, Tamil Nadu, India

Vaibhav Vyas
Department of Computer
    Science
Banasthali Vidyapith
Banasthali, Rajasthan, India

1

DEEP LEARNING TECHNIQUES IN BIG DATA-ENABLED INTERNET-OF-THINGS DEVICES

SOURAV SINGH, SACHIN SHARMA, AND SHUCHI BHADULA

Department of Computer Science & Engineering, Graphic Era (Deemed to be University), Dehradun, Uttarakhand, India

Contents

DOI: 10.1201/9781003264545-1

1.1 Introduction

The basic aim of the Internet of Things (IoT) concept is to enhance quality of life by transforming ordinary objects into smart devices. This is done by exploiting and adapting the advancements in new emerging and evolving technologies, like embedded systems, cloud computing architectures, sensor innovations, and so on. These IoT devices generally sense the surroundings with the merger and integration of various sensors into them, and, thus, produce a huge amount of data, referred to as IoT big data [1]. The data have certain properties, such as being heterogeneous in nature, as this data are generated by different sensors and different devices deployed for different applications [2]. Data can also be generated by faulty or improperly calibrated sensors or when the device itself is placed in an extreme environment, which is responsible for unexpected readings and frequent outliers. Thus, it is very difficult to analyse this type of data and extract useful information from it by using traditional approaches.

So, what if we exploit, adapt, and integrate new evolving and emerging technologies in the artificial intelligence (AI) domain, technology such as deep learning (DL), to solve the problem of IoT big data analytics. Using DL techniques would be useful in extracting hidden knowledge from IoT big data. This may help the developers and researchers to develop new innovations in IoT domain that can actuate real-time decisions, based on the hidden facts in data and situation around. The integration of AI in IoT seems to be promising, but it is not an easy task because today's IoT infrastructure is not designed for running complex and resource-intensive AI algorithms. There is a huge demand for the development of lightweight algorithms, tailored to IoT characteristics.

The terms IoT and DL were becoming more popular day by day with the future is of AI-enabled smart devices. With the rise and

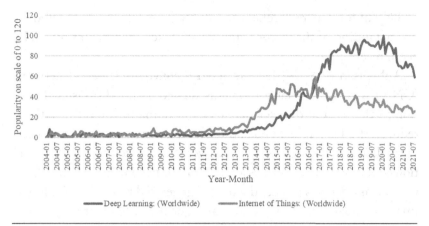

Figure 1.1 "Google Trend" showing the increase in the popularity of Internet of Things and deep learning in recent years.

development of capable hardware and 5G technology adaptation in recent times, the implementation of highly capable IoT devices becomes feasible [3]. Figure 1.1 shows the recent trends in IoT and DL, observed by Google Trends. The growing popularity of IoT and DL is capable of creating new jobs in the domain of IoT and AI. Thus, it can have a great economic impact. Many IoT applications came into existence in recent years in different domains, such as smart cities, agriculture, smart home, smart cars, etc. The main crux of these applications is the implementation of AI techniques for prediction or data analytics. Among them all, DL techniques were mainly utilized in IoT for encountering tasks such as pattern recognition, object detection, classification of sensor data, clustering, etc. This is because traditional machine learning (ML) algorithms and models were unable to solve the complex analytics issues related to IoT-generated data.

1.2 Literature Review

Our survey focused on the recent innovations in the field of IoT using DL techniques by different researchers. This helps us in building an understanding of various DL techniques that can integrate with IoT. Here, we have discussed the contributions of different authors, with DL techniques or DL tools utilized in smart systems. We also highlight the various outcomes from different studies done by different independent groups of researchers for DL-IoT integration. This may be helpful for new researchers and developers who wants to build an understanding of the various approaches taken by different researchers in recent times.

Anbarasan et al. [4] have utilized a convolution neural network (CNN) with IoT to solve problems related to flood disaster detection in the natural disaster management domain. First, the authors reduced the IoT big data related to flood disaster. The data was then normalized and all missing values were pre-processed. A combination of attributes method was applied to this pre-processed data. Then CNN classifier was provided with the generated rules. The result was finally compared with other similar algorithms. Shah et al. [5] proposed an "urban noise monitoring" system using IoT. This system can classify real-time audio data, and create a log of that data in the Google cloud. Authors also developed an advanced fusion technique by using various factors and normalization techniques. Time stretch, dynamic range compression, and pitch shifting were some of the factors included. Normalization and augmentation are integrated with CNN. A TensorFlow framework with Raspberry Pi development board is utilized for the task. Tariq et al. [6] proposed a method to develop a real-time human-speech inputted human-emotion detection system. It was used to help elderly people in nursing homes. The authors developed an IoT-DL solution with the model for data augmentation techniques and normalization techniques. The CNN is used in the development and the system recorded an accuracy value of 95%. Fang et al. [7] developed a procedure for jobs remaining time (in the production domain) prediction using DL techniques. IoT is used in shops to collect historical data. A stacked sparse autoencoder (S-SAE) DL model is used to learn features of big data from manufacturing. It helped in time prediction of remaining jobs. Muthu et al. [8] developed a wearable IoT-based solution with DL techniques to overcome issues in health support systems. The Boltzmann belief network is used to train the data collected. Generalized approximate reasoning-based intelligence control (GARIC) is designed with IoT with regression rules to gather information about patients. The outcome is that the system is capable of a 96% prediction rate with accuracy of 96.33%. Jeyaraj et al. [9] worked on patient monitoring in medical IoT. Prototyping includes a smart sensor to measure signals. The National Instrument's myRIO development board is used. The

DL algorithm was developed for feature extraction of signals and abnormality detection. WEKA tools were utilized during the implementation and the results show 97% accuracy with a computation time of 65 seconds.

Hossain et al. [10] proposed an emotion-detection system using DL techniques. The inputs were in the form of video and audio, which were processed and classified using CNN DL-related techniques. The system evaluation is done under the eNTERFACE database. The authors' work is for detecting emotion using big data. This is a new idea that can be analyzed to easily produce new ideas for similar IoT implementations in the emotion-detection field with DL. Yao et al. [11] also proposed a DL model for diagnosing gallbladder stone composition. Analytics were performed on IoT big data. CNN model techniques were utilized to learn the data features, and different characteristics of gallstone chemical compositions were analysed. The work done helps in understanding recent developments in the Internet of Medical Things (IoMT) with DL. Chowdury et al. [12] proposed a water-quality monitoring system. The data is collected by using sensors, and remote monitoring of IoT is performed. The input data is in video data format, which is analyzed and compared under using streaming analytics. Features of the Spark MLlib library were also included and utilized. Ali et al. [13] also worked on streaming analytics but provided an IoT edge-based solution for processing data close to sensors for fast object detection scenarios. Also, it has been observed that instead of using the traditional remote server analytics-based approach, the new IoT-edge technology seems to be more efficient for utilizing DL for IoT. Chauhan et al. [14] presents tree-based deep neural network framework utilization for face acknowledgement in the cloud. The proposed method accomplished 99% precision. Zhou et al. [15] also worked on IoMT and developed a human-activity detection system using IoMT-DL. The designed framework is semi-supervised in nature. Multiple IoT sensors' data were infused for analyzing and long short-term memory (LSTM) was utilized. Garg et al. [16] developed a hybrid anomaly detection system in a cloud data centre network using DL and IoT using a modified CNN model for the cloud network anomaly detection. Results show comparatively better performance when tested with the DARPA 1998 dataset and KDE 1999 dataset.

1.2.1 Motivation and Contributions

Our idea for this chapter is based on summarizing the key DL techniques under the IoT domain, which can be utilized by researchers, firms, and independent developers who want to work on DL-IoT integration. Also, this may be helpful in exploring the universe of IoT big data analytics. The key contributions of this chapter are as follows:

- We summarize and compare some recent work and develop an understanding for state-of-the-art techniques.
- We present the overview of big data-enabled IoT devices and discuss the "10 V" features (discussed next) of IoT big data.
- We highlight and briefly discuss some DL models for IoT big data analytics.
- We summarize some frameworks for IoT-DL development.
- We also summarize some "supportive" techniques for IoT-DL integration.
- We briefly discuss Fog-Cloud architecture.
- We also list some commercial products and development boards for the development and quick prototyping of IoT-DL projects.
- We discuss the importance of DL techniques for big data-enabled IoT devices.
- We also briefly discuss the importance of DL in real-time IoT.
- We point out some impacts, challenges, and applications of DL-IoT integration.
- Lastly, we compare and analyse the key facts found in this survey.

1.3 Overview of Big Data-Enabled IoT Devices

IoT is basically all about generating huge amounts of data, which is called big data of IoT or simply IoT big data. The process of finding hidden patterns, facts, and new intelligent insight from this huge data is known as analytics of IoT big data. This extracted new information is helpful in making critical decisions in the IoT environment. Also, in general, this information can be used to improve the throughput of various businesses globally. Ciampi et al. [17] show that big

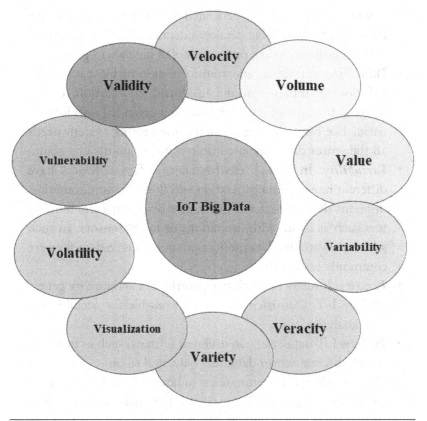

Figure 1.2 The basic "10 V" features of IoT big data.

data analytics can be useful for creating value for a company and its stakeholders.

The IoT generates data by sensing the environment with the help of various sensors integrated with different devices. These sensors were designed to generate different formats and types of data. IoT big data naturally has some characteristics associated with it. Understanding these characteristics would be useful in understanding IoT big data and IoT-DL integration. There are several researchers who have previously defined and described these characteristics very beautifully [18]–[20]. Figure 1.2 shows the "10 V" features of IoT-big data, however, here, we consider the most commonly known "10 V" features:

- *Velocity:* This feature points toward the rate of IoT data generation. Also, in a new data-driven world scenario, this also refers to the need of fast processing with respect to the data production.

- *Volume:* Quantity of data generated by IoT devices is the determining factor of IoT big data consideration. The IoT generated data is much more than other sources of big data in general.
- *Value:* The extraction and transformation of big data in the IoT domain into useful and insightful information. It also refers to the type of data captured in a given IoT service scenario. For example, a greenhouse monitoring system needs all the sensor data generated from different points of a plant.
- *Variability:* In an IoT environment, different devices have different rates of data generation and flow. In some scenarios, different devices perform differently based on common factors such as bandwidth limitations or faulty sensors. In such scenarios, variable data production and variable data flow are commonly observed.
- *Veracity:* It refers to data's trustworthiness and quality generated by IoT. Consistent data is responsible for accurate big data analytics.
- *Variety:* IoT data can be in different formats, such as in audio, visual, discrete sensor data, text data, and so on.
- *Visualization:* This feature refers to how difficult it is to visualize IoT big data. Sometimes visualization tools face some challenges due to poor functionality and sometimes poor response time. We cannot maintain billions of GB data from simple visualization techniques, such as a graph visualization technique.
- *Volatility:* Sometimes, IoT big data becomes irrelevant and obsolete at a certain period of time. It is important to keep track of such events of data irrelevancies for proper maintenance and functionality of the IoT system.
- *Vulnerability:* Around the world, hackers continuously seek some sort of data breach in IoT systems. Big data related to IoT is worth millions of dollars, and, thus, needs to be secured properly.
- *Validity:* Similar to veracity, the validity feature of IoT big data refers to the correctness of data and its accuracy for a specific intended use. Most of the time and efforts of developers are spent in cleansing big data before even analyzing it. So, some new techniques, such as DL techniques, should be adapted in the IoT scenario to make things easy and effective.

1.4 New Technologies for Big Data-Enabled IoT Devices

DL rests on the interconnection of networks formed by neurons (their computing nodes), which are known widely as neural networks. It also consists of various DL-architectures designed to conduct either supervised or unsupervised learning. In IoT big data scenarios, these techniques can be very useful for analytic purposes. In this section, we first discuss different DL architectures that can be utilized for IoT big data analytics, then we also mention some of the frameworks used to implement DL models in IoT setups. Lastly, we discuss different techniques for DL in the newly introduced fog-edge scenario. The advantage of DL architectures is that there are "hidden features", and DL can learn from them. Each layer is trained based on the previous layer's outputs.

1.4.1 DL Models for IoT Big Data Analytics

A deep neural network (DNN) starts from the input layer, then several "hidden layers" are present and then last is the output layer. Each layer consists of basic computing units, popularly known as neurons, which receive inputs and perform a basic weighted summation. This sums then goes through an activation function, which, finally, produces the output. A bias is also associated with each unit with vector of weight to input size.

Training is done through the process of assigning random weights to input data, which then is further passed to the next layer. Each other layer also does the same, providing their output to the next layer as input. At the last layer, the final output is considered. An "error rate" is flowed and propagated back to the initial input layer from across the neural network. The network repeats this cyclic process until the error rate comes under and below a value of desire or below a certain threshold. Figure 1.3 provides a visualization of DL models. Each basic DL model useful for IoT big data analytics is discussed below [21]–[23]:

1. **Convolutional neural network (CNN):** A variety of DNN that can accept image data as input and assign biases with weights to a variety of objects in that particular image [24]. A CNN can also distinctly identify various objects in that image. The pre-processing and complexity is much lower or

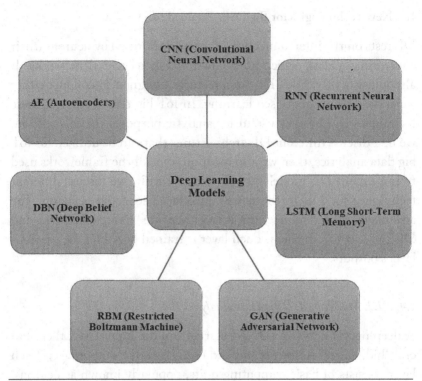

Figure 1.3 Visual representation of deep learning models.

less, if faced off with other algorithms, which is useful for IoT-DL implementation. Its architecture is based on the neurons present in the human brain and the receptive field is where individual neurons respond to the stimulus, which were solely (or only) in the region of the restricted visual field. In IoT, CNN can be useful in capturing dependencies, which are temporal and spatial dependencies in an image input, through filters of relevance.

2. **Recurrent neural network (RNN):** RNN uses sequential data (or time series data). It is useful in language translation, natural language processing, image captioning, and speech recognition [25]. Like CNN, RNN also utilizes training data for learning purposes. The output is dependent on the prior elements of sequence. The output of the previous layer is pumped (or fed) as input to the current (or present) layer. A key point to RNNs is the introduction of hidden layers, which were capable of remembering some sequence information.

3. **Long short-term memory (LSTM):** An improvement on RNN. The concept of a gate is introduced in it, which forms its building blocks. Every gate computes an output of value within 1 and 0, depending on the input value provided [26]. A feedback-loop is also present. In addition, read gate, forget gate, and write gate are present in each neuron in LSTM. The neuron tends to write its data to itself when the forget gate is active. When the forget gate sends 0 and turns off, the neuron forgets its content. LSTM performs better compared to RNN when data is characterized with a long-time dependency.

4. **Generative adversarial network (GAN):** This is based on a type of game known as minimax in which two different networks try to compete with each other by minimizing and maximizing the function value of one another [27]. In each step, the "generator" works to scam the "discriminator" by trying to play with sample data production from the random noise. In an IoT scenario, GAN can be used when we have to create something from available data.

5. **Restricted Boltzmann machine (RBM):** RBM is an artificial neural network (ANN), which is stochastic in nature. It has two layers in its structure, one is the hidden layer and another is the visible layer. The hidden layer contains the variables known as latent variables and the visible layer consists of the inputs [28]. Compared to the Boltzmann machine, the restrictions in RBM were applied to neuron connectivity. These should form a graph known as the bipartite graph, such that each hidden neuron should connect to the visible neurons (no same-layer unit connections were allowed). All hidden and visible neurons were connected with the bias. RBMs were useful in feature extraction from input data and can easily find applications in IoT big data analytics.

6. **Deep belief networks (DBN):** A DBN consists of many hidden layers that correspond to latent variables and also to the visible layers that correspond to inputs. In an IoT scenario, they can be used to juice (or extract) a hierarchical-representation of the data that is exposed at the time of training and rebuild the data used as input data [29]. It can also be used for prediction purposes with the addition a classifier layer.

7. **Autoencoder (AE):** AE consists of input and output layers. These layers are connected to one hidden layer or, in some cases, more than one hidden layers. Input and output units are of the same number in AE [30]. AE behaviour is to construct input at output layers. Due to this, AE can be useful in fault detection in an IoT big data scenario.

1.4.2 DL Frameworks for IoT-DL Development

The previous section offers a brief discussion and introduction to some commonly used DL models, with a discussion on IoT-DL integration purposes. Figure 1.4 shows some important frameworks. Next, we have a brief introduction of some of these frameworks:

1. **TensorFlow:** TensorFlow is a machine learning library system designed by Google. It is open source. Developers can use its visualization capability to visualize models. It is also a

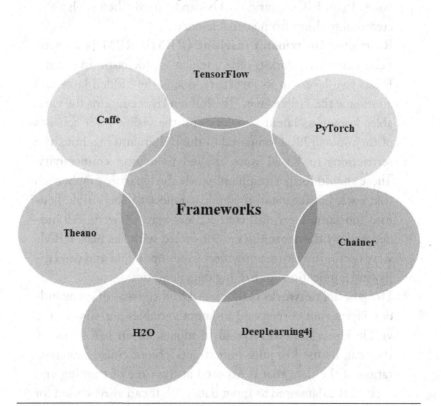

Figure 1.4   Frameworks for DL-IoT integration.

full package of DL models and algorithms for IoT-DL technology developers [31].

2. **Pytorch:** Previously known as "Torch", PyTorch now supports Python. Both CPU and GPU learning models development are supported. It is developed by the famous Facebook AI (now Meta AI) research lab [32]. Other languages supported were C and C++.

3. **Chainer:** It is also an open-source DL framework. It is developed in Python. It is popularly used for PaintsChainer, which supports automatic colourization [33].

4. **Deeplearning4J (D4J):** It is a tool for running DL in a Java virtual machine (JVM). As Java is a well-known programming language, D4J is easy to adapt by new IoT and DL developers [34].

5. **H2O:** It provides interfaces for Java, Scala, R, and Python. It can be operated in Hadoop mode, Spark mode, or in stand-alone mode [35].

6. **Theano:** It runs on CUDA libraries for complicated code. It uses mathematical graph representations [36].

7. **Caffe:** It is based on C++. It supports GPU support for CUDA and also has MATLAB integration [37].

1.4.3 Supportive Techniques/Technologies for IoT-DL Integration

A typical IoT device is a type of device that is supposed to be installed and left abandoned for years. The IoT device already has limited computational resources and runs on a typical lithium-ion battery system. However, DL techniques generally dealt with heavy computational processes, which require more computing cores and, thus, more battery power. Therefore, researchers should continuously focus on designing and developing new supportive techniques that can efficiently facilitate or at least make possible the IoT-DL integration for IoT big data analytics. Table 1.1 summarizes such supportive technologies and next is a brief description:

1. **Tinymotes:** This microcontroller-based IoT is not generally developed for running DL tasks. Tinymotes were the concept of designing tiny microprocessors customized for DL

Table 1.1 Summary of IoT-DL Supportive Technologies

METHOD/TECH	PROS	CONS	REFERENCES
Tinymotes	Good in time-critical IoT systems, energy-efficient	Special purpose networks	[44]
Edge architecture	Low latency, facilitates real-time computing	Requires dedicated devices connected to sensors	[45]
5G technology	Ability to connect huge amounts of IoT devices, reduces bandwidth issues	Still in the implementation phase	[46]
Network compression	Reduces storage, reduces computation	Not for all DL models	[47]
Accelerators	DL-model integration with hardware, efficient computations	Doesn't work with traditional hardware	[48]
Approximate computing	Saves energy	Not suitable for precise systems	[49]

needs. These processors use much less energy. By using this technique, the developers can perform on-board analytics of IoT big data. This facilitates in developing real-time scenario-based IoT applications [38].

2. **Edge architecture:** An edge device brings computing "near" to the IoT data generation sensors and "away" from the cloud servers. Generally, cloud servers were more than capable of running analytics on big data. But in IoT scenarios, these cloud servers come with a price of bandwidth considerations, low latency, privacy issues, and latent response times [39]. The development of edge-based IoT architecture has reduced these cloud issues to some extent.

3. **5G technology:** The true expansion of telecommunication network techniques like 5G gave hope to the future of an IoT-driven world. Present-day 5G promises to connect a huge number of future IoT devices with ease [40]. It also promises to meet and resolve bandwidth considerations related to IoT conduction in real scenarios. 5G can also make IoT big data analytics a more doable task, and provide support for its architecture. It also will make the cloud more accessible in real time, for a DL-based IoT device.

4. **Network compression:** Under this technique, a crowded or dense network is converted to a less dense or sparse network. Storage and computational requirements were notably reduced under this technique. The networks that can afford such sparsity were eligible for such implementations of network compression in an IoT scenario [41].
5. **Accelerators**: Specific embedded hardware design is an intuitive approach for the optimization of memory and energy requirements in IoT devices. This approach also associates embedded hardware with DL. This whole approach results in efficient computations [42].
6. **Approximate computing:** After the formation of an approximate network, a trade-off is carried out under which accuracy and energy requirements are considered for optimal output. In the real world, the outputs from these devices running AI techniques do not need to be perfect every time. Rather, these outputs should fall under a specific threshold or range to be considered correct. These approximate considerations in computing can greatly impact the performance and existence of resource-constrained IoT devices that run DL tasks [43].

1.4.4 *Fog and Cloud Architectures for DL-Computing on IoT Big Data*

Under cloud architecture of IoT, the data is sent to a remote cloud server with the help of a wired or wireless connection. The cloud then processes the data, analyses it, or just stores it for proper service delivery of IoT devices. The cloud also has its own limitations in the present-day world, such as it depends on bandwidth limitations, latency issues, and data privacy and data security issues. But the cloud is presently the most capable computing unit and can deliver any task with ease on its hardware. These features make the cloud a strong DL-computing unit in IoT applications.

Also, fog technology is a relatively new term. It uses a centralized system that interacts with embedded systems, gateways, and local area networks (LANs). Unlike edge nodes, a fog node is not directly attached to sensors [50]. It also reduces latency and can also be used for DL in IoT real-time applications. Figure 1.5 shows the cloud-fog architecture.

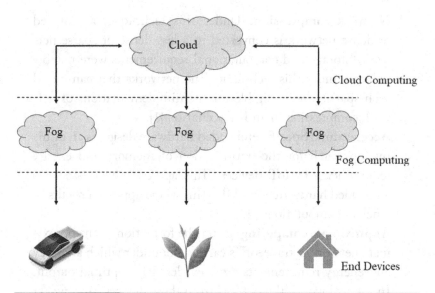

Figure 1.5   The fog-cloud architecture.

1.4.5 Some Commercial Products for Development and Quick Prototyping of DL-IoT Analytics Projects

a. **Development boards:** To physically experience the services of DL-enabled IoT devices, developers must create microcontrollers printed circuit boards (PCBs) that can run DL tasks. These generally consist of a main microcontroller (example: ARM Cortex-M), which is selected according to the developer's need. It also consists of some supporting electronics soldered on the same board. This task is exciting but it is a part of further phases in product development. Using a commercial development board is preferable for quick prototyping in the initial phases of product development [51]. Some of the microcontroller development boards commercially available are summarized in Table 1.2 (but not limiting to only these).

b. **Products that utilize IoT-DL idea:** These technologies were developed mainly for commercial purposes. On the other hand, these technologies also provide some flexibility for developers to develop their own DL-based IoT projects [52]. Table 1.3 shows some such home assistant/automation commercial products.

Table 1.2   Summary of Some Hand-Picked DL-IoT Development Boards

DEVELOPMENT BOARD	MICROCONTROLLER	RAM	STORAGE TYPE
BeagleBone AI	Texas Instruments Sitara AM5729	1 GB	16GB onboard eMMC flash
Raspberry Pi 4	Broadcom BCM2711, quad-core Cortex-A72 (ARM v8) 64-bit SoC at 1.5GHz	2 GB/4 GB/8 GB	Memory card slot
NVIDIA Jetson Nano	Quad-core ARM Cortex-A57 MPCore processor	4 GB, 64-bit LPDDR4, 1600MHz, 25.6 GB/s	16 G eMMC 5.1
Google Coral	NXP i.MX 8M SoC (quad-Cortex-A53, Cortex-M4F)	1 GB, LPDDR4	8 GB eMMC, MicroSD slot
Intel Neural Compute Stick 2	Intel Movidius Myriad X Vision Processing Unit 4 GB	1 GB	4 GB
Arduino Portenta H7	STM32H747XI dual Cortex-M7+M4 32-bit low power Arm MCU		Memory card slot

1.4.6 Some Datasets for Easy DL-IoT Integration

Sometimes training our DL system requires a huge cost. This cost is charged by some dataset provider companies [53]. This may be needed for some big enterprises, but common developers can make use of easily available datasets within Internet communities. Table 1.4 shows some common datasets.

1.4.7 The Importance of DL Techniques for Big Data-Enabled IoT Devices

In recent times, IoT has emerged as a huge source of data generation. This data, thus, needs to be analysed to get new insights from the generated data. The problem is that this data is huge in size and heterogeneous with its own characteristics. Thus, there is a need for new innovations in field of IoT big data analytics. One such innovation is to integrate DL and IoT into a single-performing system for

Table 1.3   Products Used DL in the IoT Domain

PRODUCT	DESCRIPTION	PLATFORM	APPLICATION
Google Assistant	Personal assistant	Fog	Smart home
Amazon Alexa	Personal assistant	Fog	Smart home
IBM Watson	Cognitive framework	Cloud	IoT
Microsoft Cortana	Personal assistant	Fog	Smart car, XBox

Table 1.4 Some DataSets for DL-IoT Integration

DATASET	NATURE OF DATA	SIZE	WEB LINK
MNIST	Handwritten digits	Size: 50 MB	http://yann.lecun.com/exdb/mnist/
Microsoft COCO	250,000 people with key points	328K Size: 25 GB	https://cocodataset.org/#home
ImageNet	Images according to worldNet hierarchy	Size: 150 GB	https://www.image-net.org/
Open Images Dataset	9,011,219 images with more than 5k labels	Size: 500 GB	https://opensource.google/projects/open-images-dataset
VisualQA	Containing open-ended questions about images	Size: 25 GB	https://visualqa.org/
Street View House Numbers	630,420 images in 10 classes	Size: 2.5 GB	http://ufldl.stanford.edu/housenumbers/
CIFAR-10	60,000 images in 10 classes	Size: 170 MB	https://www.cs.toronto.edu/~kriz/cifar.html
Fashion-MNIST	Fashion products	Size: 30 MB	https://github.com/zalandoresearch/fashion-mnist
IMDB reviews	25,000 highly polar movie reviews for training and 25,000 for testing	Size: 80 MB	https://www.kaggle.com/lakshmi25npathi/ imdb-dataset-of-50k-movie-reviews
20 Newsgroups	20,000 messages taken from 20 newsgroups	Size: 2 MB	https://scikit-learn.org/0.19/datasets/twenty_newsgroups.html
Sentiment140	160,000 tweets	Size: 80 MB	http://help.sentiment140.com/for-students/
WordNet	117,000 synsets are linked to other synsets by a small number of conceptual relations	Size: 10 MB	https://wordnet.princeton.edu/
Yelp Reviews	5,200,000 reviews, 174,000 business attributes, 200,000 pictures, and 11 metropolitan areas	2.66 GB JSON, 2.9 GB SQL, and 7.5 GB photos	https://www.yelp.com/
The Wikipedia Corpus	4,400,000 articles containing 1.9 billion words	Size: 20 MB	https://www.english-corpora.org/wiki/
The Blog Authorship Corpus	681,288 posts with over 140 million words	Size: 300 MB	https://cs.biu.ac.il/

(Continued)

Table 1.4 Some DataSets for DL–IoT Integration *(Continued)*

DATASET	NATURE OF DATA	SIZE	WEB LINK
Machine Translations of Various Languages	30,000,000 sentences and their translations	Size: 15 GB	http://statmt.org/wmt18/index.html
Free open-digit dataset	1,500 audio samples	Size: 10 MB	https://github.com/Jakobovski/free-spoken-digit-dataset
Free Music Archive	100,000 tracks	1000 GB	https://github.com/mdeff/fma
Ballroom	700 audio samples	Size: 14 GB	http://mtg.upf.edu/ismir2004/contest/tempoContest/node5.html
Million Song Dataset	Songs	280 GB	https://labrosa.ee.columbia.edu/millionsong/

IoT big data analysis [54]. Next, we point out some advantages of DL techniques for big data-enabled IoT devices:

- DL analytics techniques are capable of extracting useful information, new facts, and new patterns from huge IoT big data.
- IoT data have their own characteristics, such as every IoT device and sensor being capable of generating highly heterogeneous data in huge amounts. DL techniques are useful in handling such analytics issues.
- It improves quality of IoT service in general, as DL analytics help IoT to perform such tasks that were not possible before due to the lack of analytics techniques for IoT big data.
- It also helps businesses grow more significantly, as it provides new insights into their interest through IoT big data.
- DL techniques combined with IoT can solve issues regarding highly noisy data produced by different sensors in a harsh environment.
- DL techniques can give new abilities to IoT devices, making real-time decisions efficiently.
- IoT can generate streams of data continuously and for over a highly extended period of time. It is not possible for a human to analyze such big data by traditional techniques, therefore, DL techniques can be very effective in solving this issue.

1.4.8 Importance of DL Techniques in Real–Time IoT

1.4.8.1 Implementation Issues of DL Techniques in Real–Time IoT

- **Hardware issues:** Real-time IoT implementation demands CPU- and GPU-intensive tasks to be performed rapidly, as to keep pace with the built-in clock. So less capable or lightweight hardware resources can be a primary issue in DL-IoT integration in real-time scenarios [55].
- **Limited Bandwidth:** Real-time IoT requires a high-bandwidth network to work in the real world. Presently, we are living in the 5G and 6G age, but underdeveloped countries still uses the 3G and 4G infrastructure. Also, remote-area connectivity is a major hurdle. One solution of this problem

is through direct-to-home satellite Internet technology infrastructure advancements [56].

- **Complexity:** Developing real-time IoT devices for a complex network introduces new network design issues. These issues can be resolved by new developments in real-time node integration standards into an existing network [57].
- **Scalability:** Small companies usually cannot make a big pre-investment in infrastructure, such as a high-speed capable cloud, edge nodes, connectivity etc., which leads to new issues of scalability in a real-time IoT environment [58].
- **Interoperability standards:** People don't necessarily want to use those IoT products that do not add huge value to their lives. The developers keep this fact in mind while designing new projects that require other IoT devices to work in conjunction for proper analytics [59]. On the other hand, the integration with other common IoTs, such as a light bulb, washing machine, etc. in the smart home environment, for example, does not have proper compatibility standards presently, which could add real value.
- **Power issues:** High computation of DL tasks requires more energy. The batteries require more reliability to run continuously for extended periods to serve real-world projects [60].

1.4.8.2 Challenges in Implementing DL Techniques in Real-Time IoT Networks

- **Communication infrastructure:** DL applied to IoT big data requires a proper connection with other devices and servers for various tasks. Moreover, it is technically a good idea to connect IoT devices with existing cellular networks, as, theoretically, 4G-LTE is a good technology for IoT, but the incompatibility in getting phone reception with present-day cellular techniques in developing nations proves that present-day cellular infrastructure is not ready for IoT-DL implementations. So, real-time IoT requires a different approach for IoT device communication [61].
- **Underdeveloped IoT network standards:** Present-day IoT protocols and standards are not fully developed so they can

serve the compatibility and implementation needs of real-time IoT. The developers struggle with these issues during their IoT-DL project design phase.

- **Consumer expectations:** Due to high competition among IoT products, developers risk not meeting high customer expectations. This challenge may affect the overall project funding by the organisation, which may create obstacles for the innovative product development of real-time IoT.
- **Privacy:** Data breaches in users' private information is a major challenge in IoT development.

1.4.8.3 Future Considerations for Real-Time IoT-DL Integration

- **Security:** As IoT is a concept of connecting various things with the Internet, these "things" constantly remain under a security risk due to active hackers. Present-day security techniques were not designed to meet real-time IoT requirements. In the future, developers should create new lightweight techniques for real-time IoT that can run DL algorithms and models more efficiently and with security of IoT devices and data.
- **Software vulnerability:** Software vulnerability is a serious present-day consideration. Loopholes present in IoT software must be checked properly. In the future, open-source communities must be appreciated for constantly pointing out software vulnerabilities in real-time IoT.

1.4.9 Impact, Challenges, and Applications

1.4.9.1 Impact

- All application areas of IoT-DL integration seem to be improved. One such area is agriculture, which notices crop yield increases because of smart farming practices by farmers due to better prediction techniques.
- The economic impact is huge for industries also, as new insights were discovered from data, which further attracted new investors.

1.4.9.2 Challenges

- **Design factors**: Today's IoT infrastructure is not designed to handle resource-intensive DL tasks, as IoT devices were expected to be running on light hardware and utilize a small amount of energy for an extended period of time. It is a challenge under the present scenario to introduce new capable IoT designs that can run DL models and tasks efficiently.
- **Exploiting edge and fog IoT Architecture**: As edge-assisted IoT is presently available everywhere, these edge devices can run DL techniques near the IoT sensors per their architecture. Designing DL-IoT implementation architectures should also grow in the direction of edge computing.
- **DL service node discovery**: Designing new DL algorithms and models is required to fulfil the distributed fog scenarios in different IoT systems. These newly developed techniques should also be capable of discovering required nodes in an IoT network, which run a certain DL service, whenever needed. Use either SI (MKS) or CGS as primary units (SI units are encouraged.) English units may be used as secondary units (in parentheses). An exception would be the use of English units as identifiers in trade, such as "3.5-inch disk drive".

1.4.9.3 Applications

- **Smart home:** IoT in smart homes utilized the DL-tools under computer vision, natural language processing, etc., to improve quality of life.
- **Agriculture:** DL can be used for crop-yield predictions, crop-disease monitoring, soil monitoring, rain-pattern predictions, farm security applications, etc.
- **Healthcare:** IoMT is improving day by day. DL in IoMT has a great impact on patient monitoring, heart-rate pattern detection, tumour detection, fracture detection, smart medical boxes, etc.
- **Industry:** Smart manufacturing is the new trend. The advent of "Industry 4.0" has led IoT in the industrial scenario toward new horizons. DL on industrial IoT were extensively used in product selection on conveyer belts, packaging, etc.

- **Transportations:** Today's world has witnessed smart connected cars acting on IoT, running DL data processing in real-time, and becoming driverless. Smart public transport and delivery systems are few of the examples of IoT-DL integration.
- **Sports:** Various IoT fitness bands are a reality now. Almost all data related to any sport or even individuals' activities were monitored in real-time and through cloud-server big data analytics.
- **Retail:** Amazon Go stores are famous for walk-in and walk-out shopping, without any checkout. The process of shopping is becoming seamless through IoT and DL real-time analytics. Smart cart is a well-known example.

1.5 Comparative Study and Analysis

In this research, we reviewed the techniques like IoT, DL, and IoT big data analytics. We observed a huge trend in DL analytics and IoT big data. Figure 1.6 shows recent trends in IoT big data analytics and DL, among researchers. Tables 1.5 and 1.6 give a summary and comparison of the extracted features from our survey about various techniques of DL-IoT integration.

In the work Khan et al. [69], the authors use CNN to solve the challenges of segmentation of a brain tumour, which usually shows

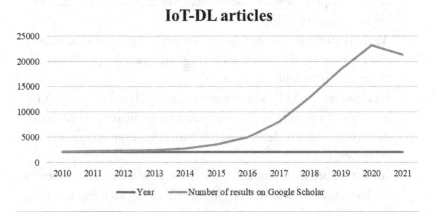

Figure 1.6 Number of results displayed on Google Scholar from 2010 to 2021 for "IoT big data analytics and DL" keywords.

Table 1.5   Summary of Some Useful Frameworks for IoT-DL Integration

FRAMEWORK	ADVANTAGE	DISADVANTAGES
TensorFlow [62]	Supports visualization of data	Slow in training compared to some other frameworks
PyTorch [63]	Supports various models	Consists of low-level APIs
Chainer [64]	Supports easy implementation of architectures	Slower computation in selected scenarios
D4J [65]	Contains visualization tools	Requires longer training time
H2O [66]	Consists of a wide interface range	Not flexible
Theano [67]	Supports various models	Too many low-level APIs
Caffe [68]	Good at CNNs	Poor at RNNs

variations in its appearance. The authors found that basic CNN approaches did not meet the system requirements, so they developed and proposed a novel method which combined CNN and hand-crafted features. The first three hand-crafted features (1: Mean intensity; 2: Histogram of oriented gradients; and 3: Local binary pattern) were computed. Then confidence surface modality is resulted by support vector machine pixel classification. Provided magnetic resonance

Table 1.6   Summary of DL Models

MODEL	IOT DATA INPUT TYPE	NOTES	SUGGESTED IOT APPLICATION DOMAIN ACCORDING TO SUITABILITY
CNN [69]	2D-image, sound etc.	For visual projects, large dataset required for its training	Agriculture, education, medical, etc.
RNN [70]	Time-series, serial data	Uses an internal memory system for processing	Pattern detection
LSTM [71]	Time-series, serial data	Gates protect access to memory cells	Activity recognition of individuals
GAN [72]	Multiple formats and types	Compares between discriminator and generator networks	Image-to-text conversion
RBM [73]	Multiple formats and types	Good in feature extraction and classification	IoT device's energy consumption prediction
DBN [74]	Multiple formats and types	Greedy approach in layer-by-layer training	Fault detection in industrial IoT
AE [75]	Multiple formats and types	Same count of input and output units in its structure. Suitable for unlabelled IoT data	Emotion detection

imaging is then passed through the proposed three-pathway CNN architecture. This shows that most of the time the problem can be resolved by new methods of integration with present technologies. In [70], the authors used DeltaRNN on Xilinx Zynq-7100 FPGA to achieve low-latency computing. The proposed network used consist of single-layer RNN with 256 gated recurrent unit neurons. The microphone setup is also used. The result in microphone setup has achieved 7.1 ms minimum latency and 177 fps maximum throughput. The authors were convinced that RNN makes their system suitable as an IoT computing platform. Authors in [71], used LSTM for air-quality forecasting through IoT. It is difficult to predict accurately from non-linear smog data, so a new algorithm was proposed using LSTM, which is a two-layer prediction model. Sample data was collected over 96 hours in four cities. The author achieved satisfactory results in prediction. In [72], the authors used GAN for an intrusion-detection system using IoT. In the proposed work, every IoT monitor observed itself and also neighbouring nodes to detect external and internal attacks. Moreover, the proposed system does not require any shared datasets among nodes, which is why it can be used in the privacy-sensitive applications of IoT. The proposed system achieved 25% higher precision, 20% higher accuracy, and a 60% lower false-positive rate.

In [73], the authors proposed a network traffic prediction system. They used an enhanced echo-state restricted Boltzmann machine (eERBM). The following functional components of features learning is used, namely supervised nonlinear approximation, information compensation, and input superposition. Theoretical analysis shows that eERBM achieved superior nonlinear approximation. This work was the first attempt in applying eERBM in network-traffic prediction. The authors in [74] proposed a secured architecture for an industrial control system, using DBN and a standard classifier with a support vector machine. The architecture develops two ensemble-based detection algorithms. It uses the network traffic and payload features for the detection model. The proposed solution is useful in large training data scenarios. Lastly, in [75], the authors worked on anomaly detection in industrial edge devices. They used squeezed convolutional variational autoencode for time-series data anomaly detection. The developed model is applied to UCI-datasets, for performance evaluations and further applied to real-world data for indirect model performance comparisons. Fire modules from SqueezeNet are also used.

1.6 Conclusion

IoT and big data are in high demand, as are DL analytics methodologies. This IoT-DL connection has a long way to go from here. With the help of new research in accordance with the integration of the IoT domain with DL techniques, we may achieve tremendous development in the respective domains, which will certainly improve the quality of life of future and present generations. To develop a knowledge of state-of-the-art techniques, we conducted an exhaustive assessment of previous publications on DL approaches in the IoT sector in this chapter. We then discussed the "10 Vs" of IoT big data and several new DL approaches for IoT-DL integration, such as CNN, RNN, LSTM, and GAN. We have included a list of various key DL frameworks that can be used in the IoT arena. Following that, we reviewed some supporting technologies such as tinymotes, edge technology, 5G, etc. Then, we briefly mentioned fog architecture. For rapid IoT-DL prototyping, we also mentioned several development boards, commercial devices, and online datasets. Under real-time IoT, we also explored DL implementation concerns, obstacles, and future considerations. Finally, we conducted a comparison analysis of the various data and facts we discovered during our literature review. According to the findings, IoT-DL integration is becoming a much-needed trend in smart settings, leading to a technology-driven future. The security and privacy concerns with DL-IoT devices must be addressed in the future. Blockchain, for example, must be evaluated and implemented. To combat software vulnerabilities, some hardware-based security solutions should also be created. For IoT networks, an intrusion-detection system with firewalls and authentication must be developed. These types of measures are required for future IoT-DL deployments in the real world.

References

1. Hajjaji, Y., Boulila, W., Farah, I. R., Romdhani, I., & Hussain, A. (2021). Big data and IoT-based applications in smart environments: A systematic review. *Computer Science Review*, *39*, 100318.

2. Xu, T., Fu, Z., Yu, M., Wang, J., Liu, H., & Qiu, T. (2021, May). Blockchain Based Data Protection Framework for IoT in Untrusted Storage. In *2021 IEEE 24th International Conference on Computer Supported Cooperative Work in Design (CSCWD)* (pp. 813–818). IEEE.

3. Serrano, W. (2021). The blockchain random neural network for cyber-secure IoT and 5G infrastructure in smart cities. *Journal of Network and Computer Applications, 175*, 102909.

4. Anbarasan, M., Muthu, B., Sivaparthipan, C. B., Sundarasekar, R., Kadry, S., Krishnamoorthy, S., & Dasel, A. A. (2020). Detection of flood disaster system based on IoT, big data and convolutional deep neural network. *Computer Communications, 150*, 150–157.

5. Shah, S. K., Tariq, Z., & Lee, Y. (2019, December). IoT Based Urban Noise Monitoring in Deep Learning Using Historical Reports. In *2019 IEEE International Conference on Big Data (Big Data)* (pp. 4179–4184). IEEE.

6. Tariq, Z., Shah, S. K., & Lee, Y. (2019, December). Speech Emotion Detection Using IoT Based Deep Learning for Health Care. In *2019 IEEE International Conference on Big Data (Big Data)* (pp. 4191–4196). IEEE.

7. Fang, W., Guo, Y., Liao, W., Ramani, K., & Huang, S. (2020). Big data driven jobs remaining time prediction in discrete manufacturing system: A deep learning-based approach. *International Journal of Production Research, 58*(9), 2751–2766.

8. Muthu, B., Sivaparthipan, C. B., Manogaran, G., Sundarasekar, R., Kadry, S., Shanthini, A., & Dasel, A. (2020). IOT based wearable sensor for diseases prediction and symptom analysis in healthcare sector. *Peer-to-Peer Networking and Applications, 13*(6), 2123–2134.

9. Rajan Jeyaraj, P., & Nadar, E. R. S. (2019). Smart-monitor: Patient monitoring system for IoT-based healthcare system using deep learning. *IETE Journal of Research, 68*(2), 1435–1442.

10. Hossain, M. S., & Muhammad, G. (2019). Emotion recognition using deep learning approach from audio–visual emotional big data. *Information Fusion, 49*, 69–78.

11. Yao, C., Wu, S., Liu, Z., & Li, P. (2019). A deep learning model for predicting chemical composition of gallstones with big data in medical Internet of Things. *Future Generation Computer Systems, 94*, 140–147.

12. Chowdury, M. S. U., Emran, T. B., Ghosh, S., Pathak, A., Alam, M. M., Absar, N., ... Hossain, M. S. (2019). IoT based real-time river water quality monitoring system. *Procedia Computer Science, 155*, 161–168.

13. Ali, M., Anjum, A., Yaseen, M. U., Zamani, A. R., Balouek-Thomert, D., Rana, O., & Parashar, M. (2018, May). Edge Enhanced Deep Learning System for Large-Scale Video Stream Analytics. In *2018 IEEE 2nd International Conference on Fog and Edge Computing (ICFEC)* (pp. 1–10). IEEE.

14. Chauhan, D., Kumar, A., Bedi, P., Athavale, V. A., Veeraiah, D., & Pratap, B. R. (2021). An effective face recognition system based on Cloud based IoT with a deep learning model. *Microprocessors and Microsystems, 81*, 103726.

15. Zhou, X., Liang, W., Kevin, I., Wang, K., Wang, H., Yang, L. T., & Jin, Q. (2020). Deep-learning-enhanced human activity recognition for Internet of healthcare things. *IEEE Internet of Things Journal, 7*(7), 6429–6438.
16. Garg, S., Kaur, K., Kumar, N., Kaddoum, G., Zomaya, A. Y., & Ranjan, R. (2019). A hybrid deep learning-based model for anomaly detection in cloud datacenter networks. *IEEE Transactions on Network and Service Management, 16*(3), 924–935.
17. Ciampi, F., Demi, S., Magrini, A., Marzi, G., & Papa, A. (2021). Exploring the impact of big data analytics capabilities on business model innovation: The mediating role of entrepreneurial orientation. *Journal of Business Research, 123*, 1–13.
18. Rathore, M. M., Shah, S. A., Shukla, D., Bentafat, E., & Bakiras, S. (2021). The role of AI, machine learning, and big data in digital twinning: A systematic literature review, challenges, and opportunities. *IEEE Access, 9*, 32030–32052.
19. Rehman, A., Naz, S., & Razzak, I. (2021). Leveraging big data analytics in healthcare enhancement: Trends, challenges and opportunities. *Multimedia Systems, 28*(4), 1339–1371.
20. Biermann, O., Koya, S. F., Corkish, C., Abdalla, S. M., & Galea, S. (2021). Food, big data, and decision-making: A scoping review—The 3-D commission. *Journal of Urban Health, 98*(1), 69–78.
21. Minaee, S., Boykov, Y. Y., Porikli, F., Plaza, A. J., Kehtarnavaz, N., & Terzopoulos, D. (2021). Image segmentation using deep learning: A survey. IEEE Transactions on Pattern Analysis and Machine Intelligence, *44*(7), 3523–3542.
22. Ye, M., Shen, J., Lin, G., Xiang, T., Shao, L., & Hoi, S. C. (2021). Deep learning for person re-identification: A survey and outlook. *IEEE Transactions on Pattern Analysis and Machine Intelligence, 44*(6), 2872–2893.
23. Wang, W., Lai, Q., Fu, H., Shen, J., Ling, H., & Yang, R. (2021). Salient object detection in the deep learning era: An in-depth survey. *IEEE Transactions on Pattern Analysis and Machine Intelligence,* 44(6), 3239–3259.
24. Albawi, S., Mohammed, T. A., & Al-Zawi, S. (2017, August). Understanding of a Convolutional Neural Network. In *2017 International Conference on Engineering and Technology (ICET)* (pp. 1–6). IEEE.
25. Yin, C., Zhu, Y., Fei, J., & He, X. (2017). A deep learning approach for intrusion detection using recurrent neural networks. *IEEE Access, 5*, 21954–21961.
26. Le, X. H., Ho, H. V., Lee, G., & Jung, S. (2019). Application of long short-term memory (LSTM) neural network for flood forecasting. *Water, 11*(7), 1387.
27. Creswell, A., White, T., Dumoulin, V., Arulkumaran, K., Sengupta, B., & Bharath, A. A. (2018). Generative adversarial networks: An overview. *IEEE Signal Processing Magazine, 35*(1), 53–65.
28. Wang, G., Qiao, J., Bi, J., Jia, Q. S., & Zhou, M. (2019). An adaptive deep belief network with sparse restricted Boltzmann machines.

IEEE Transactions on Neural Networks and Learning Systems, 31(10), 4217–4228.

29. Zhao, L., Zhou, Y., Lu, H., & Fujita, H. (2019). Parallel computing method of deep belief networks and its application to traffic flow prediction. *Knowledge-Based Systems, 163,* 972–987.

30. Huang, F., Zhang, J., Zhou, C., Wang, Y., Huang, J., & Zhu, L. (2020). A deep learning algorithm using a fully connected sparse autoencoder neural network for landslide susceptibility prediction. *Landslides, 17*(1), 217–229.

31. Dokic, K., Martinovic, M., & Mandusic, D. (2020, September). Inference Speed and Quantisation of Neural Networks with TensorFlow Lite for Microcontrollers Framework. In *2020 5th South-East Europe Design Automation, Computer Engineering, Computer Networks and Social Media Conference (SEEDA-CECNSM)* (pp. 1–6). IEEE.

32. Jain, A., Awan, A. A., Subramoni, H., & Panda, D. K. (2019, November). Scaling Tensorflow, Pytorch, and Mxnet Using Mvapich2 for High-Performance Deep Learning on Frontera. In *2019 IEEE/ACM Third Workshop on Deep Learning on Supercomputers (DLS)* (pp. 76–83). IEEE.

33. Ruedeeniraman, N., Ikeda, M., & Barolli, L. (2019, July). Tensorflow: A Vegetable Classification System and its Performance Evaluation. In *International Conference on Innovative Mobile and Internet Services in Ubiquitous Computing* (pp. 132–141). Springer, Cham.

34. Lang, S., Bravo-Marquez, F., Beckham, C., Hall, M., & Frank, E. (2019). Wekadeeplearning4j: A deep learning package for weka based on deeplearning4j. *Knowledge-Based Systems, 178,* 48–50.

35. KB, S. K., Krishna, G., Bhalaji, N., & Chithra, S. (2019). BCI cinematics–A pre-release analyser for movies using H2O deep learning platform. *Computers & Electrical Engineering, 74,* 547–556.

36. Chung, Y., Ahn, S., Yang, J., & Lee, J. (2017). Comparison of deep learning frameworks: About theano, tensorflow, and cognitive toolkit. *Journal of Intelligence and Information Systems, 23*(2), 1–17.

37. Awan, A. A., Hamidouche, K., Hashmi, J. M., & Panda, D. K. (2017, January). S-Caffe: Co-Designing MPI Runtimes and Caffe for Scalable Deep Learning on Modern GPU Clusters. In *Proceedings of the 22nd ACM SIGPLAN Symposium on Principles and Practice of Parallel Programming* (pp. 193–205).

38. Asci, M., Ileri, C. U., & Dagdeviren, O. (2019, September). Performance Evaluation of Capacitated Minimum Spanning Tree Algorithms for Wireless Sensor Networks. In *2019 4th International Conference on Computer Science and Engineering (UBMK)* (pp. 1–5). IEEE.

39. Kaleem, Z., Yousaf, M., Qamar, A., Ahmad, A., Duong, T. Q., Choi, W., & Jamalipour, A. (2019). UAV-empowered disaster-resilient edge architecture for delay-sensitive communication. *IEEE Network, 33*(6), 124–132.

40. Ahmad, W. S. H. M. W., Radzi, N. A. M., Samidi, F. S., Ismail, A., Abdullah, F., Jamaludin, M. Z., & Zakaria, M. (2020). 5G technology: Towards dynamic spectrum sharing using cognitive radio networks. *IEEE Access, 8,* 14460–14488.

41. Tung, F., & Mori, G. (2018). Deep neural network compression by in-parallel pruning-quantization. *IEEE Transactions on Pattern Analysis and Machine Intelligence, 42*(3), 568–579.

42. Song, L., Chen, F., Zhuo, Y., Qian, X., Li, H., & Chen, Y. (2020, February). Accpar: Tensor Partitioning for Heterogeneous Deep Learning Accelerators. In *2020 IEEE International Symposium on High Performance Computer Architecture (HPCA)* (pp. 342–355). IEEE.

43. Liu, W., Lombardi, F., & Schulte, M. (2020). Approximate computing: From circuits to applications. *Proceedings of the IEEE, 108*(12), 2103–2107.

44. Bang, S., Wang, J., Li, Z., Gao, C., Kim, Y., Dong, Q., ... Sylvester, D. (2017, February). 14.7 a 288µw Programmable Deep-Learning Processor with 270kb On-Chip Weight Storage Using Non-Uniform Memory Hierarchy for Mobile Intelligence. In *2017 IEEE International Solid-State Circuits Conference (ISSCC)* (pp. 250–251). IEEE.

45. Li, H., Ota, K., & Dong, M. (2018). Learning IoT in edge: Deep learning for the Internet of Things with edge computing. *IEEE network, 32*(1), 96–101.

46. Wang, D., Chen, D., Song, B., Guizani, N., Yu, X., & Du, X. (2018). From IoT to 5G I-IoT: The next generation IoT-based intelligent algorithms and 5G technologies. *IEEE Communications Magazine, 56*(10), 114–120.

47. Hwang, J., Uddin, A. S., & Bae, S. H. (2021). A layer-wise extreme network compression for super resolution. *IEEE Access, 9*, 93998–94009.

48. Kong, H., Huai, S., Liu, D., Zhang, L., Chen, H., Zhu, S., ... Lewis, M. A. (2021). EDLAB: A benchmark for edge deep learning accelerators. *IEEE Design & Test, 39*(3), 8–17.

49. Masadeh, M., Hasan, O., & Tahar, S. (2021). Machine-learning-based self-tunable design of approximate computing. *IEEE Transactions on Very Large Scale Integration (VLSI) Systems, 29*(4), 800–813.

50. Kimovski, D., Ijaz, H., Saurabh, N., & Prodan, R. (2018, May). Adaptive Nature-Inspired Fog Architecture. In *2018 IEEE 2nd International Conference on Fog and Edge Computing (ICFEC)* (pp. 1–8). IEEE.

51. Plaza, P., Sancristobal, E., Carro, G., Castro, M., & Ruiz, E. (2018). Wireless Development Boards to Connect the World. In Online Engineering & Internet of Things (pp. 19–27). Springer, Cham.

52. Hoy, M. B. (2018). Alexa, Siri, Cortana, and more: An introduction to voice assistants. *Medical Reference Services Quarterly, 37*(1), 81–88.

53. Tajbakhsh, N., Jeyaseelan, L., Li, Q., Chiang, J. N., Wu, Z., & Ding, X. (2020). Embracing imperfect datasets: A review of deep learning solutions for medical image segmentation. *Medical Image Analysis, 63*, 101693.

54. Coccia, M. (2020). Deep learning technology for improving cancer care in society: New directions in cancer imaging driven by artificial intelligence. *Technology in Society, 60*, 101198.

55. Aggarwal, S., & Sharma, S. (2021). Voice Based Deep Learning Enabled User Interface Design for Smart Home Application System. *2nd International Conference on Communication, Computing & Industry 4.0(C214)*, 1–6, https://doi.org/10.1109/C2I454156.2021.9689435.

56. Juyal, A., Sharma, S., & Matta, P. (2021). Deep Learning Methods for Object Detection in Autonomous Vehicles. In *2021 5th International Conference on Trends in Electronics and Informatics (ICOEI)* (pp. 751–755). IEEE.

57. Agarwal, V., & Sharma, S. (2021). A Survey of Deep Learning Techniques to Improve Radio Resource Management in Vehicular Communication Network. In *International Conference on Sustainable Advanced Computing* (ICSAC).

58. Ghildiyal, A, Sharma, S., & Kumar, A. (2021). Street Cleanliness Monitoring System Using Deep Learning. In *2021 Third International Conference on Intelligent Communication Technologies and Virtual Mobile Networks (ICICV)* (pp. 868–873). IEEE.

59. Juyal, P., & Sharma, S. (2020). Detecting the Infectious Area Along with Disease Using Deep Learning in Tomato Plant Leaves. In *2020 3rd International Conference on Intelligent Sustainable Systems (ICISS)* (pp. 328–332). IEEE.

60. Juyal, P., & Sharma, S. (2020). Estimation of Tree Volume Using Mask R-CNN Based Deep Learning. In *2020 11th International Conference on Computing, Communication and Networking Technologies (ICCCNT)* (pp. 1–6). IEEE.

61. Sharma, S., Ghanshala, K. K., & Mohan, S. (2018). A Security System Using Deep Learning Approach for Internet of Vehicles (IoV). In *2018 9th IEEE Annual Ubiquitous Computing, Electronics & Mobile Communication Conference (UEMCON)* (pp. 1–5). IEEE.

62. Haghighat, E., & Juanes, R. (2021). Sciann: A keras/tensorflow wrapper for scientific computations and physics-informed deep learning using artificial neural networks. *Computer Methods in Applied Mechanics and Engineering, 373*, 113552.

63. Ashraf, M., Ahmad, S. M., Ganai, N. A., Shah, R. A., Zaman, M., Khan, S. A., & Shah, A. A. (2021). Prediction of Cardiovascular Disease Through Cutting-Edge Deep Learning Technologies: An Empirical Study Based on TensorFlow, Pytorch and Keras. In *International Conference on Innovative Computing and Communications* (pp. 239–255). Springer, Singapore.

64. Hagargi, P. A. (2021). The Effective Use of Deep Learning Network with Software Framework for Medical Healthcare. In Techno-Societal 2020 (pp. 225–240). Springer, Cham.

65. Shah, B., & Bhavsar, H. (2021). Overview of Deep Learning in Food Image Classification for Dietary Assessment System. In Intelligent Systems, Technologies and Applications (pp. 265–285). Springer, Singapore.

66. Indulkar, Y. (2021, March). PUBG Winner Ranking Prediction Using R Interface 'h2o' Scalable Machine Learning Platform. In *2021 International Conference on Emerging Smart Computing and Informatics (ESCI)* (pp. 300–305). IEEE.

67. Bhargavi, K. (2021). Deep learning architectures and tools: A comprehensive survey. *Deep Learning Applications and Intelligent Decision Making in Engineering*, 55–75. https://doi.org/10.4018/978-1-7998-2108-3.ch002.

68. Yang, C. T., Liu, J. C., Chan, Y. W., Kristiani, E., & Kuo, C. F. (2021). Performance benchmarking of deep learning framework on Intel Xeon Phi. *The Journal of Supercomputing, 77*(3), 2486–2510.
69. Khan, H., Shah, P. M., Shah, M. A., ul Islam, S., & Rodrigues, J. J. (2020). Cascading handcrafted features and convolutional neural network for IoT-enabled brain tumor segmentation. *Computer Communications, 153,* 196–207.
70. Gao, C., Braun, S., Kiselev, I., Anumula, J., Delbruck, T., & Liu, S. C. (2019, May). Real-Time Speech Recognition for IoT Purpose Using a Delta Recurrent Neural Network Accelerator. In *2019 IEEE International Symposium on Circuits and Systems (ISCAS)* (pp. 1–5). IEEE.
71. Wang, B., Kong, W., Guan, H., & Xiong, N. N. (2019). Air quality forecasting based on gated recurrent long short term memory model in Internet of Things. *IEEE Access, 7,* 69524–69534.
72. Ferdowsi, A., & Saad, W. (2019, December). Generative Adversarial Networks for Distributed Intrusion Detection in the Internet of Things. In *2019 IEEE Global Communications Conference (GLOBECOM)* (pp. 1–6). IEEE.
73. Sun, X., Ma, S., Li, Y., Wang, D., Li, Z., Wang, N., & Gui, G. (2019). Enhanced echo-state restricted Boltzmann machines for network traffic prediction. *IEEE Internet of Things Journal, 7*(2), 1287–1297.
74. Huda, S., Yearwood, J., Hassan, M. M., & Almogren, A. (2018). Securing the operations in SCADA-IoT platform based industrial control system using ensemble of deep belief networks. *Applied Soft Computing, 71,* 66–77.
75. Kim, D., Yang, H., Chung, M., Cho, S., Kim, H., Kim, M., … Kim, E. (2018, March). Squeezed Convolutional Variational Autoencoder for Unsupervised Anomaly Detection in Edge Device Industrial Internet of Things. In *2018 International Conference on Information and Computer Technologies (ICICT)* (pp. 67–71). IEEE.

2

IoMT-Based Smart Health Monitoring

The Future of Health Care

INDRASHIS MITRA, YASHI SRIVASTAVA, KANANBALA RAY, AND TEJASWINI KAR

School of Electronics Engineering, KIIT Deemed to be University, Bhubaneswar, Odisha, India

Contents

2.1 Introduction to IoMT

The worldwide population of elderly people is expected to more than quadruple over the next three decades, reaching 1.5 billion in 2050. In this scenario, there is an epidemiological and demographic shift that is affecting the health state of the entire population. The Internet of Medical Things (IoMT) plays an important role in this scenario by ensuring remote monitoring of elderly patients during crucial times. The IoT is a notion that encompasses anyone, at any time, in any location, with any service, on any network. It is a megatrend in next-generation technologies that has the potential to influence the whole business continuum. It may be defined as the connectivity of uniquely

DOI: 10.1201/9781003264545-2

identified smart items and devices inside today's Internet infrastructure, with additional benefits. Readers can further refer to a variety of journal articles [1–4] for a deeper, more vivid understanding of IoT. In the present era, IoMT-based smart monitoring techniques for health conditions are gaining popularity. The IoT-based smart health monitoring framework is a new paradigm in the healthcare industry toward better medical-care administration for individuals [5]. Currently, hospitals and medical-care organizations are transforming from a customary way to a modernized patient-focused methodology. Conventionally, specialists are required during medical emergencies for the physical examination of patients. Likewise, real-time readings from IoT-based devices provide the professionals with necessary data to guide and monitor a patient's health on a regular basis [6].

IoT has turned into one of the most influential communication paradigms of the 21st century. In the IoT environment, all items in our everyday life become part of the World Wide Web because of their correspondence and processing capacities. Through prompt detection, continuous fitness monitoring can save up to 60% of human lives and aid in real-time monitoring of patients' health indicators [7, 8]. Heart rate is one of the fundamental physiological points, essential for observing and providing results for each patient, thereby assisting in the maintenance of good health [9]. To keep people motivated and healthy, a quick, open, and modern medical-care framework is increasingly important, and it turns out to be more effective in saving money and decreasing sickness. In this chapter, an upgraded medical-care observation framework is portrayed, which is an advanced mobile phone-based system intended to offer remote methodology and social help to members. IoT, by and large, has arisen as a popular answer for many day-to-day issues. Intensive care and critical care units require broad consideration of patients having critical conditions and continuous administration of specialists along with attendants, which isn't generally conceivable because of the enormous number of patients [9, 10].

With an improvement in innovation and the scaling down of sensors, there have been endeavours to implement innovation in different areas to enhance human life. Developments have made it easier to distinguish between daily life actions and accidents, thus, helping in delivering timely assistance to the needy [10]. Lindemann et al. integrated a tri-axial accelerometer into a hearing aid device and used thresholds for acceleration and velocity to judge whether a fall had occurred [11]. One principal zone of exploration is the medical services area. Subsequently, this venture is an endeavor to tackle the medical services issue that is prevalent currently [12, 13]. The fundamental goal of the undertaking was to plan a distant medical-care framework. It is divided into three main sections. The first phase involved using sensors to locate the patient's vitals; the second involved sending information to a Bluetooth-connected Android app on a mobile phone and displaying data on a dashboard; and the third involved transmitting the recognized data to faraway individuals.

2.2 Related Work and Findings

Many articles can be found in the literature in the field of smart health monitoring. Tamilselvi et al. [7] built a health-monitoring system that can track fundamental symptoms of a patient such as heart rate, oxygen saturation percentage (SpO_2), body temperature, and eye movement. Heartbeat, SpO_2, temperature, and eye-blink sensors were employed as capturing components, while an Arduino UNO was used as a processing device. Although the designed system was deployed, no specific performance measurements for any patient were given. Trivedi et al. [8] proposed a mobile device-controlled Arduino-based health parameter monitoring system. The analogue sensor data was captured and delivered to the Arduino UNO board. The captured analogue values are transformed into digital data via the inbuilt analogue to digital converter. The physical properties were transferred to the designed gadget through Bluetooth. The Bluetooth gadget made use of a module that didn't cover a large region.

In an IoT setting, Acharya et al. [9] presented a healthcare monitoring kit. Heartbeat, electrocardiogram (ECG), body temperature, and respiration were among the fundamental health metrics tracked by the designed system. The main hardware components employed here are the pulse sensor, temperature sensor, blood pressure sensor, ECG sensor, and Raspberry Pi. Sensor data was captured and forwarded to a Raspberry Pi for processing before being sent back to the IoT network. The system's main flaw is that no data visualization interfaces have been created. Bourke [10] used two tri-axial accelerometers on the trunk and thigh to derive four thresholds–upper and lower thresholds for the trunk and thigh, respectively. A decline would happen if any of the four thresholds were exceeded. The difficulty with this strategy is that other activities of daily living (ADLs), such as sitting down quickly and leaping also involve significant vertical acceleration. As a result, relying just on acceleration to identify falls leads to a high number of false positives [14–16].

It is observed from the literature review that most of the works include a set of sensors for monitoring health parameters and displaying them on a Web page. But that has its own set of challenges, such as the Web page may not be calibrated for display on any screen size, like that of laptops and mobile phones. Or the sensors measuring the parameters might take up a lot of space and lead to a cumbersome, uncomfortable device that must be worn by the patient. Various fall-detection technologies have been offered in the past to establish a dependable monitoring system for senior persons with high accuracy, sensitivity, and specificity criteria [17]. Table 2.1 shows the description of the sensors.

Table 2.1 Description of the Sensors

SL. NO.	SENSOR	FEATURES
1.	MLX 90614 [15]	Touchless InfraRed Digital Temperature Sensor Range: −70°C to 382°C Voltage range: 3–5V Dimensions: 11mm × 17mm $S_M$bus compatible interface
2.	MAX 30102 [16]	Integrated heartrate monitor and pulse oximeter biosensor Power: 1.8 V; 5.0 V supply for internal LEDs Dimensions: 20.3 × 15.2 mm Weight: 1.1 g I2C compatible communication interface LED peak-to-peak wavelength: 660 nm/880 nm LED power supply voltage: 3.3~5 V Detection signal type: light reflection signal (PPG) Output signal interface: I2C communication interface Voltage: 1.8~3.3V~5V (optional) Board reserved assembly hole size: 0.5 x 8.5 mm Main power input terminal: 1.8–5 V 3-bit pad
3.	MPU 6050 [17]	3-axis gyroscope and a 3-axis accelerometer I2C interfacing: 2 aux pins Resistor: 4.7K (pull-up), 4.7K (pull-down) Data propagation: I2C bus Voltage change detector: 16-bit ADC

Fall-detection mechanisms will continue evolving in the next few years [18]. Therefore, in our proposal, we presented a less bulky display that is also easier to grasp than what is presented in [5]. Overall, the ideation is similar to what is presented in Ref. [6], but it vastly improves upon the presentation by enabling a seamless transition between laptop as well as mobile screens. The dashboard and mobile connectors are new features that allow sharing patient data with others who are far away in a simple and painless way.

2.3 Proposed Model and Approach

2.3.1 Objective of the Work

The most important idea behind this project is to design, develop, and implement a smart patient healthcare monitoring system. The sensors used here are embedded in the body of the patient to sense parameters like heartbeat and temperature. These sensors are connected to a master unit that calculates all the values. These values are then transmitted by leveraging IoT cloud technology to the base [19]. From the base station, these can be easily accessed by the doctor at some other location. Thus, based on the temperature and heartbeat values that the doctor can easily refer to, using Web as well as phone applications, the physician can determine the state of the patient and necessary measures can be taken. Furthermore, the methodology also includes a system to detect if an aged patient falls down and alert the caregivers so that they can receive immediate help. A pre-fall phase, a falling phase, an impact phase, a resting phase, and a recovery phase can all be classified as phases of a fall [20].

2.3.2 System Approach

The complete system for monitoring the required parameters is shown in Figure 2.1. The first step for the functioning of the system is to initialize the sensors for the collection of data for monitoring. The patient data, i.e., temperature and blood pressure, are then read and compared with predetermined values. If the values are found to violate them, the data are sent and respective people are alerted through a buzzer sound. The doctor receives this data and can take necessary action, thus, not wasting the golden hour, which is vital for the patient's immediate care.

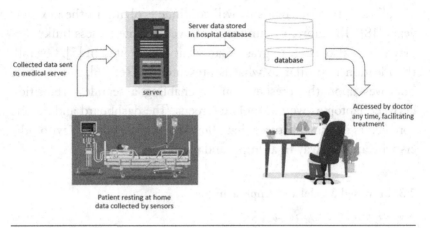

Figure 2.1   Patient monitoring workflow.

The second part of the project is the fall detection mechanism, which is based on classical physics. The reasons behind choosing the Cartesian coordinate system are:

   i. Gravity is always perpendicular to the ground.
  ii. If a vest is worn on the body, then the orientation of the vest and trunk are always the same. The origin is assumed to be near the neck, aligned to the geodetic system.

At any given time t, acceleration along the three axes are denoted as $A_x(t)$, $A_y(t)$ and $A_z(t)$ separately, namely A(t) = {Ax(t), Ay(t), Az(t)} [21]. The resulting acceleration $\alpha(t)$ can be found using Equation (2.1)

$$A(t) = \sqrt{Ax(t)^2 + Ay(t)^2 + Az(t)^2} \tag{2.1}$$

The gravitational components are essentially an approximation. The trunk angle $\theta(t)$ can be calculated using Equation (2.2):

$$\theta(t) = \cos^{-1}\left(\frac{Ax(t)}{\sqrt{Ax(t)^2 + Ay(t)^2 + Az(t)^2}}\right) \tag{2.2}$$

2.3.3 Data Acquisition

A sensor board, measuring 65 mm × 40 mm × 7 mm, is appropriate for use in a vest. It has a class 2 Bluetooth module and a low-power micro-controller. The default transmission rate of the module is 15,200 bps with the maximum range being 10 m. The tri-axial accelerometer can measure up to ±16 g with full-scale reading of the gyroscope being ±2000°/s. The sampled data from both of these are acquired and transmitted to a smartphone.

Human activities tend to occur at frequencies less than 20 Hz, hence the sampling frequency of human activities can be set at 100 Hz. The board can acquire tri-axial accelerations and angular velocity, which can be relayed directly to a smartphone. As falls are distinguished by great angular velocity and rapid acceleration, four subcategories of ADLs and two types of falls are proposed so that the difference between ADLs and falls can be found. ADLs include Sitting (S_d), Squatting down (S_q), Walking (W_k), and Bowing (B_w). Falls include Backward fall ($B_{w\text{-Fall}}$) and Sideward fall ($S_{w\text{-Fall}}$). Figure 2.2 illustrates an overview of the complete algorithm. Figure 2.2(a) indicates the patient metric monitoring and Figure 2.2(b) indicates the fall detection workflow.

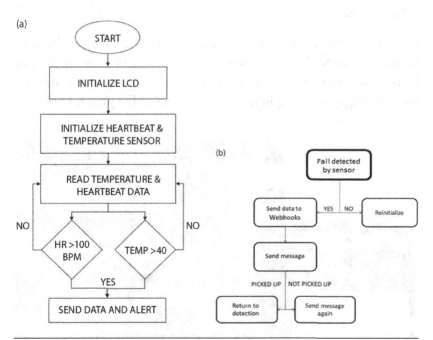

Figure 2.2 Overview of the complete algorithm. Flow diagram of metrics monitoring (a); fall detection flow chart (b).

2.3.4 IFTTT Integration

If This Then That (IFTTT) is an Internet service through which sequences of conditional statements, called applets, can be created. Using these applets, emails can be exchanged, music played, messages exchanged, notifications received and sent, etc. The information exchange is facilitated in real time through Webhooks. This is a huge benefit since it alerts the caregivers about the condition of the elderly and makes it easier for them to take prompt action. This is achieved by using IFTTT to send SMS notifications to a mobile phone when a fall is detected.

After setting up the desired connection and step-by-step execution of the instructions, the results can be displayed on the mobile interface. The complete experimental set up and the display of the output message in response to a sample fall detection on the mobile interface are depicted in Figure 2.3. The parameters that are being monitored by the sensors are checked via a Website that will display the sensor data in a graphical way for better understanding and to keep check on the threshold limits of the parameters.

2.3.5 IoT–Dashboard

Dashboards are a means to visualize data, giving all users the ability to understand the analytics essential for their business or project. Generic users can use this to participate in and understand the analytics through data compilation and see trends. The plan is to make a

Figure 2.3 Notifications from MPU6050 via IFTTT integration displayed on a cellphone.

Web-based dashboard for effective and easy monitoring and understanding of the various health parameters of the patient, such as blood pressure and temperature.

Thinger.io is a free, cloud IoT platform that helps to prototype, scale, and manage connected products in an easy way. The aim is to regularize IoT usage, making it reachable to the whole world and modernizing the evolution of big IoT projects. It has a connected platform that expedites communication between devices, software architecture, and various data toolkits, plugins, and integrations to manage and work with generated information. The complete connectivity structure of the thinger.io platform is given in Figure 2.4.

The thinger.io dashboard system is a property that lets us design data presentation interfaces easily. While eliminating the need for coding, it is made in such a way that various elements from an inventory can be selected. Moreover, the entire layout can be configured using point-and-click methodology. Using the configuration forms, it is possible to set the sampling interval, data sources, and other characteristics for each widget.

Normal Website coding (using HTML, CSS, and JS) could have been used to design a Website for displaying the parameters. But since it was open source, easy to use, and most importantly, it was convenient to create simple, attractive dashboards using this platform, the choice was obvious. Moreover, there is a vast array of devices supported by thinger.io. So, a wide variety of devices can be easily integrated into the project, irrespective of the manufacturers or properties.

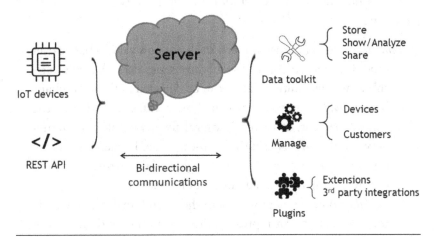

Figure 2.4   Connectivity of the thinger.io platform.

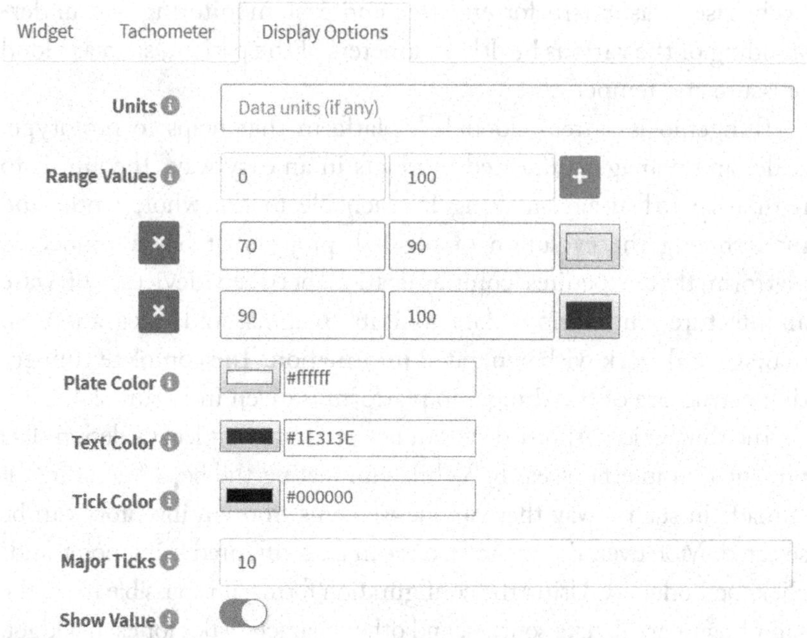

Widget	Tachometer	Display Options

Units ⓘ	Data units (if any)		
Range Values ⓘ	0	100	+
✕	70	90	☐
✕	90	100	■
Plate Color ⓘ	☐ #ffffff		
Text Color ⓘ	■ #1E313E		
Tick Color ⓘ	■ #000000		
Major Ticks ⓘ	10		
Show Value ⓘ	◯		

Figure 2.5　Illustration of widget selection.

Figure 2.5 is an illustration of defined widgets and how they can be configured for displaying customized results, such as colour, text type, units, etc. It is possible to share dashboards with others through a hyperlink. To analyse data from different devices of the same type, dashboards can be configured using appropriate templates.

The following is a description of various widgets and their parameters:

Time-series chart: A time-series chart shows how values change over time. It is convenient to display time-series data. A single variable as well as multiple values can be depicted in the same chart.

A Donut chart: A graph that can show a value, rounded to the nearest percent. It is highly useful for a variable fluctuating between the largest and the smallest value. In such a scenario, it is appropriate to represent a single variable whilst updating it in real-time from a data bucket or a gadget.

Text/Value: A convenient widget to show random data, especially text that is unfit for representation with other widgets. It can display data from connected devices as well as data buckets.

Clock: Can display the present time in the local time zone or in UTC. It is convenient when processes are being monitored in real time.

Dashboard Tab: An extra page that helps to simplify navigation between interlinked consoles and helps to arrange the data visualization. Each tab might have varying widgets and data sources, but all the tabs have the same configuration settings (widget border-radius, column index, etc.). There is also the benefit of keeping all unused tabs open so that no real-time data are lost when switching tabs.

2.3.6 IoT–Blynk

The parameters that are being monitored by the different sensors are visualized remotely on smartphones via the Blynk app, which has a back-end server that provides data on request and is supported by a wide array of libraries integrating various features, such as different connections, no laptop needed, etc. The entire organization of the Blynk app is demonstrated in Figure 2.6. Thus, a quality GUI experience can be provided to the customers, i.e., the relatives and family members of the patient. By using the Blynk app, anyone who has been

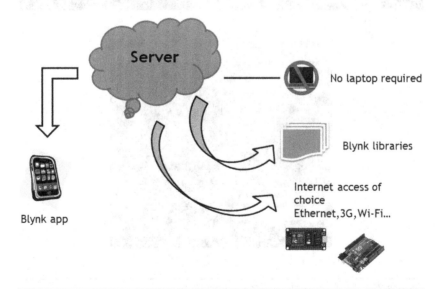

Figure 2.6   Organization of the Blynk cloud.

given the QR code can download the app, which will contain the required project for metrics monitoring. This approach will reduce the amount of panic within family members and will provide a suitable environment and time duration for the best possible outcome.

Blynk helps to plot the graphical representation of data that will be given by the sensors that are being used. It uses a virtual pin concept through which data can be pushed from the Node MCU to the Blynk mobile app widgets. The data can also travel from the widgets to the Node MCU via the ESP8266 Wi-Fi module present. Blynk Inc.'s Virtual Pin is a feature that facilitates data exchange between hardware and the Blynk mobile app. Sample layout illustrations of the Blynk app are shown in Figures 2.7a and b.

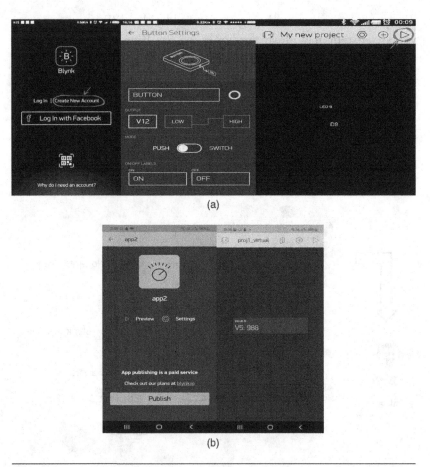

(a)

(b)

Figures 2.7   Sample Blynk app layout illustrations (a) and (b).

2.4 Conclusions

This chapter described a system to effectively use technology for the benefit of the healthcare domain. The entire focus was mainly on two objectives. The first one was a smart health-monitoring system to collect the health history of patients with a unique ID and store it in a database so that doctors did not need to spend much time in search of the report and be able to give analysis right from the dashboard. The monitoring of all patients from multiple locations is one of the major obstacles in the introduction of IoT for healthcare applications [22]. Any healthcare procedure being done will be updated and reflected in the dashboard itself. The latter is the wearable sensor-based fall-detection system for elderly people that tracks their movements and identifies falls by analysing deviations in readings from daily activities, automatically sending a request or an alert for help to the caregivers. The capacity to identify falls when patients are unsupervised might enhance the prognosis for victims of falls [23]. In today's mobile-connected world, it's more convenient to receive notifications on a phone than through a Web-based site, which is exactly what this device did. Furthermore, with the vivid crystal-clear display, the combination of the Blynk app platform and the thinger.io dashboard feature makes it simple for a lay person to grasp the variations in patient data. The features of the dashboard allow presentation of the data using various charts that are instrumental in conveying and displaying the results over a period of time, thus, helping doctors to understand any fluctuations in health parameters and make effective decisions for the patient treatment.

Exploratory work based on Wireless Sensor Network (WSN) is the initial IoT-based healthcare research effort [12, 24]. This is an expansion of existing work that has already been carried out. However, there are a few shortcomings to this, too. A basic knowledge of the operation must be learned by the caregivers. More sensors can be connected to collect more information. Also, both the caregiver and the wearer should know how to protect the sensors from water damage or other physical damage. Though the medical sector was slow to adopt the first stage of IoT technology as compared to other sectors, the new interest in the Internet of Medical Things (IoMT) proved to be revolutionary in today's world. It is set to transform how we keep people healthy and safe, while bearing costs in mind. The IoMT is an amalgamation of applications and medical devices that connect Medicare IT systems via different network technologies. The technology can reduce needless hospital visits along with decreasing the load on the healthcare sector by connecting patients and physicians. The suggested project is reasonable and is market-based. With easily available, secure data at their fingertips, it is possible for the healthcare sector to take huge strides toward progress and development for the betterment of humanity. Thus, it can be deduced that this will have a huge impact on the available healthcare scene.

References

[1]. J. Höller, V. Tsiatsis, C. Mulligan, S. Karnouskos, S. Avesand and D. Boyle, From Machine-to-Machine to the Internet of Things: Introduction to a New Age of Intelligence, Amsterdam, The Netherlands: Elsevier, 2014.

[2]. G. Kortuem, F. Kawsar, D. Fitton and V. Sundramoorthy, "Smart objects as building blocks for the Internet of Things", *IEEE Internet Computing.*, vol. 14, pp. 44–51, Jan./Feb. 2010.

[3]. K. Romer, B. Ostermaier, F. Mattern, M. Fahrmair and W. Kellerer, "Real-time search for real-world entities: A survey", *Proceedings of the IEEE*, vol. 98, no. 11, pp. 1887–1902, Nov. 2010.

[4]. D. Guinard, V. Trifa and E. Wilde, "A resource oriented architecture for the Web of Things", *Proceedings of the Internet Things (IOT)*, pp. 1–8, 2010, https://doi.org/10.1109/IOT.2010.5678452.ookref>

[5]. Md. M. Islam, A. Rahaman and Md. R. Islam, *Development of Smart Healthcare Monitoring System in IoT Environment*, Springer Nature Singapore Pte Ltd. https://doi.org/10.1007/s42979-020-00195-y.

[6]. N. Deepak, C. H. Rajendra Prasad and S. Sanjay Kumar, "Patient health monitoring using IOT", *International Journal of Innovative Technology and Exploring Engineering*, vol. 8, 454–457, 2018.

[7]. V. Tamilselvi, S. Sribalaji, P. Vigneshwaran, P. Vinu and J. Geetharamani, IoT based health monitoring system. In: *2020 6th International conference on advanced computing and communication systems (ICACCS)*, IEEE, pp. 386–9, 2020.

[8]. S. Trivedi and A. N. Cheeran, Android based health parameter monitoring. In: *2017 International conference on intelligent computing and control systems (ICICCS)*, IEEE, pp. 1145–9, 2017.

[9]. A. D. Acharya and S. N. Patil, IoT based health care monitoring kit. In: *2020 Fourth international conference on computing methodologies and communication (ICCMC)*, IEEE, pp. 363–8, 2020.

[10]. A. K. Bourke, J. V. O'Brien and G. M. Lyons, "Evaluation of a threshold-based tri-axial accelerometer fall detection algorithm", *Gait and Posture*, vol. 26, pp. 194–199, 2007.

[11]. U. Lindemann, A. Hock, M. Stuber, W. Keck and C. Becker, "Evaluation of a fall detector based on accelerometers: A pilot study", *Medical and Biological Engineering and Computing*, vol. 43, no. 5, pp. 548–551, 2005.

[12]. S. M. Riazul Islam, D. Kwak, M. D. Humaun Kabir, M. Hossain and K.-S. Kwak, "The Internet of Things for health care: a comprehensive survey", *IEEE Access*, vol. 3, pp. 678–708, 2015.

[13]. A. Rahaman, Md. M. Islam, Md. R. Islam, M. S. Sadi, and S. Nooruddin, "Developing IoT based smart health monitoring systems: A review", *Revue d'Intelligence Artificielle*, vol. 33, pp. 435–440, 2019. doi: 10.18280/ria.330605.

[14]. Q. Li, J. A. Stankovic, M. A. Hanson, A. T. Barth, J. Lach and G. Zhou, Accurate, fast fall detection using gyroscopes and accelerometer derived posture information. In: *Body sensor networks; international workshop on wearable & implantable body sensor networks*, Berkeley, CA, USA, pp. 138–43, 2009.

[15]. M. S. Islam, M. T. Islam, A. F. Almutairi, G. K. Beng, N. Misran and N. Amin, "Monitoring of the human body signal through the Internet of Things (IoT) based LoRa wireless network", *System Journal of Applied Sciences*, vol. 9, no. 9, pp. 1884, https://doi.org/10.3390/app9091884. lref>

[16]. P. H. Patil, P. Singh, S. Biradar and P. Rane, "Design and implementation of wireless patient health monitoring system", *International Journal of Engineering Research and Technology*, vol. 2, no. 6, 2013.

[17]. J. Wang, Z. Zhang, B. Li, S. Lee and R. S. Sherratt, "An enhanced fall detection system for elderly person monitoring using consumer home networks", *IEEE Transactions on Consumer Electronics*, vol. 60, pp. 23–28, 2014.

[18]. G. Vavoulas, M. Pediaditis, E. G. Spanakis and M. Tsiknakis, The MobiFall dataset: An initial evaluation of fall detection algorithms using smartphones. In: *Proceedings of the IEEE 13th international conference on bioinformatics and bioengineering*, Chania, Greece, 10–13 November, pp. 1–4, 2013.

[19]. S. P. Kumar, V. R. R. Samson, U. B. Sai, P. L. S. D. M. Rao and K. K. Eswar, Smart health monitoring system of patient through IoT. In: *2017 International conference on I-SMAC (IoT in social, mobile, analytics and cloud) (I-SMAC)*, IEEE, pp. 551–6, 2017.

[20]. C. Becker, L. Schwickert, S. Mellone, F. Bagalà, L. Chiari, J. L. Helbostad, W. Zijlstra, K. Aminian, A. Bourke and C. Todd, et al., Proposal for a multiphase fall model based on real-world fall recordings with body-fixed sensors, In Zeitschrift Für Gerontologie Und Geriatrie, Berlin, Germany: Springer International Publishing, pp. 707–715, 2012.

[21]. J. He, C. Hu and X. Y. Wang, "A smart device enabled system for autonomous fall detection and alert", *International Journal of Distributed Sensor Networks*, vol. 12, pp. 1–10, 2016.

[22]. R. Kumar and M. Rajakesan, An IoT based patient monitoring system using raspberry Pi, In: *International conference on computing technologies and intelligent data engineering(ICCTIDE'16)*, 2016.

[23]. F. Bianchi, S. J. Redmond, M. R. Narayanan, S. Cerutti and N. H. Lovell, "Barometric pressure and triaxial accelerometry-based falls event detection", *IEEE Transactions on Neural Systems and Rehabilitation Engineering*, vol. 18, no. 6, pp. 619–627, 2010.

[24]. M. R. Desai and S. Toravi, A smart sensor interface for smart homes and heart beat monitoring using WSN in IoT environment. In: *2017 International conference on current trends in computer, electrical, electronics and communication (CTCEEC)*, IEEE, pp. 74–7, 2017.

3

A REVIEW ON INTRUSION DETECTION SYSTEMS AND CYBER THREAT INTELLIGENCE FOR SECURE IoT-ENABLED NETWORKS

Challenges and Directions

PRABHAT KUMAR, GOVIND P. GUPTA, AND RAKESH TRIPATHI

Department of Information Technology, National Institute of Technology Raipur, Chhattisgarh, India

Contents

3.1 Introduction

The rapid growth of the Internet and proliferation of low-cost and low energy-consuming sensors are responsible for the emergence of the Internet of Things (IoT) [1]. The IoT is a concept invented by British inventor Kevin Ashton in 1999 to depict a system in which the real world is linked to the Internet via pervasive sensors and can be defined as:

> The IoT is a self-configuring, adaptable, dynamic network that uses standard communication protocols to connect 'things' with Internet. The objects provide services with or without human involvement by using unique address, data gathering, and connectivity. The service is accessed via sophisticated interfaces and made available anywhere, anytime, and for anything [2].

The IoT market has grown rapidly over the last decade, with the total economic potential exceeding $120 billion in 2016 and potentially reaching $6.2 trillion by 2027. As anticipated by Cisco and Ericsson in 2020, the IoT forms a vision of the future Internet that leverages the sensing and processing capabilities of multiple objects to improve human-environment interaction [3]. The IoT paradigm is recognized as a key enabling technology in realizing smart environments. The goal of such pervasive computing is to make human existence more valued and productive by addressing issues related to living conditions [4]. The *Padova Smart City* in Italy is a fantastic example of an IoT system [5, 6]. A few examples of IoT applications such as smart home, smart city, smart grids, smart farming, and smart healthcare, etc., are shown in Figure 3.1.

As illustrated in Figure 3.2, a typical IoT system consists of three fundamental elements, a set of front-end devices that can detect, compute, and transmit; a back-end storage and processing unit that can give insights and intelligence; and a communication infrastructure that links front-end sensors to back-end servers [7]. In IoT applications, front-end equipment performs a range of tasks and is adapted to a specific purpose. These devices are resource-constrained and include sensors, actuators, microprocessors with limited storage, computing, communication, and even energy capacity for those powered by batteries [8, 9]. The back-end servers, on the other hand, are significantly more powerful. Many services have been deployed in the cloud as a result of the rapid growth of cloud computing to take advantage of the inexpensive and easily accessible storage and computing capabilities [10]. The major cloud vendors, such as Amazon Web Services and

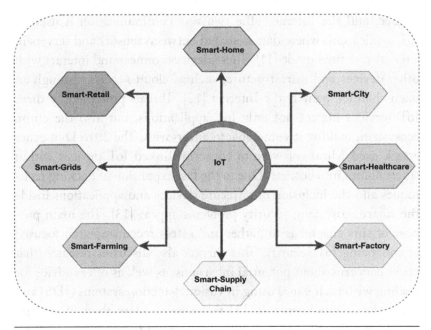

Figure 3.1   Real-world IoT applications.

Microsoft Azure, offer an IoT suite to help clients gather and transfer data to the cloud, make it simple to load and analyze that data, and expedite IoT development. Finally, the communication infrastructure connects front-end devices to back-end servers and each other via wired and wireless networks such as Wi-Fi, LTE, Bluetooth,

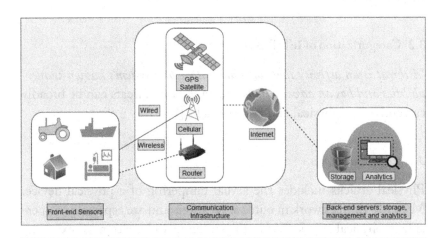

Figure 3.2   IoT three-tier architecture.

Zigbee, and the Internet. The two-way communication is used in IoT applications where data is shared between sensors and servers in a (near) real-time mode [11]. These devices connect and interact with other devices and infrastructure, such as cloud servers, through an open channel, namely the Internet [12]. Threats presented by these IoT services impact not only IoT applications, but also the entire ecosystem, making it vulnerable to adversaries. The 2016 Dyn cyber attack used Mirai software to conscript linked IoT devices within smart homes into botnets. Due to the fast expansion of hacking techniques and the inclusion of unsecure devices and applications inside the smart ecosystem, security problems appear [13]. The main purpose of this chapter is to gather and assess recent research focused at enhancing IoT security. This chapter also discusses research that raises concerns about potential intrusions, as well as offers advice for dealing with such issues using intrusion detection systems (IDS) and cyber threat intelligence (CTI) techniques. More than 65 articles addressing a broader area related to security in IoT-enabled networks are reviewed.

This chapter is structured as follows: Section 3.2 discuss various threats found in IoT networks. Section 3.3 presents the security mechanisms available for IoT-enabled networks. Section 3.4 contains a literature review of IDS and CTI with their advantages and disadvantages. In Section 3.5, some research challenges with future directions are highlighted. Lastly, Section 3.6 discusses the conclusion of this chapter.

3.2 Categorization of IoT Threats

"A threat is an activity that takes advantage of a system's known vulnerabilities and has an adverse impact upon it". IoT threats can be broadly categorized as physical and cyber attacks [14].

3.2.1 Physical Attacks

Physical attacks includes the actual tampering of a physical device. Most IoT devices work in outdoor locations and are especially vulnerable to physical attacks due to the scattered and unattended existence of IoT. Such attacks include radio frequency jamming, side channel attacks, permanent denial of service, sleep denial attacks, malicious node injections, etc. [15].

a. *Radio frequency jamming:* This type of attack disrupts communication by emitting signals, proactively or reactively, that cause packets to be damaged or IoT users to be denied the ability to send data packets during while the signals are being sent. In the IoT, jamming drastically lowers bandwidth availability [16].

b. *Side channel attack:* An exploit of the information leakages (such as timing, power, electromagnetic signals, sound, light, etc.) in the system. This attack is carried out by observing, collecting, and analyzing information leakages in the device as it is being processed. Any sensitive information on the device can be retrieved using these attacks. The majority of the time, they are employed to attack cryptographic devices [17].

c. *Permanent denial of service (PDoS):* Also called a phlashing attack, it causes extensive damage to the physical device, which most likely will need replacement or reinstallation. In general, detection of a security lapse by the hacker is required for the spread of this attack [18].

d. *Sleep denial attack:* The goal of these attacks is to drain the batteries of devices by increasing their duty cycle. These attacks try to reduce the projected lifetime of the established IoT network by compelling nodes to wake up at inconvenient times or inducing additional responsibility (e.g., listening, retransmissions) [19].

e. *Malicious node injection:* In this attack, the attacker physically places a new compromised node between two or more authentic nodes. The data is subsequently altered, and inaccurate data is sent to the other nodes. Using a large number of nodes, the attacker launches a malicious node injection attack. To begin, the adversary first inserts a replica of an actual node. Then, more malicious nodes are added to this mix and the cyber attack is carried out by both of these nodes working together. As a result, the victim node experiences a collision, and is unable to receive or transmit packets [20].

3.2.2 Cyber Attacks

In cyber attacks, the attacker attempts to insert malware or malicious software to gain unauthorized access of network component. This includes denial-of-service (DoS), distributed DoS (DDoS), ransomware, and man-in-the-middle (MitM) attacks [21].

   a. ***Denial-of-service (DoS):*** In this attack, the malicious user behaviour prevents registered IoT devices from accessing network information, servers, or other infrastructures. A DoS condition is generated by overwhelming the targeted server or network connection with data until the victim is unable to respond or ultimately fails, effectively blocking access to legitimate IoT devices [22].

   b. ***Distributed denial-of-service (DDoS):*** When several IoT devices collaborate to attack a single target, this is known as a DDoS attack. For large-scale attacks, DDoS adversaries also utilize a botnet, which is a network of infected IoT devices connected to the Internet. Attackers use various commands and control tools to exploit IoT devices, taking advantage of security vulnerabilities or application weaknesses. As more and more devices become connected through IoT, DDoS attacks are becoming increasingly severe. In addition, IoT devices come with default keys with no security system, which makes them easy targets for attackers. Consumers generally overlook IoT device penetration and, as a result, these systems are easily exploited to launch a large-scale attack without security administrator awareness [23].

   c. ***Man-in-the-middle (MitM):*** When a third party intercepts a user communication, it is termed as MitM attack. An attacker may desire to read the contents of a communication; alternatively, the attacker may wish to manipulate the contents of the message or otherwise affect the connection, such as infecting a victim with malware. The first is an ability to violate the secrecy of the communication, while the latter is an effort to compromise its integrity [24].

   d. ***Ransomware attacks:*** The name "ransomware" is a combination of the terms "ransom" and "ware", with the term ransom referring to a payment and ware indicating a malware attack.

In a ransomware attack, the attacker locks the victim's data with powerful encryption technology and seeks a ransom in exchange for the decryption key. This can result in the loss of data, the disruption of normal system operations, and financial damages [25].

e. *Theft attacks:* A sequence of intrusions in which an attacker tries to get sensitive data by breaching the security of an IoT system. Stealing records and key logging are two examples of theft attacks. During data-theft cyber attacks, an intruder attempts to breach a remote IoT system, acquiring illegal access to data that can be delivered to a distant attack computer. The attacker hacks the remote host to record the user's keystrokes, potentially stealing confidential credentials through key-logging activities [26].

3.3 Security Mechanisms in IoT-enabled Networks

3.3.1 Intrusion Detection System

An intrusion is a purposefully or unlawfully carried out operation in a network's infrastructure to steal important network resources, and it usually differs from the system's routine activity [27]. An IDS can be defined as:

> An IDS is a collection of tools, resources, and methodologies that monitor network traffic and protect authorized users from behaviors that threaten the information system's availability, confidentiality, and integrity. [28]

IDS may be categorized into two categories based on *position* and *detection*, as stated below:

a. ***IDS based on position:*** IDS can be classified based on where the detection takes place and can be classified into two types host-based IDS (HIDS) and network-based IDS (NIDS).
   - *Host-based IDS (HIDS):* HIDS is a type of monitoring software that tracks and protects a single host machine. These threats can have a variety of effects on a system, including gaining access to it, altering system files, using

system RAM needlessly, and keeping the CPU active at all times. To avoid such attacks, HIDS constantly monitors log files on the host. This provides HIDS with good system knowledge, but at the price of poor network isolation. The high construction cost of HIDS, especially for bigger networks, is a disadvantage. An attacker can also confuse or deactivate the HIDS if they have illegal access [29].

- *Network-based IDS (NIDS):* NIDS are generally physically separate instruments that are located on the "upstream" network of the system being monitored, and they usually analyze many independent networks on a typical network. However, these programmes have little to no knowledge about the internal condition of the systems they manage, making it more difficult to spot [30]. Any of the three layers of the IoT architecture depicted in Figure 3.3 can identify intrusions. The network layer

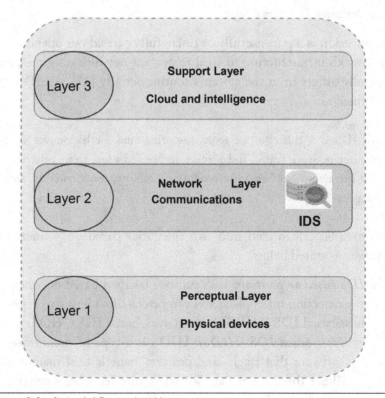

Figure 3.3 A generic IoT network architecture.

serves as a backbone for linking various IoT devices and commonly used for its deployment.

b. *IDS based on detection:* The analytical method employed by the IDS based on the system infrastructure can be used to identify malicious activities and invasive behaviours of the system. Depending on how they analyze data, IDS are categorized as signature-based or anomaly-based.

- *Signature or knowledge-based IDS (SIDS):* A signature is a pattern (string) or a set of patterns that refers to a previously identified threat (such as byte sequences in network traffic or known dangerous instruction patterns of malware). If a stored pattern matches the observed threat, intrusion is recognized. Since the system employs information stored in its database to recognize intrusions, it is also called knowledge-based IDS. This kind of IDS is effective for known attacks; however, due to a lack of signatures, it is unable to detect zero-day or unknown or unseen attacks. Cyber security systems prefer signature-based detection since it is simple to set up and effective at detecting known attacks (high detection with low false-alarm rate) [31].

- *Anomaly or behaviour-based IDS (AIDS):* In *AIDS*, a typical user profile is created by observing genuine user network connections and behaviours on a regular basis. When there is a difference in behaviour between ongoing actions and the developed model, it is considered as an intrusion [32]. Statistical data analysis, mining, and algorithmic learning methodologies are used to identify anomalies. The anomaly detector is effective at detecting and preventing unknown threats. However, they have a significant false-alarm rate as the previously unobserved (legitimate) actions can be classified as anomalies.

3.3.2 Cyber Threat Intelligence

The passive monitoring of data for potential security vulnerabilities is a typical intrusion detection process. An IDS begins by passively examining all traffic and logs for anything it recognizes when it is deployed. This "matching" might be as basic as a unique string found in a malware sample, connections made through odd ports, unexpected flow volumes, etc. When an IDS finds a match, it generates an alert [33]. CTI or threat hunting is not the same as intrusion detection. Instead of depending on an IDS, hunting actively seeks out and investigates risks. There is a chance to "search" for a specific behaviour when threatening actors develop new methods of attack and new vulnerabilities in technology are uncovered. Threat hunting analyzes all current and previous data with the aim of spotting "new" (or "unknown") threats in their close surroundings [34]. Technically, we can define CTI as:

> A process of analysing data using tools and procedures to provide actionable knowledge about existing or emerging threats aimed at a company in order to reduce risk. To combat attacks, it enables organizations to make faster, more informed security decisions and shift their behaviour from reactive to proactive approach. [35]

CTI is broadly classified as: Tactical, operational, technical, and strategic [36].

a. *Strategic CTI:* Includes high-level information related to the monetary impact of various cyber activities, attack trends, the budget required to mitigate them, and the impact of high-level business selections. Although strategic CTI is useful, identifying relevant information and valuable insights regarding cyber threats requires a significant amount of effort [37].

b. *Operational CTI:* Includes information on specific threats to an organization. It assists enterprises in identifying potential threat actors, as well as their intent, capability, and ability to attack susceptible IT infrastructure. This CTI can help less sophisticated threat groups as they often discuss their plans in unprotected channels. For more advanced groups that generally take great measures in their talks and communications, obtaining such intelligence is difficult [38].

c. *Tactical CTI:* Provides information related to tactics, techniques, and procedures (TTPs) used by threat actors (attackers) to perform attacks. Intelligence provides them with information on how to develop a defence strategy to counter these attacks. The report details the security system flaws that attackers could exploit, as well as how to spot such attacks. The information is used to improve existing security controls and defence mechanisms, as well as to identify and eliminate network vulnerabilities [39].

d. *Technical CTI:* It is related to the Indicator of Compromise (IoC), i.e., pieces of forensic data, such as data found in system log entries or files, that identify potentially malicious activity on a system or network. This acts as the main source of producing intelligence to feed the investigating and mentoring functions of an organization, such as intrusion detection and prevention systems [40]. The research toward CTI models, particularly for IoT networks is still in its early stage.

An effective CTI should provide information that is trustworthy and actionable [41]. A CTI's major purpose is to provide an attack-detection method that allows security measures to be adjusted in a real scenario, increasing the likelihood of detecting and blocking harmful conduct before it occurs [42]. The trial-and-error approach to decode login data, spam URLs, ransomware, and botnet node activity are vulnerabilities to domain infrastructure.

3.4 Literature Review

3.4.1 Intrusion Detection System for Safeguarding IoT

We review key works from state-of-the-art research on IDS for IoT security. We start with a detailed description of the authors' solutions to get a better understanding of IDS architectures and implementations. For instance, Al-Shaher *et al.* [43], suggested an IDS for identifying regular and malicious actions using a multi-layer perceptron (MLP) and a neural network. The proposed approach obtained 93% accuracy with two hidden layers. However, few other important evaluation metrics, i.e., detection rate (DR), FAR, F1 score, were not considered and the dataset used for the experiment was not mentioned.

Marwan *et al.* [44], presented a machine-learning (ML)-enabled security system for IoT-based healthcare. The main objective of this work was to prevent unauthorized access to health information and medical data. This model used fuzzy C-means clustering (FCM) and support vector machines (SVM) at the first level and a CloudSec component at the second level to ensure data integrity. The model based on SVM achieved effective results. However, the proposed approach lacked implementation details.

Kaur *et al.* [45], used ML techniques to design a four-layer hybrid architecture for a secure healthcare system. This method allowed the integration and analysis of unstructured information, which can aid patients in receiving better treatment and healthcare professionals in making informed decisions. The proposed strategy, however, lacked implementation details.

For remote healthcare systems, Begli *et al.* [46], developed an IDS. SVM was used in this approach to prevent User to Root (U2R) and DoS attacks. The proposed framework was tested on the NSL-KDD dataset and reported a 95.01% DR. However, the proposed IDS was tested using an out-of-date dataset that did not include any IoT network traffic or telemetry data.

Newaz *et al.* [47], designed a security framework named HealthGuard for healthcare data. To differentiate between normal and abnormal instances, this model calculates the change in a patient's physiological function. In addition, ML techniques such as artificial neural network (ANN), decision tree (DT), k-Nearest Neighbour (k-NN) and Random Forest (RF) were employed. The model outperforms using DT by 93% accuracy. However, one of the important evaluation metrics, i.e., FAR, was not considered in this experiment.

He *et al.* [48], presented an IDS for healthcare networks. For feature selection, the proposed model employed the stacked autoencoder. The methods k-NN, naive Bayes (NB), XGBoost and SVM were used to identify intrusive actions. The detection system with XGBoost surpassed the competition and obtained 97.83% accuracy. However, instead focusing on security, this strategy mainly concentrated on performance issues. Almiani *et al.* [49], presented an intelligent IDS for fog computing security based on multi-layered recurrent neural networks. The traffic processing engine and the recurrent ANN classification engine were the two phases of this model. To effectively classify normal and abnormal occurrences, an adaptive variant of the back-propagation method was utilized for training. The suggested model was tested on the NSL-KDD dataset, which lacked contemporary IoT attacks.

Kumar et al. [50], designed Unified IDS (UIDS), and deployed it on gateway nodes and cluster heads for threat detection in IoT systems. The suggested model was tested on the UNSW-NB15 dataset and demonstrated an improvement in accuracy of 88.92% using the C5 approach. An anomaly IDS for IoT network infrastructures was presented in [51]. Linear discriminant analysis (LDA) and principal component analysis (PCA) were utilized in the suggested model for dimension reduction, while the NB and certainty factor versions of k-NN were employed for classification. U2R and R2L attacks were the primary targets of this model. Despite the fact that this model had an 84.66% DR for binary classification, it was developed using the NSL-KDD dataset, which contained obsolete threats.

Khan et al. [52] used stacked autoencoder and a soft-max classifier to design a two-stage deep learning (TSDL) IDS. In the first step, this model learns feature representations based on likelihood scores to discriminate between normal and malignant behaviours. This score was utilized as a feature to detect unusual traffic in the second stage. Using the KDD99 and UNSW-NB15 datasets, this model was able to achieve high identification rates of up to 99.996% and 89.134%, respectively. However, one hot encoding approach was employed during data pre-processing, resulting in a sparse and complicated dataset.

Alrashdi et al. [53], designed a fog-based anomaly detection (FBAD), system that could distinguish between attack and normal instances. For healthcare threat detection, this model employs an online sequential extreme learning machine. Furthermore, as fog computing is closer to IoT devices at the network edge, the suggested distributed attack detection framework was used there due to its high accuracy and low latency. The suggested experiment used an out-of-date NSL-KDD dataset and achieved a 97.09% accuracy rate.

Swarna et al. [54], proposed a deep neural network (DNN)-based IDS in an IoT-based healthcare system to categorize and detect unseen cyber attacks. For feature extraction, this model employed Grey-wolf optimization (GWO) mixed with PCA. The suggested hybrid PCA-GWO dimensionality reduction was subsequently integrated with

DNN, resulting in a 99.90% accuracy rate. However, the suggested model was tested using the obsolete NSL-KDD dataset and was implemented in cloud computing.

3.4.2 Cyber Threat Intelligence for Securing IoT

Various research for threat hunting and intelligence has been undertaken in recent years. The most fundamental criteria for any cyber threat protection and warning system should certainly include CTI modelling and threat type identification for a network. Artificial intelligence (AI)-based CTI models has received substantial attention from industry and academics due to its efficient power to understand large-scale data and combat undetected threat occurrences. This review makes use of multiple current research topics based on ML and DL-based CTI solutions.

For instance, Koloveas *et al.* [55] proposed a ML-based framework named "intime" that enabled a security team to find, gather, analyze, and share CTI from various popular social networks such as trusted structured sources (e.g., known security databases), clear/deep/dark forums, Web sites and popular social networks, marketplaces, or other data store types (e.g., pastebins). However, this model used a traditional ML approach and achieved low overall accuracy, i.e., 87.51%. In Ref. [56], the authors used *doc2vec*, a neural network-based threat extraction tool and MLP model to detect threats from the dark Web social network. In the proposed model, datasets were collected using a Web crawler and then manually categorized into critical posts and non-critical posts. The MLP-based CTI obtained very low 79.4% overall accuracy on unseen data.

Atluri *et al.* [57], designed a ML-based CTI framework for an industrial control system (ICS) using a bagging decision trees (BDT) model and achieved 94.24% accuracy and outperformed other traditional ML approaches. However, this model did not discuss the technique used for feature extraction or the steps used in data pre-processing. Sentuna *et al.* [58], designed an enhanced posterior probability-based naive Bayes (ENBPP) technique. This approach combined the posterior probability function of naive Bayes with a modified risk assessment function to optimize the threat prediction accuracy and processing time. The model provided 92–96% improvement in overall accuracy but lacked attack-type identification.

Usman *et al.* [59], presented a novel technique using dynamic malware analysis, CTI, ML, and data forensics to identify malicious Internet protocol (IP) during communication. The underlying approach efficiency was accessed using various ML models, where DT obtained 93.5% accurate predictions. However, model lacked attack-type identification.

Deliu *et al.* [35], integrated SVM and latent Dirichlet allocation (LDA) to design a two-stage hybrid process to automatically extract information about various threats, such as leaked credentials, malicious proxy servers, and identified threats. However, the proposed scheme was evaluated based on time analysis and lacked various evaluation metrics to access its effectiveness.

Zhou *et al.* [37], designed an ensemble Bayesian network using majority voting to identify Cross-site scripting (XSS) attack. In this model, features were extracted from the domain knowledge, i.e. the created XSS attack ontology. In the experiment, different percentages of sampled malicious records were inserted, and the problem was modelled as a binary classification and achieved overall 98.54% accuracy. However, the model lacked attack-type identification.

Noor *et al.* [40], proposed an ML-based security framework to identify cyber threats based on observed attack patterns. This work generated a semantic network of TTPs and detection mechanisms by correlating threat incidents among themselves to recognize the existence of a TTP in a network and obtained 92% accuracy.

Alsaedi *et al.* [60], proposed ToN-IoT, a new IIoT-based dataset that includes both conventional sensor measurement data and various forms of cyber attacks aimed at IIoT applications. A data driven security solution that used various ML algorithms were proposed and the model outperformed using Classification and Regression Trees (CART) technique and obtained 88.00% accuracy but model lacked specific attack type identification.

HaddadPajouh *et al.* [61], presented a secured layered design named AI4SAFE-IoT for IoT edge layer infrastructure. The primary components provided in this design were cyber threat hunting, cyber threat attribution, an intelligent firewall for web application, and cyber TI. The recommended modules, which are based on the Cyber Kill Chain model, identify, assign, and further describe the phase of a threat lifespan. However, various evaluation parameters were not used.

Noor *et al.* [62] designed an ML-based system that accepts TTPs as input; further, it uses the information gain-based feature selection technique to select the most common TTPs. Finally, using association rule mining (ARM) technique, the selected features from TTPs are mined for threat detection. However, the proposed model used a manual procedure to extract features and lacked various evaluation metrics.

Naik *et al.* [63], designed a threat detection solution that combined two different fuzzy approaches, i.e., FCM and fuzzy hashing (FH), and suggested an efficient fuzzy analytic methodology to cluster ransomware sample. Without requiring additional transformational processes to establish distance between items for clustering, the proposed FCM used replication scores provided by a FH algorithm and clustered them into uniformity groups.

Moustafa *et al.* [64], used beta mixture models (BMM) and hidden Markov models (HMM), to develop new threat intelligence system in industrial settings. ICS was utilized to reduce the dimensions of power system and UNSW-NB15 datasets, achieving 96.32% and 98.45% accuracy on both datasets, respectively. However, to effectively estimate the BMM and HMM parameters, this technique required a large number of normal and threat cases.

Ebrahimi *et al.* [65], proposed a semi-supervised threat identification framework. In this work, the transductive approach based on the lexical and structural characteristics was used to label the unlabelled data. Further, for cyber-threat identification tasks, a DL-based long short-term memory (LSTM) technique was used and the model achieved 94.70% accuracy, but the model lacked specific attack-type identification.

Husari *et al.* [66], presented *ActionMiner*, a framework for converting each unstructured CTI report into a structured list of threat actions for subsequent study. This model used entropy and mutual information techniques to accurately extract each cyber threat action and achieved improved 93% DR. However, the proposed scheme lacked various evaluation metrics to assess its effectiveness.

Al-Hawawreh *et al.* [36], suggested a CTI based on DL approaches. In this work, features were extracted using a deep sparse auto-encoder and threats were identified using a gated recurrent neural network.

3.5 Challenges and Research Directions

The majority of current security mechanisms rely on access control and performance factors. These security systems lack a deployment method that can be employed in an IoT setting. Tables 3.1 and 3.2 highlight the key points of different studies available in literature based on which of following main research directions are identified:

- The majority of IDS research either utilized outdated intrusion datasets (e.g., KDD CUP99 or NSL-KDD) or failed to specify the source of datasets used to assess their work [44, 46–48, 53, 54]. Thus, evaluation of the IDS using the latest IoT-based intrusion dataset is a challenging research issue.
- Most of the existing IDS works on centralized architecture and suffers low accuracy, detection, and high FAR. Thus, design of a distributed IDS using machine or DL techniques for IoT is challenging issue.
- Most of the existing solutions for designing an intelligent CTI are based on statistical and classical ML techniques [12, 35, 37, 38, 40, 67] and these existing solutions suffered from lower detection accuracy, high FAR, and were also very complex. In addition, these solutions suffered from lack of generalization. Due to this, the latest and most dynamic threats are not effectively detected. Thus, designing of an efficient CTI model with high generalization capability and accuracy is a challenging research issue.
- Most of the previous studies have used manual labelling or feature extraction processes. Unfortunately, these process are time consuming and error-prone procedures that necessitate a large investment of resources and are still heavily used in threat-type analysis to provide insight of attack behaviours. Thus, there is a requirement of an automated feature extraction process [56, 59, 64, 65].

Table 3.1 Summary of Investigated Methods to Design IDSs

AUTHORS	AREA	DETECTION METHOD	DATASET	FEATURE SELECTION	STATISTICAL ANALYSIS	DEPLOYMENT SOLUTION	DISTRIBUTED
Al-Shaher et al. [43]	Healthcare	MLP	NA	✕	✕	✕	✕
Marwan et al. [44]	Healthcare	SVM+FCM	NA	✕	✕	✕	✕
Kaur et al. [45]	Healthcare	ML	NA	✕	✕	✕	✓
Begli et al. [46]	Healthcare	SVM	NSL-KDD	✕	✕	✕	✕
Newaz et al. [47]	Healthcare	DT	NA	✕	✕	✕	✕
He et al. [48]	Healthcare	XGBoost	NA	✓	✕	✕	✕
Almiani et al. [49]	IoT	ANN	NSL-KDD	✓	✕	✕	✓
Kumar et al. [50]	IoT	UIDS	NA	✓	✕	✕	✓
Pajouh et al. [51]	IoT	TDTC	NSL-KDD	✓	✓	✕	✕
Khan et al. [52]	NIDS	TSDL	KDD99	✓	✓	✕	✕
Alrashdi et al. [53]	IoT	EOS-ELM	NSL-KDD	✓	✕	✕	✓
Swarna et al. [54]	IoMT	DNN	NSL-KDD	✓	✕	✕	✕

Note: Terms and abbreviations: NA denotes that there is no information available; MLP: Multi-layer perceptron; SVM: Support vector machines; FCM: Fuzzy C-means clustering; DT: Decision tree; ANN: Artificial neural network; UIDS: Unified IDS; TSDL: Two-stage deep learning; EOS-ELM: Ensemble of online sequential extreme learning machine; DNN: Deep neural network.

Table 3.2 Summary of Investigated Methods to Design CTI

AUTHORS	AREA	APPROACH	DATASET	AUTOMATIC ANALYSIS	THREAT DETECTION	ATTACK-TYPE IDENTIFICATION	DEPLOYMENT SOLUTION
Koloveas et al. [55]	IoT	RF	SEDD	×	✓	×	×
Kadoguchi et al. [56]	Online forum	MLP	DARK WEB	×	✓	×	×
Atluri et al. [57]	IIoT	BDT	ICS	×	✓	×	×
Sentuna et al. [58]	CTI	ENBPP	NSL-KDD, CICIDS-2017	✓	✓	×	✓
Usman et al. [59]	IoT	DT	NA	×	✓	×	✓
Deliu et al. [35]	Online forum	SVM	NA	×	✓	×	×
Zhou et al. [37]	Online forum	EBN	XSS Payloads	×	✓	×	×
Noor et al. [40]	CTI	TTD	ATT&CK	×	✓	✓	×
Alsaedi et al. [60]	IIoT	CART	ToN-IoT	×	✓	×	×
HaddadPajouh et al. [61]	IoT	AI4SAFE-IoT	NA	×	×	×	✓
Noor et al. [62]	CTI	ARM	ATT&CK	✓	✓	×	×
Naik et al. [63]	CTI	FCM	NA	✓	✓	×	×
Moustafa et al. [64]	IIoT	HMM	UNSW-NB15	×	✓	✓	✓
Ebrahimi et al. [65]	Online forum	LSTM	DNM	✓	✓	×	×
Husari et al. [66]	CTI	ActionMiner	NA	×	✓	×	×
Al-Hawawreh et al. [36]	IoT	GRNN	ToN-IoT	✓	✓	✓	×

Note: Terms and abbreviations: NA denotes that there is no information available; RF: Random forest; SEDD: Stack exchange data dump; MLP: Multi-layer perceptron; IIoT: Industrial Internet of Things; BDT: Bagging decision trees; ICS: Industrial control system; CTI: Cyber threat intelligence; ENBPP: Enhanced posterior probability-based naive Bayes; DT: Decision tree; SVM: Support vector machines; EBN: Ensemble Bayesian networks; TTD: ThreatTTP-Detection; CART: Classification and regression trees; ARM: Association rule mining; FCM: Fuzzy C-means; HMM: Hidden Markov models; LSTM: Long short-term memory; GRNN: Gated recurrent neural network.

3.6 Conclusion

In this survey chapter, we explored the security requirements and numerous attacks that occur in the IoT-enabled network. The works reviewed in this study mainly focused on the issue and numerous efforts made by the scientific community as well as industry to design optimized security measures that provide reasonable protection for IoT networks. Various comparisons including DR, false alarm rate, and the application of state-of-the-art techniques in IoT were conducted. Finally, several future research directions in the design of effective intrusion detection and cyber threat intelligence methods for IoT-enabled networks have been suggested.

References

[1] P. Kumar, G. P. Gupta, and R. Tripathi, "An ensemble learning and fog-cloud architecture-driven cyber-attack detection framework for IoMT networks," *Computer Communications*, vol. 166, pp. 110–124, 2021.

[2] R. Ahmad and I. Alsmadi, "Machine learning approaches to IoT security: A systematic literature review," *Internet of Things*, vol. 14, p. 100365, 2021.

[3] P. Kumar, G. P. Gupta, and R. Tripathi, "A distributed ensemble design based intrusion detection system using fog computing to protect the Internet of Things networks," *Journal of Ambient Intelligence and Humanized Computing*, vol. 12, no. 10, pp. 9555–9572, 2021.

[4] X. Yao, F. Farha, R. Li, I. Psychoula, L. Chen, and H. Ning, "Security and privacy issues of physical objects in the IoT: Challenges and opportunities," *Digital Communications and Networks*, vol. 7, no. 3, pp. 373–384, 2021.

[5] P. Kumar, G. P. Gupta, and R. Tripathi, "PEFL: Deep privacy-encoding based federated learning framework for smart agriculture," *IEEE Micro*, vol. 42, no. 1, pp. 33–40, 2021.

[6] P. Kumar, G. P. Gupta, R. Tripathi, S. Garg, and M. M. Hassan, "DLTIF: Deep learning-driven cyber threat intelligence modeling and identification framework in IoT-enabled maritime transportation systems," IEEE Transactions on Intelligent Transportation Systems, 2021, https://doi.org/10.1109/TITS.2021.3122368.

[7] P. Kumar, G. P. Gupta, and R. Tripathi, "Design of anomaly-based intrusion detection system using fog computing for IoT network," *Automatic Control and Computer Sciences*, vol. 55, no. 2, pp. 137–147, 2021.

[8] R. Kumar, P. Kumar, R. Tripathi, G. P. Gupta, S. Garg, and M. M. Hassan, "BDTwin: An integrated framework for enhancing security and privacy in cybertwin-driven automotive industrial Internet of Things," *IEEE Internet of Things Journal*, vol. 9, no. 18, pp. 17110–17119, 2022, https://doi.org/10.1109/JIOT.2021.3122021.

[9] P. Kumar, R. Kumar, G. P. Gupta, and R. Tripathi, "A distributed framework for detecting DDOS attacks in smart contract-based blockchain-IoT systems by leveraging fog computing," *Transactions on Emerging Telecommunications Technologies*, vol. 32, no. 6, p. e4112, 2021.

[10] J. Frahim, C. Pignataro, J. Apcar, and M. Morrow, "Securing the Internet of Things: A proposed framework," Cisco White Paper, 2015.

[11] N. Chaabouni, M. Mosbah, A. Zemmari, C. Sauvignac, and P. Faruki, "Network intrusion detection for IoT security based on learning techniques," *IEEE Communications Surveys Tutorials*, vol. 21, no. 3, pp. 2671–2701, 2019.

[12] P. Kumar, G. P. Gupta, and R. Tripathi, "TP2SF: A trustworthy privacy-preserving secured framework for sustainable smart cities by leveraging blockchain and machine learning," *Journal of Systems Architecture*, vol. 115, p. 101954, 2021.

[13] R. Kumar, P. Kumar, R. Tripathi, G. P. Gupta, N. Kumar, and M. M. Hassan, "A privacy-preserving-based secure framework using blockchain-enabled deep-learning in cooperative intelligent transport system," *IEEE Transactions on Intelligent Transportation Systems*, vol. 23, no. 9, pp. 16492–16503, 2022, https://doi.org/10.1109/TITS.2021.3098636.

[14] H. Tab rizchi and M. K. Rafsanjani, "A survey on security challenges in cloud computing: Issues, threats, and solutions," *The Journal of Supercomputing*, vol. 76, no. 12, pp. 9493–9532, 2020.

[15] M. Keshk, E. Sitnikova, N. Moustafa, J. Hu, and I. Khalil, "An integrated frame- work for privacy-preserving based anomaly detection for cyber-physical systems," *IEEE Transactions on Sustainable Computing*, vol. 6, no. 1, pp. 66–79, 2019.

[16] H. A. B. Salameh, S. Almajali, M. Ayyash, and H. Elgala, "Spectrum assignment in cognitive radio networks for internet-of-things delay-sensitive applications under jamming attacks," *IEEE Internet of Things Journal*, vol. 5, no. 3, pp. 1904–1913, 2018.

[17] A. T. Lo'ai and T. F. Somani, "More secure Internet of Things using robust encryption algorithms against side channel attacks," in *2016 IEEE/ACS 13th International Conference of Computer Systems and Applications (AICCSA)*. IEEE, 2016, pp. 1–6.

[18] N. S. S. Ahmed and D. Acharjya, "Detection of denial of service attack in wireless network using dominance based rough set," *International Journal of Advanced Computer Science and Applications*, vol. 6, no. 12, pp. 267–278, 2015.

[19] A. Gallais, T.-H. Hedli, V. Loscri, and N. Mitton, "Denial-of-sleep attacks against IoT networks," in *2019 6th International Conference on Control, Decision and Information Technologies (CoDIT)*. IEEE, 2019, pp. 1025–1030.

[20] J. Deogirikar and A. Vidhate, "Security attacks in IoT: A survey," in *2017 International Conference on I-SMAC (IoT in Social, Mobile, Analytics and Cloud)(I- SMAC)*. IEEE, 2017, pp. 32–37.

[21] M. Keshk, B. Turnbull, N. Moustafa, D. Vatsalan, and K. R. Choo, "A privacy-preserving-framework-based blockchain and deep learning for protecting smart power networks," *IEEE Transactions on Industrial Informatics*, vol. 16, no. 8, pp. 5110–5118, 2020.

[22] R. Khader and D. Eleyan, "Survey of DoS/DDoS attacks in IoT," *Sustainable Engineering and Innovation*, vol. 3, no. 1, pp. 23–28, 2021.

[23] K. Tsiknas, D. Taketzis, K. Demertzis, and C. Skianis, "Cyber threats to industrial IoT: A survey on attacks and countermeasures," *IoT*, vol. 2, no. 1, pp. 163–188, 2021.

[24] J. J. Kang, K. Fahd, S. Venkatraman, R. Trujillo-Rasua, and P. Haskell-Dowland, "Hybrid routing for man-in-the-middle (MitM) attack detection in IoT networks," in *2019 29th International Telecommunication Networks and Applications Conference (ITNAC)*. 2019, pp. 1–6.

[25] M. Humayun, N. Jhanjhi, A. Alsayat, and V. Ponnusamy, "Internet of Things and ransomware: Evolution, mitigation and prevention," *Egyptian Informatics Journal*, vol. 22, no. 1, pp. 105–117, 2021.

[26] P. Kumar, R. Kumar, G. P. Gupta, and R. Tripathi, "A distributed framework for detecting DDoS attacks in smart contract-based blockchain-IoT systems by leveraging fog computing," *Transactions on Emerging Telecommunications Technologies*, vol. 32, no. 6, e4112, 2021.

[27] P. Kumar, R. Tripathi, and G. P. Gupta, "P2idf: A privacy-preserving based intrusion detection framework for software defined Internet of Things-fog (sdiot-fog)," in *Adjunct Proceedings of the 2021 International Conference on Distributed Computing and Networking*. 2021, pp. 37–42.

[28] H. P. S. Sasan, and M. Sharma, "Intrusion detection using feature selection and machine learning algorithm with misuse detection," *International Journal of Computer Science and Information Technology*, vol. 8, no. 1, pp. 17–25, 2016.

[29] J. Ren, J. Guo, W. Qian, H. Yuan, X. Hao, and H. Jingjing, "Building an effective intrusion detection system by using hybrid data optimization based on machine learning algorithms," *Security and Communication Networks*, vol. 2019, p. 7130868, Jun 2019. [Online]. Available: https://doi.org/10.1155/2019/7130868.

[30] B. A. Tama, and K.-H. Rhee, "HFSTE: Hybrid feature selections and tree-based classifiers ensemble for intrusion detection system," *IEICE Transactions on Information and Systems*, vol. 100, no. 8, pp. 1729–1737, 2017.

[31] P. Kumar, G. P. Gupta, and R. Tripathi, "Toward design of an intelligent cyber attack detection system using hybrid feature reduced approach for IoT networks," *Arabian Journal for Science and Engineering*, vol. 46, no. 4, pp. 3749–3778, 2021.

[32] S. M. Tahsien, H. Karimipour, and P. Spachos, "Machine learning based solutions for security of Internet of Things (IoT): A survey," *Journal of Network and Computer Applications*, vol. 161, p. 102630, 2020.

[33] T. Qiu, Z. Zhao, T. Zhang, C. Chen, and C. P. Chen, "Underwater Internet of Things in smart ocean: System architecture and open issues," *IEEE Transactions on Industrial Informatics*, vol. 16, no. 7, pp. 4297–4307, 2019.

[34] M. K. Kagita, N. Thilakarathne, T. R. Gadekallu, P. K. R. Maddikunta, and S. Singh, "A review on cybercrimes on the Internet of Things," *CoRR*, 2020. [Online]. Available: https://arxiv.org/abs/2009.05708.

[35] I. Deliu, C. Leichter, and K. Franke, "Collecting cyber threat intelligence from hacker forums via a two-stage, hybrid process using support vector machines and latent Dirichlet allocation," in *2018 IEEE International Conference on Big Data (Big Data)*. IEEE, 2018, pp. 5008–5013.

[36] M. Al-Hawawreh, N. Moustafa, S. Garg, and M. S. Hossain, "Deep learning- enabled threat intelligence scheme in the Internet of Things networks," *IEEE Transactions on Network Science and Engineering*, vol. 8, no. 4, pp. 2968–2981, 2020.

[37] Y. Zhou, and P. Wang, "An ensemble learning approach for XSS attack detection with domain knowledge and threat intelligence," *Computers & Security*, vol. 82, pp. 261–269, 2019.

[38] Y. Ghazi, Z. Anwar, R. Mumtaz, S. Saleem, and A. Tahir, "A supervised machine learning based approach for automatically extracting high-level threat intelligence from unstructured sources," in *2018 International Conference on Frontiers of Information Technology (FIT)*. IEEE, 2018, pp. 129–134.

[39] S. Bromander, "Understanding cyber threat intelligence: Towards automation," 2021.

[40] U. Noor, Z. Anwar, A. W. Malik, S. Khan, and S. Saleem, "A machine learning framework for investigating data breaches based on semantic analysis of adversary's attack patterns in threat intelligence repositories," *Future Generation Computer Systems*, vol. 95, pp. 467–487, 2019.

[41] S. Samtani, M. Abate, V. Benjamin, and W. Li, "Cybersecurity as an industry: A cyber threat intelligence perspective," *The Palgrave Handbook of International Cybercrime and Cyberdeviance*, Palgrave Macmillan, Cham, pp. 135–154, 2020, https://doi.org/10.1007/978-3-319-78440-3_8.

[42] I. Deliu, C. Leichter, and K. Franke, "Extracting cyber threat intelligence from hacker forums: Support vector machines versus convolutional neural networks," in *2017 IEEE International Conference on Big Data (Big Data)*. IEEE, 2017, pp. 3648–3656.

[43] M. A. Al-Shaher, R. T. Hameed, and N. Ţăpuş, "Protect healthcare system based on intelligent techniques," in *2017 4th International Conference on Control, Decision and Information Technologies (CoDIT)*. IEEE, 2017, pp. 0421–0426.

[44] M. Marwan, A. Kartit, and H. Ouahmane, "Security enhancement in healthcare cloud using machine learning," *Procedia Computer Science*, vol. 127, pp. 388–397, 2018.

[45] P. Kaur, M. Sharma, and M. Mittal, "Big data and machine learning based secure healthcare framework," *Procedia Computer Science*, vol. 132, pp. 1049–1059, 2018.

[46] M. Begli, F. Derakhshan, and H. Karimipour, "A layered intrusion detection system for critical infrastructure using machine learning," in *2019 IEEE 7th International Conference on Smart Energy Grid Engineering (SEGE)*. IEEE, 2019, pp. 120–124.

[47] A. I. Newaz, A. K. Sikder, M. A. Rahman, and A. S. Uluagac, "Healthguard: A machine learning-based security framework for smart healthcare systems," in *2019 Sixth International Conference on Social*

Networks Analysis, Management and Security (SNAMS). IEEE, 2019, pp. 389–396.

[48] D. He, Q. Qiao, Y. Gao, J. Zheng, S. Chan, J. Li, and N. Guizani, "Intrusion detection based on stacked autoencoder for connected health-care systems," *IEEE Network*, vol. 33, no. 6, pp. 64–69, 2019.

[49] M. Almiani, A. AbuGhazleh, A. Al-Rahayfeh, S. Atiewi, and A. Razaque, "Deep recurrent neural network for IoT intrusion detection system," *Simulation Modelling Practice and Theory*, vol. 101, pp. 102031, 2019.

[50] V. Kumar, A. K. Das, and D. Sinha, "UIDS: A unified intrusion detection system for IoT environment," *Evolutionary Intelligence*, vol. 14, no. 1, pp. 47–59, 2021.

[51] H. H. Pajouh, R. Javidan, R. Khayami, D. Ali, and K.-K. R. Choo, "A two-layer dimension reduction and two-tier classification model for anomaly-based intrusion detection in IoT backbone networks," *IEEE Transactions on Emerging Topics in Computing*, vol. 7, no. 2, pp. 314–323, 1 April-June 2019, https://doi.org/10.1109/TETC.2016.2633228.

[52] F. A. Khan, A. Gumaei, A. Derhab, and A. Hussain, "A novel two-stage deep learning model for efficient network intrusion detection," *IEEE Access*, vol. 7, pp. 30373–30385, 2019, https://doi.org/10.1109/ACCESS.2019.2899721.

[53] E. Aloufi, M. A. Zohdy, and H. Ming, "FBAD: Fog-based attack detection for IoT healthcare in smart cities," in *2019 IEEE 10th Annual Ubiquitous Computing, Electronics & Mobile Communication Conference (UEMCON)*. IEEE, 2019, pp. 0515–0522.

[54] Swarna Priya R.M., Praveen Kumar Reddy Maddikunta, Parimala M., Srinivas Koppu, Thippa Reddy Gadekallu, Chiranji Lal Chowdhary, Mamoun Alazab, "An effective feature engineering for DNN using hybrid PCA-GWO for intrusion detection in IoMT architecture," *Computer Communications*, vol. 160, pp. 139–149, 2020.

[55] P. Koloveas, T. Chantzios, S. Alevizopoulou, S. Skiadopoulos, and C. Tryfonopou-los, "Intime: A machine learning-based framework for gathering and leveraging web data to cyber-threat intelligence," *Electronics*, vol. 10, no. 7, p. 818, 2021.

[56] M. Kadoguchi, S. Hayashi, M. Hashimoto, and A. Otsuka, "Exploring the dark web for cyber threat intelligence using machine leaning," in *2019 IEEE International Conference on Intelligence and Security Informatics (ISI)*. IEEE, 2019, pp. 200–202.

[57] V. Atluri, and J. Horne, "A machine learning based threat intelligence frame- work for industrial control system network traffic indicators of compromise," in *SoutheastCon 2021*. IEEE, 2021, pp. 1–5.

[58] A. Sentuna, A. Alsadoon, P. Prasad, M. Saadeh, and O. H. Alsadoon, "A novel enhanced naïve bayes posterior probability (ENBPP) using machine learning: Cyber threat analysis," *Neural Processing Letters*, vol. 53, no. 1, pp. 177–209, 2021.

[59] N. Usman, S. Usman, F. Khan, M. A. Jan, A. Sajid, M. Alazab, and P. Watters, "Intelligent dynamic malware detection using machine

learning in IP reputation for forensics data analytics," *Future Generation Computer Systems*, vol. 118, pp. 124–141, 2021.

[60] A. Alsaedi, N. Moustafa, Z. Tari, A. Mahmood, and A. Anwar, "Ton IoT telemetry dataset: A new generation dataset of IoT and IIoT for data-driven intrusion detection systems," *IEEE Access*, vol. 8, pp. 165 130–165 150, 2020.

[61] H. HaddadPajouh, R. Khayami, A. Dehghantanha, K.-K. R. Choo, and R. M. Parizi, "AI4SAFE-IoT: An AI-powered secure architecture for edge layer of Internet of Things," *Neural Computing and Applications*, vol. 32, no. 20, pp. 16119–16133, Oct 2020. [Online]. https://doi.org/10.1007/s00521-020-04772-3

[62] U. Noor, Z. Anwar, U. Noor, Z. Anwar, and Z. Rashid, "An association rule mining-based framework for profiling regularities in tactics techniques and procedures of cyber threat actors," in *2018 International Conference on Smart Computing and Electronic Enterprise (ICSCEE)*. 2018, pp. 1–6.

[63] N. Naik, P. Jenkins, N. Savage, and L. Yang, "Cyberthreat hunting - part 2: Tracking ransomware threat actors using fuzzy hashing and fuzzy c-means clustering," in *2019 IEEE International Conference on Fuzzy Systems (FUZZ-IEEE)*. 2019, pp. 1–6.

[64] N. Moustafa, E. Adi, B. Turnbull, and J. Hu, "A new threat intelligence scheme for safeguarding industry 4.0 systems," *IEEE Access*, vol. 6, pp. 32910–32924, 2018, https://doi.org/10.1109/ACCESS.2018.2844794.

[65] M. Ebrahimi, J. F. Nunamaker Jr, and H. Chen, "Semi-supervised cyber threat identification in dark net markets: A transudative and deep learning approach," *Journal of Management Information Systems*, vol. 37, no. 3, pp. 694–722, 2020.

[66] G. Husari, X. Niu, B. Chu, and E. Al-Shaer, "Using entropy and mutual information to extract threat actions from cyber threat intelligence," in *2018 IEEE International Conference on Intelligence and Security Informatics (ISI)*. IEEE, pp. 1–6, 2018.

[67] P. Kumar, R. Kumar, G. Srivastava, G. P. Gupta, R. Tripathi, T. R. Gadekallu, and N. N. Xiong, "PPSF: A privacy-preserving and secure framework using blockchain-based machine-learning for IoT-driven smart cities," *IEEE Transactions on Network Science and Engineering*, vol. 8, no. 3, pp. 2326–2341, 2021.

4

SELF-ADAPTIVE APPLICATION MONITORING FOR DECENTRALIZED EDGE FRAMEWORKS

MONIKA SAXENA, KIRTI PANDEY, VAIBHAV VYAS, AND C.K. JHA

Department of Computer Science, Banasthali Vidyapith, Banasthali, Rajasthan, India

Contents

DOI: 10.1201/9781003264545-4

4.1 Introduction

Self-adaptive applications assess their own conduct and behavioral changes. The assessment shows self-adaption gives better functionality and performance. This means the applications have multiple ways to achieve their objectives and have sufficient knowledge to make effective changes in time. In addition, self-adaptive application must contain a set of components for each major function together with component descriptions so that system components may be selected and planned in response to the evaluators at runtime. Edge computing refers to the processing of data on and near the device. This huge amount of data could be difficult to handle completely in the cloud network. However, Edge offers the complete calculation or part of the calculation, which can handle data near data in the Edge network. It allows low latency, quicker response, and more detailed data analysis. The self-adaption has the ability to impede sequenced component input/output and to produce some of this code out of the specifications. An application seeks to implement this new adjustment basis in runtime rather than during design and maintenance activities [1].

4.1.1 Self-Adaptive Systems

Self-adaptive systems (SAS) are able to modify their runtime to achieve system goals. Some reasons for adjustment actions to an auto-adaptive system are unpredictable conditions such as system changes, system defects, new requirements, and changes in requirement priorities [1].

A SAS continuously monitors itself, collects data, and analyzes these uncertainties to determine if adaptation is necessary. The challenging aspect of a SAS design and implementation is not only that changes must be made during runtime but the system must meet the requirements to the extent that they are satisfactory [2]. It is often difficult to develop these systems, as available knowledge is not sufficient to foresee all runtime conditions at design time. Therefore, when more knowledge is available, designers often prefer to address this uncertainty at runtime.

The architecture of SAS has been taken into account by researchers and developers (including) as fields of study. The proposed architecture is performed in the following ways:

a. *Monitoring*: To have sufficient awareness of a situation.

b. *Analysis*: The appropriate system quality measures that take several dimensions of concern into consideration (e.g. cost, performance, security, availability).

c. *Planning*: Establishing an appropriate adaptation strategy that takes into account the trade-offs that could be affected between different quality dimensions.

d. *Execution*: Building systems to give the adaptive process greater flexibility and support concurrent adaptations with their actuation interface.

e. *Knowledge*: For the process of adaptation and balance between abstract system views and detailed information, different types of information are most helpful to make informed adaptation decisions.

4.1.2 Evaluation of Self-Adaptive Applications

There are various points of view that could be analyzed in method of evaluation for SAS in scientific literature. Any system that adapts itself is supposed to consist of a system and a management system. The assessment of SAS is based on their scale in both main sections [2].

a. *Assessment of management system (Controller)*: This section concerns the assessment of the quality of autonomous mechanisms by the controller or managing unit. This part focuses on the mechanisms of self-adaptation and high performance to be dealt with in the development process. The quality of the design in this category affects the all-in-one quality and overall performance of the SAS significantly.

b. *Assessment of the implementing system*: It is concerned with assessing the qualities of the SAS that are often based on self-adaptation performance. It concerns issues of quality that are measured during system performance.

Evaluation mechanisms can also be dependent on the various quality attributes and software metrics of self-adapting applications. The quality characteristics are used for the assessment of system quality, with emphasis on such qualities as performance and optimization and are relevant for autonomous systems. The software metrics used to evaluate adjustment quality, both local and global, include adaptive services, adaptation time, and degree of decentralization [2].

4.1.3 Selection of Approaches for Available Assessment

The following premises are considered for selecting various approaches for evaluation. Our goals are to provide general and definite guidance on the assessment of autonomous systems by drawing upon the evaluation approaches available. Therefore, some of the approaches studied by researchers to identify available assessment approaches identified their shared values and differences for SAS. The performance is evaluated by some basic parameters like evaluation, adaptively, quality, metric. The main study is identified using various quality attributes and different software metrics as assessment mechanisms. To achieve the same, many of the studies are examined [2].

The aim of this chapter is to address three main challenges. First, the different adaptive applications in Edge framework still to be fully resolved. Second, we will discuss the new taxonomy of adaptive applications monitoring requirements orchestrated in accordance with basic Edge frameworks. Third, we will discuss the use of widely employed monitoring technologies for the cloud and compare them in terms of reliability and high performance.

4.2 The Framework

Various software solutions have proposed cloud-based systems, including the Internet of Things (IoT) applications. So, as a result, thousands of users and various devices are connected to Internet applications, resulting in the generation and processing of trillions of gigabytes of data in cloud data centres. However, because of the large heterogeneous volume of data generated by various users and devices and transmitted to central cloud data centres, communication bandwidth and computing resources are used inefficiently. Given that all the resources and computer intelligence required to process data are mainly located in cloud-central data centres, data analytics are still an ongoing problem in research on current cloud solutions, such as Amazon Web Services IoT or Google' Cloud Dataflow. Modern cloud structures, such as Edge [3] and fog [4] computing, are defined as increasing the capacity and responsibility of resources on the network in comparison to the traditional and centralized available cloud architectures. In Edge framework, delays and response times are low for different Edge applications [3].

4.2.1 Edge Computing Framework

Edge computing allows systems to process data to the data source on the middle edge of the network. The analysis and knowledge generation at or near the data source reduces the communication bandwidth between the sensor and the central data centre. Edge computing solutions are mostly based on an IoT gateway model and soft-level corporate stacks, and operate as an aggregate and controller at the edge of IoT deployment [5].

The self-adaptive Edge framework application enables developers to visually develop and manage apps, connected protocols, and dial-up data flows to manage, analyze, and transmit data. The Edge framework's overall functionality may be broken into: field device connection, applications development, and fog, edge, and cloud connections [6].

a. **Field Devices Connection**: The communication between devices and the entrance is simplified by this framework. Initially, it encapsulates protocols such as Modbus and OPC- UA to be able to reuse the common format on different devices, and then creates an automated digital image of a device to connect it easily to the gateway and to the cloud. It offers a wide range of APIs, such as RS 232/485, Bluetooth, and BLE for interfaces with the I/O and gateway.

b. **Applications Development**: An IoT Edge application container used on gateways, where the user can create applications.

c. **Connectivity**: Provides the full connectivity manager for remote cloud servers in which telemetry data are stored and promoted, and a policy-oriented publisher system that sums up applications from the complexity of the network layer and the publishing protocol is used. It provides full administration of the network [6].

Edge computing refers to the processing of data on and near the device. This huge amount of data could be difficult to handle completely in the cloud network. Edge computing offers the complete calculation or part of the calculation, which can handle data close to data in the Edge network. It allows low latency, quicker response, and more detailed data analysis [7].

IoT-connected devices typically provide healthcare, smart city, smart grid, transport, multimedia, and security services. These services are generally dependent on AI methods, which are intensive in calculations and which use massive data. These devices had been sending data to the cloud or a local data centre for data processing a few years ago. The Edge node data part can be processed with ongoing developments in Edge computing, which minimizes the total latency of the application [7].

4.2.2 Why Edge Computing?

Currently the whole world is being digitized and data are generated in several fields. In most cases, this information needs to be processed quickly to facilitate current technology (real-time applications). A few years ago, cloud technologies were introduced, which gradually reduced the need for computers to be owned by small- to medium-sized companies and research institutes. Edge computing is an alternative way to calculate the data location and is especially suited for real-time use. Part of the IoT, in particular, may require short response times, private data, and large data that may be difficult for the network [6].

This chapter focuses on the monitoring of these SAS in an Edge-based environment, where the data processing takes time. Consequently, it is necessary to monitor and auto-adjust this processing to ensure that the centralized cloud and Edge facilities, border devices, and the complete infrastructure is compatible with each other and utilized efficiently [5]. Figure 4.1 provides as an example of a modern computing framework scheme architecture with a variety of layers: a) Central cloud computing [8], b) software-defined network (SDN) and virtualization network functions (NFV) technology [9], c) Edge computing framework [5], and d) IoT objects, sensors, or users [6]. Below is an example of pioneering cloud computing frameworks of the multi-layer architecture presented in the figure:

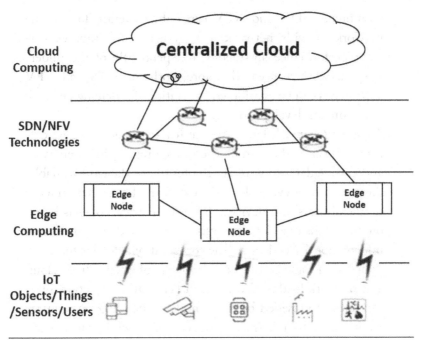

Figure 4.1   Different layers of four-layered IoT framework [5, 7].

The complete task of the IoT data communication procedure is divided into four layers, each with its own task.

a. ***Centralized data analytics over cloud***: This layer contains cloud data centres that may be part of different providers. For storage, application, and data processing operations, the centralized cloud computing layer can typically be used. Applications in this layer can be made up of various modular services [5] with an individual application conducting different high-quality data processing for various user requirements [3].

b. ***SDN/NFV technologies***: New ways of designing, creating, and operating a network are emerging, with the development of NFV and SDN [10]. These two additional technologies can facilitate the data transition between the cloud and Edge nodes. Implementation can easily improve the management and dynamics of the network. For example, if the current quality of the network is not satisfactory, the path between the Centralized Cloud Layer (CCL) (the first layer) and the Edge Computing Layer (ECL) can be altered.

Combined, SDN and NFV can define overall flow of the network, provide network management, and improve network performance abstraction independently of the underlying network devices. Therefore, both the SDN and NFV approaches can be considered as solutions for driving network environment development [1].

c. *Edge computing*: Edge nodes are IoT gateways and data collection services that can be used to aggregate, filter, encrypt, and encode data streams. Attributes to raw data are available. Here, resources available in the cloud are distributed, moving near end users and devices. The use of Edge nodes is based on time-sensitive data analysis for which these streams of information are collected. The computational load is therefore removed in some cases from computers of a centralized cloud and network load is also reduced [11]. Other functionalities can also be provided by Edge nodes depending on requirements for each case. These nodes consist of services in an early warning system that captures direct sensor link data, filters the data, adds the various calculated values, and then sends the data to the "warning trigger", the other service that runs in a centralized cloud layer. An ECL can therefore download substantial amounts data from the base network and data centres. As an enlargement of the centralized cloud, this new paradigm gives low latency, position awareness of devices, and optimizes user experience under quality of services [1, 11].

d. *Field objects/sensors/users*: Connected devices are present on the Internet in this layer. Sensors may able to evaluate different network parameters and users also are able to use constrained devices like mobile phones using online software solutions. They may be able to control objects [1].

4.2.3 Characteristics

The previously discussed framework has many characteristics over the classical model, some of them include:

a. *Reduced network traffic levels*: Edge nodes at the Edge layer can filter unnecessary information into a CCL and only aggregate important information to the first layer [7].

b. *Enhanced application performance*: Instead of using the centralized cloud computing layer, data processing locally at the Edge of ECL next to users or devices can be used to reduce latency, reduce response time, thus, improving the quality of services [5].

c. *New load balance applications*: This paradigm introduced new service functions such as the operating services movement between the CCL and the ECL to support on-demand load balance. By localizing the strength of the calculation at Edge nodes as compared with the traditionally centralized calculation, it can produce a highly improved load balance conduct [11].

d. *Locality, network, and context information awareness*: As a result of its advanced computing architecture, end-user information can now be traceable in order to provide customized services efficiently, such as mobility, networking condition, behaviour, environment, and location. These ensure that user requirements and quality of experience (QoE) preferences (as a direct user satisfaction measurement) are taken into account [1].

e. *Reduced energy use*: The demand for maximizing energy efficiency has always been connected to the rapid growth of Internet-connected objects and users. Tasks not far from node Edge devices, such as central cloud data centres, can be downloaded. This reduces their use in terminals, central computer infrastructures, and network points between the ECL and CCL [1].

4.3 Literature Review

The main aim of this chapter is to explore the fundamental issues that are still not properly addressed in different academic literatures and industry to develop surveillance in the context of Edge computing. The focus is on the analysis of the elemental features of existing cloud technologies, to understand how these challenges can currently be addressed, and to determine precisely their strengths and weaknesses in this field [2]. The review is based on the different application monitoring level of SAS.

In particular, it is possible to summarize the principal contribution of this article as follows: a) Systematic analysis of different concepts of monitoring and b) identifying the main technical and open challenges for monitoring.

4.3.1 Analysis of Monitoring Levels

A better monitoring system is needed to address the complete spectrum of demands, including the underlying infrastructures and the Edge computing systems. A changing operations environment to fulfil that QoS is a requirement of the application [1].

4.3.1.1 Virtual Machine Level Monitoring Virtualization is possible for all physical resources, including computer processor units, computer memory, discs, and network. On a single physical machine, multiple virtual machines (VMs) can be deployed and, thus, share physical resources. Here, we must control both the CCL and ECL that have configurable virtualized resource levels. Such resources should have little or no self-sufficient intervention from a request provider [6].

Monitoring the virtual machines in different cloud data centres and various Edge nodes is done in order to make efficient use of resources. By monitoring efficiently, the use of these virtualized resources and optimization of performance can be best achieved. These resources are monitored using mainly the computer processor unit, computer memory, storage, and network monitoring tools; the computer processor unit displays the number of computer processor units as a percentage used of the all-computer processor units in one virtual machine [1]. The processing capacity is not available if processor use reaches 100% and the computer processor unit run queues start to fill in. The large number of data that is used by a virtual machine is recorded or the percentage of drive space used can be indicated. Further storage of the virtual machine and allocation to the corresponding partition can frequently solve disc space problems. Network use is the volume of traffic, including external and internal high-volume data, on a particular network of a virtual machine [3].

In order to ensure that monitoring as a service (MAAS) is available for various cloud-based application providers and clients that have data monitoring in a multitenant environment, Hume et al. [12] have adopted a cloud monitoring system. They work across federated clouds but are limited to data centre monitoring tools. All infrastructures must use the same monitoring system in this approach. A cloud-based monitoring solution can be used across federated testbeds while it is one of the main requirements for state-of-the-art computer frameworks.

A mathematical model for estimating overhead resources for virtual machines was developed by Spalding et al. [12] any application on a specified platform may be used in the proposed model to approximate the virtualized resource demands. The model can also be used to calculate combined resource requirements for virtual machines that are simple host co-located. The solution sets out the minimum resources needed to avoid lower performance due to hunger from resources of a virtual machine.

Another notable aspect of this work is the use of the virtualized profiling resources that Kwon et al. [13] demonstrated in a monitoring system architecture that consists of a dashboard showing how servers and virtual machines are used in real time. It was noted that if the processor unit was overloaded, storage and memory will not normally work on virtual servers. The article, however, did not explain the experiment, and, thus, the given solution cannot be fully used for performance improvement of a virtual machine. The proposed surveillance architecture should only be utilized for a certain specification.

In Meera et al. [14] a system is proposed to monitor agent-based resources that provide the cloud-based application provider with virtual machine-related information (processor unit and memory use). A proposed alarm function triggers if the value violates a limit, which is used for various purposes, such as prediction of faults and service level access (SLA) evaluation, can improve the proposed surveillance architecture. The dependency on centralized coordination limits this architecture. In contrast, monitoring agency reporting resources should be autonomous to meet the requirements of self-adaptation solutions for Edge calculations.

Clayman et al. [15] described the lattice monitoring framework, which enables system parameters for virtual infrastructures to be measured and reported in real time for cloud-based service management. This monitoring framework provides the library necessary for implementing a custom surveillance system with APIs, considered a toolkit. The primary objective of the given framework of monitoring is to collect and share information via the User Datagram Protocol (UDP) or multi-cast protocol. In the monitoring framework, as a result, the visualization functionality of their solution proposal does not apply.

The iOverbook autonomous resource management tool was introduced by Caglar et al. [16] in heterogeneous and virtualized contexts. These provide a feed-forward neural network strategy based on an online overbooking strategy, which takes into account historical resources used to predict the mean processor units and the use of memory one step forward. But the efficient filtering of potential could improve their work, particularly on the Edge nodes in broadbands, which can quench heavy data overhead transmission. Also, to enable the proposed solution in highly dynamic environments, we need to work with a high sampling frequency.

4.3.1.2 Container-Level Monitoring   Virtual machines use of containers that do not need an operating system (as other virtual server types do) to boot, are increasing quickly [17]. One reason is that the images of the containers are much smaller than the images of the virtual machine. A number of containers have been developed to support hypervisor-based technology, including the container service Amazon EC2 and Google Container Engine (GKE).

Because container-driven services are lighter in nature, they can be implemented more efficiently and quickly than virtual machines. In framework applications, this type of agility is easier for pulling container images or migrating appliances into cloud-computer nodes using traditional machine-based virtual technology. Agility is necessary, because the migration process is an effective tool for many applications, including load balance, hardware failure, scale systems, and allocation of resources [17].

With the advanced calculation trend, which changed the dynamic cloud environment and workload, users can support self-adaptation to meet apps and users through this lightweight cloud technology. Interoperable service and orchestration packaging can also be offered, enabling the linking different software components to create the entire application. The lightweight distribution and orchestration by the decentralized Edge cloud of portable applications allows the data management and calculation to move from data centres to the end of a network [1].

Stankovski et al. [18] suggested implementing a distributed self-adjusting architecture using a container-based Edge computing concept like Docker and Kubernetes to define a high time-consuming equality for applications. The containerized application (file upload use cases) can be deployed at different locations to create, serve, and destroy the service. Each container can have the necessary resource features for the host assigned to monitoring and operational strategy data by the user, manager, or developer of application.

The performance of containers in Docker based on the use of system resources was evaluated by Preeth et al. [19]. From the criteria, authors proposed that container-based virtualization is similar to bare metal memory, processor unit, and disc operating systems. Docker's performance in relation to these three metrics is closest to the performance of the native environment. However, the host operating system has far less network bandwidth than the network usage container in Docker. But only one host in this work has been assigned to an experimental container. The performance of containers may also be judged against other technologies of virtualization [19].

Beserra et al. [20] examined the performance of container virtualization as opposed to virtualizing I/O-bound drives. Based on this assessment. Furthermore, if only one abstraction exists per physical server, both virtualized techniques perform the same. Beserra et al. [21] establishes the mechanism to ensure the quality-of-service (QoS) network for critical times using Docker. The application can give priority to network access for all host-running containers, allowing them to give greater priority to more of the total network bandwith available. Thus, a network-bandwidth intensive containerized application cannot lead to poor or unwanted implementation because a Docker host is shared with other applications. However, without regard to the current data flow requirements or on-going buffer status, the authors did experiment in a static setting.

4.3.1.3 Link-Quality Monitoring   Many cloud-based applications, such as "warning systems", require minimum delays and jitter to ensure guaranteed QoS on the network. This is a challenge because the conditions of network infrastructure change continually, making it difficult to maintain performance. Some applications are deployed at network nodes as well as other centralized data centres. This is a difficult field of research as it is not just about the live migration of services between Edges [1].

For all communication transit through Edge computing frameworks, network performance is measured by end-to-end quality monitoring. The Edge paradigm consists of four types of connections in network:

a. *Cloud data-centre and an Edge node communication*: The application of advanced principles by new enabling technologies, such as SDN and NFV, to properly develop, implement, deploy, and operate networks between cloud data centres and Edge nodes within the edges of the computing framework. A dynamic setup, migration, and scale-up of routing such as network functions, packet transmission, and services on the firewall can be efficient for the virtualization of network components such as routers, bridges, and switches [7].

b. *In between Edge nodes communications*: Edge nodes handle a stream of virtualized resources locally at various locations. This helps the individual increase its full system performance through cooperation between peered Edge nodes and the delivery of content. Communication of data between these nodes could be affected by a centralized approach like SDN [10] or a completely distributed method, such as OSPF [22] through conventional routing protocols.

c. *Within cloud data-centres communications*: Data exchanges between software components in various phases of cloud-based applications are increasing rapidly, and cloud- based applications are growing significantly. Changes in connection-related networking conditions among individually replicated and distributed applications across/out of cloud data centres have resulted in a challenge to ensure good QoS for these applications types.

d. *In between end users and Edge node communication*: Self-adapting application providers must adapt services to the IoT system and the networking conditions of the customer to ensure high performance [7].

The basic network measurement parameters are:

a. *Throughput*: Maximum utilization of data channels [23].

b. *Delay*: Indicates the length a packet travels from one end-point or node to another. The time it takes to send a message to a distant location may also be considered the time of the trip [23].

c. *Packet loss*: If you do not reach your destination; one or more data packets lost through their travel through the network [23].

d. *Jitter*: The variation received in the sequence for the end-to-end delay packet. In real-time applications, this network parameter is extremely significant as jitter affects the dimensions of connected data-stream tampers [23].

A detailed analysis of the commercial gaming systems was conducted by Jiang et al. [23]. The results show that bandwidth and packet loss limitations adversely affect the quality of graphics and rate of frames, but network delay buffering does not significantly impact the graphic quality of the game services. The authors focus on the view of cloud-based gaming systems users. The service provider's point of view can be evaluated as a further field of research, as [24] noted that computer infrastructure measurement is not sufficient to run cloud services optimally. Cloud service assessment is also of extreme importance for the network level. The author proposes an approach involving the use of different technologies without any detailed information or implementation. Furthermore, the solution relates to expensive, therefore not feasible, high-capacity Edge routers.

The approach proposed does not take into account network trade. A non-intrusive Edge monitoring approach introduced by Taherizadeh et al. [25] to evaluate critical QoS, including delays, packet losses, output, and jitter, to use the QoS user experience in streaming real-time data. The authors argue that network-based knowledge monitoring helps application providers adjust to the conditions of the user, such as network status. The key adjustment option for this work is to dynamically connect users to a set of the best trusted servers with full performance of the network.

Cervino et al. [26] conducted experiments on the advantages in point-to-point streaming of virtual machines. The authors placed network distribution nodes strategically in Amazon's global cloud infrastructure. The main goal was to increase live streaming levels in point-to-point video conference services, create connections between

Amazon's cloud data centres, and reduce the packet loss between their data centres using low latency. The authors evaluate different Amazon data centre network QoS metrics in various locations.

4.3.1.4 Application-Level Monitoring   The computer edge is an agnostic application since it is not suitable for a particular software system or application. Nonetheless, all applications need to be expanded so that the applications for measuring metrics contain information about service situations and performance. Whereas many research projects take into account the reliability of cloud infrastructures, efficient monitoring techniques are still lacking for the detection and measurement of QoS degradation at the application level.

Leitner et al. [27] proposed the CloudScale monitoring system to measure the distributed application performance during its runtime and to adopt scaling policies for virtual resource supplies and de-supply. Their proposed approach to events models the workload conduct and supports a multidimensional analysis. However, only elasticity, which can often be increased or decreased regardless of application topology and reconfiguration, is considered in the resource pool.

To run a Sentinel Twitter analysis application, Rizki et al. [28] used container- based virtualization. The application includes several containerized cloud components. These can provide Docker container reconfiguration and real-time service monitoring, informing on changing load basis, the reconfiguration module on application restructuring. The authors proposal can be scalable for dynamically duplicating running components so that the workload can be divided.

Emeakaroha et al. [29] have implemented the general-purpose monitoring framework CASViD, supporting low-level system measurement, for example, of CPU, memory use, and high-level application measurements, depending on type and performance of the application. The results suggest that CASViD's efficient measuring interval can be defined based on a non-intrusive design to monitor various metrics. It offers efficient intervals for measuring various metrics for varying working loads. As the next step, this framework can be improved to support multi-level applications.

Farokhi et al. [30] proposed a stand-alone resource controller that complies with service response times by vertical scaling of both the over and under resource supply memory and CPU. The control module automatically adjusts for interactive service performance, including the Web server, optimal memory, and CPU. As maximum storage or CPU capacity is limited, scaling both vertically and horizontally could expand so that unlimited workloads could be generated in broad Edge scenarios.

To achieve automated application performance, Xiong et al. [31] proposed the model-driven vPerfGuard framework. There are three modules to this approach that can detect performance bottlenecks: a) A sensor element for collecting system measurement time and application level metrics, such as application performance and response time; b) A model building element that allows a custom model to be created that demonstrates the relationship between application performance and system metrics; and c) An updated model for automatic detection when changing the performance model.

Mastelic et al. [32] proposed the response time and the use of the central processing unit and memory. Their monitoring system includes all application processes consumption. Those procedures have the same parent process and, therefore, list the process identifications for the application being monitored; all processes that belong to the application can be summed up in resources and calculated for total resource consumption. This model could include additional types of measurements.

Cheng et al. [33] proposed a cloud-monitoring runtime model performance guarantee approach. A performance model is built using the linear regression algorithm using runtime monitoring data. This includes the resource allocated to the VM, number of applications co-existing on the VM itself, actual use by resource application, and operational load, etc. The outcome shows that performance can control the provisioning approach efficiently to reach specified performance goals.

Casas et al. [34] discussed real-time migration of video streaming service instances to address the impact of mobility for users. Authors used an advanced computer environment to quickly replace cloud services across various borders if a user sees the video quality as inadequate. In this work, supported by the input, three application-level measurement metrics, including images for frames per second, drop images, and video quality were used as a monitoring tools for deep packet inspection. These metrics are positively related to QoE. If any

Table 4.1   Summary of Application-Level Monitoring

PAPER	REVIEW	PARAMETERS
Leitner et al. [27]	Cloud application adaption	Throughput, Response Time
Rizki et al. [28]	Twitter analysis applications based on container level adaption	Throughput, Response Time
Emeakaroha et al. [29]	Breaches in cloud apps	Throughput, Response Time
Farokhi et al. [30]	Web applications adaption for cloud	Throughput, Response Time
Xiong et al. [31]	The performance of cloud apps can be predicted using models	Throughput, Response Time
Mastelic et al. [32]	Audio/Video services of cloud apps can be predicted using models	Response time
Cheng et al. [33]	A performance model is built using the linear regression algorithm using runtime monitoring data for resource allocation	Throughput, Response Time
Casas et al. [34]	Real time migration of video streaming service based on QoE	Throughput
Rao et al. [35]	Distributed RL mechanism for resource allocation	Throughput

of these measurement thresholds are violated for a certain period of time, the service must be migrated.

Rao et al. [35] used an iBalloon distributed reinforcement learning (RL) mechanism for the supply of VM resource that is autonomous and adaptable, in which surveillance is essential. Cloud infrastructures now offer the flexibility to adapt application performance to the changes in work charge by means of horizontal or vertical scaling solutions.

Table 4.1 shows the review details of different papers based on response time and throughput parameters.

4.4 Technical and Open Challenges for Monitoring

The following are the main challenges currently facing the monitoring of adaptive applications within Edge computing frames based on our analyses:

a. *Mobility management*: Applications are managed over moving devices.
b. *Scalability and resource availability*: Applications and resources are available and scalable.

c. *Prior knowledge:* The knowledge is required to implement adaptive applications.

d. *Data management:* Data can be managed over cloud and fog.

e. *Coordinated decentralization:* Decentralization should be managed by coordination functions.

f. *Saving time, cost and energy:* SAS must be used to save time and energy.

g. *Optimal resource scheduling among Edge nodes:* Scheduling is needed to improve SAS function.

h. *Fault tolerance:* Fault monitoring is needed at the Edge point.

i. *Proactive systems:* To monitor and overcome these challenges list here, we can use proactive systems before implementing adaptive applications.

4.5 Requirement Classification

The classifications of monitoring for SAS in the respect of the Edge computing framework are divided into functional and non-functional requirements:

a. *Functional requirements:* Includes the usability of applications in multi-tenant environments and in virtualization. The application must have the capability for long-term and large-scale storing capacity. In dynamic environments, adaptive services must support different type of actions like the service migration, installation, and configuration of monitoring systems. The previously mentioned requirements are common for all different monitoring levels. If we see about the different monitoring levels. Then in the Container and in Virtual monitor level, it is required to provide quick resource management on the time and the support of hardware virtualization. In the end-to-end link monitor level, it is required to focus on QoS and on-demand network configuration as well as network quality conditions. At the application level of monitoring, the key points addressed in the related works were grouped into four topics based on their use and importance for the SAS design and are analyzed and described. Such topics highlight important evidence that must be considered in the development of these applications and frameworks. Because important elements cited in the literature are used in the design of such frameworks, understanding this evidence is useful for the design of frameworks for self-adaptive applications, according to our analysis. Furthermore, this evidence can aid in the comprehension of open issues that need to be addressed, resulting in more comprehensive and solid future solutions.

b. *Non-functional requirements*: These are necessary for the creation of any software system. These needs must be given extra attention in the self-adaptive applications domain, primarily because they appear as terms for QoS attributes in numerous SLAs and monitoring processes. As a result, we discovered that monitoring and QoS in self-adaptive applications must be addressed holistically, as the applications' QoS should not be monitored solely through specific QoS parameters (i.e., individual metrics). In this way, combining QoS qualities might provide more proof of an application's health, as different metrics can provide a complete picture of services. Although such a combination may be a viable answer for some applications, it is not for everyone.

c. *Adaptation of architecture*: Adaptation is a characteristic that allows a software system to recognize the context in which it is used or to alter itself in real time. Parallel to this, architectural adaptation was a frequent theme in other studies that needed more research. Self-adaptive applications run in a distributed environment and can interact with users of several applications at the same time to meet their needs, which can alter depending on the context in which the apps are deployed and/or used. As a result, a successful adaptation in one setting may have unintended consequences in another. As a result, concerns including performance, reliance on sub-architectures, and linkages between sub-architectures must be addressed. Representation of the goal of software development entails breaking down various objectives into a set of requirements. As a result, the execution of an adaptation activity will alter the requirements and may alter the software's aims. The software in self-adaptive applications is represented by basic or composite services, and choreography may be involved. The authors of the study published by Casas et al. [34] raised worry about the lack of support for goal representation at run-time. When an adaptation activity is undertaken, this gap has hampered the depiction of self-adaptive applications and the evolution of apps.

d. *Automated support*: The creation of tools to assist in the transfer of legacy systems to the cloud, as well as the lack of self-adaptation assistance in such tools. In autonomic systems, automated assistance tries to increase system reliability through component-level testing.

Edge computing allows for the deployment of applications at the network's edge. Applications are frequently organized as microservices to take use of available devices' dispersed resources, with tight criteria for low latency and high availability. However, a decentralized Edge system, for which the application may be designed, is characterized by high volatility due to unreliable devices that make up the system or unexpected network exits. As a result, application deployment and assurance that it will continue to function in the face of volatility is difficult. We offer an adaptive framework for deploying and sustaining microservice-based applications.

4.6 Conclusion

Monitoring solutions collect information at several levels to make things easier the self- adaptive decision-making mechanisms in the Edge computing world. To this end, other monitoring levels, including containers, network quality end-to-end and application, and virtualized resources such as processor units, memory, and discs, are important to consider. In the future, researchers can focus to improve these previously listed parameters. In this chapter, research papers were selected to be examined so all important requirements for functional and non-functional monitoring in Edge computing frameworks were mentioned for adaptive applications.

The IoT is totally dependent on applications. Services also differ according to IoT applications; low-level applications and high-level applications both have different services. The service can be supervised for this purpose. A Web application service, for example, can be monitored to ensure that the application's response time is within acceptable limits. Whether a service is monitored is in keeping with the perceived risk that an infringement occurs. If the perceived risk is low, there may be no need for surveillance and vice versa. The degree of risk perceived in connection with a service transaction may change over time. However, this change cannot be dealt with by traditional monitoring techniques. A SAS monitor adapts the perceived level of risk to noticed changes. This framework combines a conventional service monitor and a self-control protocol. Research and development are beginning to take place in the applications developed for Edge computing frameworks. Great attention has been given to the monitoring of adaptive applications of Edge framework, an area still to be examined and improved.

Acknowledgement

We would like to acknowledge Professor C.K. Jha, Head, Department of Computer Science for their support and Banasthali Vidyapith, Jaipur, who provided us a better platform to research and explore different aspects of computer science.

References

1. Weyns, D. (2020). An introduction to self-adaptive systems: A contemporary software engineering perspective. John Wiley & Sons.
2. Raibulet, C., Fontana, F. A., Capilla, R., & Carrillo, C. (2017). An overview on quality evaluation of self-adaptive systems. Managing trade-offs in adaptable software architectures, 2017, pp. 325–352.
3. Shi, W., Cao, J., Zhang, Q., Li, Y., & Xu, L. (2016). Edge computing: Vision and challenges. IEEE internet of things journal, 3(5), 637–646.
4. Bonomi, F., Milito, R., Natarajan, P., & Zhu, J. (2014). Fog computing: A platform for internet of things and analytics. In Big data and internet of things: A roadmap for smart environments (pp. 169–186). Springer, Cham.
5. Saxena, M., & Jha, D. (2019). A new pattern mining algorithm for analytics of real time internet of things data. International journal of innovative technology and exploring engineering, 9(1). doi: 10.35940/ijitee. A4506.119119
6. Saxena, M., Vyas, V., & Jha, C. K. (2021, March). A framework for multi-sensor data fusion in the context of IoT smart city parking data. In

IOP Conference Series: Materials Science and Engineering (Vol. 1099, No. 1, p. 012011). IOP Publishing.

7. Long, C., Cao, Y., Jiang, T., & Zhang, Q. (2017). Edge computing framework for cooperative video processing in multimedia IoT systems. IEEE transactions on multimedia, 20(5), 1126–1139.

8. Wang, L., Von Laszewski, G., Younge, A., He, X., Kunze, M., Tao, J., & Fu, C. (2010). Cloud computing: A perspective study. New generation computing, 28(2), 137–146.

9. Nguyen, V. G., Brunstrom, A., Grinnemo, K. J., & Taheri, J. (2017). SDN/NFV-based mobile packet core network architectures: A survey. IEEE communications surveys & tutorials, 19(3), 1567–1602.

10. Herrera, J. D. J. G., & Vega, J. F. B. (2016). Network functions virtualization: A survey. IEEE Latin America transactions, 14(2), 983–997.

11. Satyanarayanan, M. (2017). The emergence of Edge computing. Computer, 50(1), 30–39.

12. Hume, A. C., Al-Hazmi, Y., Belter, B., Campowsky, K., Carril, L. M., Carrozzo, G., ... Van Seghbroeck, G. (2012, June). Bonfire: A multi-cloud test facility for internet of services experimentation. In International Conference on Testbeds and Research Infrastructures (pp. 81–96). Springer, Berlin, Heidelberg.

13. Spalding, M. D., Fish, L., & Wood, L. J. (2008). Toward representative protection of the world's coasts and oceans—progress, gaps, and opportunities. Conservation letters, 1(5), 217–226.

14. Kwon, S. K., & Noh, J. H. (2013). Implementation of monitoring system for cloud computing environments. International journal of modern engineering research (IJMER), 3(4), 1916–1918.

15. Meera, A., & Swamynathan, S. (2013). Agent based resource monitoring system in IaaS cloud environment. Procedia technology, 10, 200–207.

16. Clayman, S., Galis, A., Chapman, C., Toffetti, G., Rodero-Merino, L., Vaquero, L. M., ... Rochwerger, B. (2010, April). Monitoring service clouds in the future internet. In Future internet assembly (pp. 115–126).

17. Caglar, F., & Gokhale, A. (2014, June). iOverbook: Intelligent resource-overbooking to support soft real-time applications in the cloud. In 2014 IEEE 7th International Conference on Cloud Computing (pp. 538–545). IEEE.

18. Tajon, C. A., Seo, D., Asmussen, J., Shah, N., Jun, Y. W., & Craik, C. S. (2014). Sensitive and selective plasmon ruler nanosensors for monitoring the apoptotic drug response in leukemia. ACS nano, 8(9), 9199–9208.

19. Stankovski, S., Ostojić, G., & Zhang, X. (2016). Influence of industrial internet of things on mechatronics. Journal of mechatronics, automation and identification technology, 1(1), 1–6.

20. Preeth, E. N., Mulerickal, F. J. P., Paul, B., & Sastri, Y. (2015, November). Evaluation of Docker containers based on hardware utilization. In 2015 International Conference on Control Communication & Computing India (ICCC) (pp. 697–700). IEEE.

21. Beserra, D., Moreno, E. D., Endo, P. T., & Barreto, J. (2016, October). Performance evaluation of a lightweight virtualization solution for HPC I/O scenarios. In 2016 IEEE International Conference on Systems, Man, and Cybernetics (SMC) (pp. 004681–004686). IEEE.
22. Dusia, A., Yang, Y., & Taufer, M. (2015, September). Network quality of service in docker containers. In 2015 IEEE International Conference on Cluster Computing (pp. 527–528). IEEE.
23. Soree, P., Gupta, R. K., Singh, K., Desiraju, K., Agrawal, A., Vats, P., ... & Singh, S. B. (2016). Raised HIF1α during normoxia in high altitude pulmonary edema susceptible non-mountaineers. Scientific reports, 6(1), 1–7.
24. Jiang, Y., Lin, C., Wu, J., & Sun, X. (2001, July). Integrated performance evaluating criteria for network traffic control. In Proceedings. Sixth IEEE Symposium on Computers and Communications (pp. 438–443). IEEE.
25. Mohit, P., Amin, R., & Biswas, G. P. (2017). Design of authentication protocol for wireless sensor network- based smart vehicular system. Vehicular communications, 9, 64–71.
26. Taherizadeh, S., Jones, A. C., Taylor, I., Zhao, Z., & Stankovski, V. (2018). Monitoring self-adaptive applications within Edge computing frameworks: A state-of-the-art review. Journal of systems and software, 136, 19–38.
27. Cervino, J., Rodríguez, P., Trajkovska, I., Mozo, A., & Salvachúa, J. (2011, July). Testing a cloud provider network for hybrid P2P and cloud streaming architectures. In 2011 IEEE 4th International Conference on Cloud Computing (pp. 356–363). IEEE.
28. Leitner, P., Satzger, B., Hummer, W., Inzinger, C., & Dustdar, S. (2012, March). CloudScale: A novel middleware for building transparently scaling cloud applications. In Proceedings of the 27th Annual ACM Symposium on Applied Computing (pp. 434–440).
29. Rizki, R., Rakhmatsyah, A., & Nugroho, M. A. (2016, May). Performance analysis of container-based hadoop cluster: OpenVZ and LXC. In 2016 4th International Conference on Information and Communication Technology (ICoICT) (pp. 1–4). IEEE.
30. Emeakaroha, V. C., Ferreto, T. C., Netto, M. A., Brandic, I., & De Rose, C. A. (2012, July). CASViD: Application level monitoring for SLA violation detection in clouds. In 2012 IEEE 36th Annual Computer Software and Applications Conference (pp. 499–508). IEEE.
31. Farokhi, S., Lakew, E. B., Klein, C., Brandic, I., & Elmroth, E. (2015, September). Coordinating CPU and memory elasticity controllers to meet service response time constraints. In 2015 International Conference on Cloud and Autonomic Computing (pp. 69–80). IEEE.
32. Xiong, X., & De la Torre, F. (2013). Supervised descent method and its applications to face alignment. In Proceedings of the IEEE Conference on Computer Vision and Pattern Recognition (pp. 532–539).
33. Mastelic, T., Emeakaroha, V. C., Maurer, M., & Brandic, I. (2012, April). M4Cloud-generic application level monitoring for resource-shared cloud environments. In CLOSER (pp. 522–532).

34. Cheng, L., Wang, S. H., Chen, Q. C., & Liao, X. M. (2011). Moderate noise induced cognition impairment of mice and its underlying mechanisms. Physiology & behavior, 104(5), 981–988.

35. Casas, P., D'Alconzo, A., Wamser, F., Seufert, M., Gardlo, B., Schwind, A., ... Schatz, R. (2017, May). Predicting QoE in cellular networks using machine learning and in-smartphone measurements. In 2017 Ninth International Conference on Quality of Multimedia Experience (QoMEX) (pp. 1–6). IEEE.

5

FEDERATED LEARNING AND ITS APPLICATION IN MALWARE DETECTION

SAKSHI BHAGWAT AND GOVIND P. GUPTA

Department of Information Technology, National Institute of Technology Raipur, Chhattisgarh, India

Contents

DOI: 10.1201/9781003264545-5

5.1 Introduction

Many organizations and industries are facing the problem of growing cyber-attacks. Malware are the programmes that, when executed, can destroy the function of a system. Malware can be classified on the basis of behaviour and execute itself as adware, spyware, worms, Trojans, viruses, rootkits, backdoors, ransomware, and browser hijackers. Computer and mobile systems are attacked to destroy resources, steal sensitive information, and user credentials. For detecting malware in machine learning (ML), the local data is collected in one aggregated server. This leads to the violation of privacy, which can be solved by using federated learning (FL), which allows for the detection of malware when local data is at the device.

FL is a new technology introduced by Google in 2016. It is also known as collaborative learning. The FL model is trained in a decentralized network from which the device has local data; the network does not need to exchange the data, which preserves its confidentiality. FL is also combined with blockchain technology and is used with IoT devices. A decentralized network is one in which the nodes have control over their data and permission to access it, while a centralized network used in ML has a single authorized server that manages all data and permissions for the access. This chapter addresses the research gap.

In Section 5.2, we review related work and identify the gap in current state-of-the-art research. We conclude this work in Section 5.3, summarizing our main findings and future work. A list of key acronyms and abbreviations used in this chapter are given in Table 5.1.

5.2 Federated Learning and its Architecture

This section presents a brief description of the FL concept and its architecture.

5.2.1 Federated Learning

With the speedy increase of data, training the ML model becomes more complex, and for large datasets, it consumes more time and resources. In the traditional ML model, various participants are required to upload their data on a central server to learn a model.

Table 5.1   List of Key Acronyms

ACRONYMS	DEFINITIONS
FL	Federated learning
IoT	Internet of Things
HFL	Horizontal federated learning
VFL	Vertical federated learning
FTL	Federated transfer learning
ML	Machine learning
SVM	Support vector machine
CNN	Convolution neural network
DNN	Deep neural network
HMM	Hidden Markov model
GRUs	Gated recurrent units
DSA	Digital signature algorithm
ECC	Elliptic curve cryptography
LSTM	Long short-term memory
HPC	Hardware performance counter
PCA	Principle component analysis

Due to this privacy issue, many organizations are not inclined to participant in centralized learning. To alleviate this drawback, another approach is used in which the training dataset is subdivided; simultaneously, a model is trained on the subset and a parameter server is used to aggregate model parameters. Author of Ref. [1] has proposed FL that merges various participants and train models aggregately without uploading data onto a server, which avoids collection of private data. The model architecture is shown in Figure 5.1.

According the authors of Ref. [2], FL has two architectures: horizontal FL (HFL) and vertical FL (VFL).

5.2.2 Federated Learning Architecture

5.2.2.1 Horizontal Federated Learning   In HFL, different participants collaborate and train an ML model; they have same data structure. Figure 5.2 represents the HFL. The following four steps are used to train a model:

- *Step 1*: Participants locally train the model, and then share the result with server use encryption, differential privacy, and secret sharing techniques to maintain privacy.

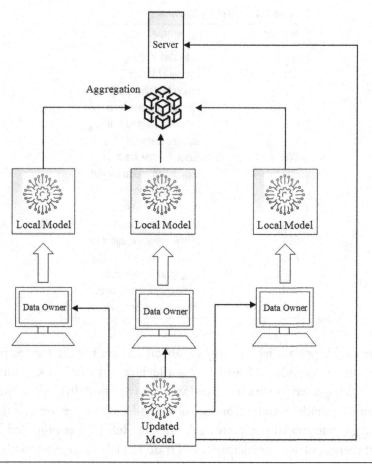

Figure 5.1   Working model of federated learning architecture.

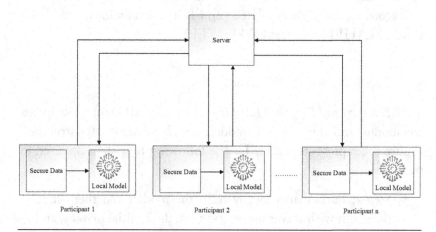

Figure 5.2   Horizontal federated learning.

- *Step 2*: The server aggregates the result from the participants without learning any information about the participants.
- *Step 3*: The server sends the aggregated result back to the participants.
- *Step 4*: The participant updates their model.

The assumption for HFL is that participants are honest and the server is honest and curious, so there is no information leakage.

5.2.2.2 Vertical Federated Learning   VFL is also known as feature-based federated learning. Figure 5.3 shows the workflow of VFL. An example includes when two companies train the model jointly, each with their own data, but they don't want to share the data due to data privacy issues. To ensure confidentiality, a collaborator is used, and it is assumed that the collaborator is honest and does not collide with either party and that the parties are honest but curious. This FL has two parts. The first is encrypted entity alignment. In this, a unique ID is given to each user in two companies based on encryption, but there are some common users of both companies; the common users must confirm but without exposing their data between companies. The second is encrypted model training. After knowing the common user model which is trained on this data. The training process of VFL is shown in Figure 5.3.

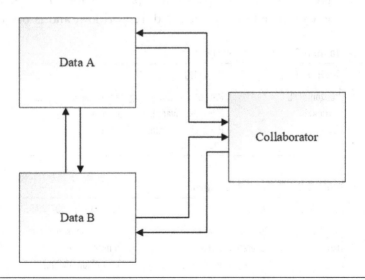

Figure 5.3   Vertical federated learning.

5.2.2.3 Federated Transfer Learning Another architecture of FL is proposed in Ref. [3], called federated transfer learning (FTL). FTL has introduced secure aggregation to protect the privacy of users. It uses data from various sources to train the model. It increases the accuracy and decreases the loss or error in predicting the label. There are three components of FTL: guest, host, and arbiter.

- *Guest*: Holds data and the server's data computation and encryption.
- *Host*: Holds data.
- *Arbiter*: Sends public keys to the guest and host. It is responsible for collecting gradient.

The guest and host consist of local data from which local models are trained and encrypted results are computed. Model training is carried out in two approaches: heterogeneous and homogenous. From the data, gradients and loss are calculated. These encrypted values are transferred to the arbiter. Modified gradient and loss are computed by the arbiter and sent to the guest and host, from which they modify their local models. This FTL workflow is iterative until the loss is minimized to the expected value.

5.3 Frameworks for Federated Learning

- *PySyft*: PySyft is the open-source platform for FL. It is a framework based on PyTorch and TensorFlow, and is based

Table 5.2   Summary of Architectures

ARCHITECTURE	BENEFITS
Horizontal FL	Provides security using independence of models
Vertical FL	Provides privacy using encryption
FTL	Reduces loss using higher accuracy encryption

Table 5.3   Summary of FL Platforms

PLATFORM	FOCUS	SUPPORTING SOFTWARE
PySyft	Preserves privacy	PyTorch, TensorFlow
TFF	Federated learning	TensorFlow, Keras
FATE	Secured Computation	TensorFlow, PyTorch
LEAF	Multi-tasking, Meta-learning	Python library

on providing privacy using differential privacy and computes encryption using multi-party computation and homomorphic encryption.

- ***TensorFlow Federated (TFF)***: TFF is a framework developed by Google for decentralized learning based on TensorFlow. It consists of two layers:
  a. Federated learning: A high-level interface that allows performing basic FL tasks such as federated training and evaluation of models.
  b. Federated core: The low-level interface that allows customization of the FL by combining communication operators with TensorFlow.

- ***Federated AI Technology Enabler (FATE)***: For secured computation in FL, the WeBank AI has started an open-source project called FATE. It provides secured computation using homomorphic encryption and multi-party computation.

- ***LEAF***: A framework allowed for FL, meta-learning, and multi-tasking. It consists of three components: datasets, reference implementation, and metrics. It is used for different datasets, such as Federated Extended MNIST (FEMNIST) for image classification, Twitter for sentiment analysis, Shakespeare for next character prediction, CelebA for image classification, and a synthetic dataset for classification.

5.4 Malware and its Types

In this modern age, use of mobile devices is increasing. This growth of mobile devices has led to privacy and security threats. As the Android operating system is open-source, it becomes easy for hackers to attack mobile devices. SMS spam, malware, and phishing are all cybercrimes that have increased. Cybercrime has increased by 600% since the beginning of the COVID-19 global pandemic. In first half of 2021, 1.3 million malicious Android apps are found, which leads to a total of 23.4 million Android-based malwares. This makes Android malware detection essential.

Malware is any software programme that can harm a computer system. It is a programme written by a hacker to attack a client's PC and harm it in different manners. Antivirus is unable to protect the system, if it is attacked by malwares. New tools are available on the Internet for hackers to develop malware, requiring fewer skills. To protect the system of an organization or of individual from malware is the responsibility of cybersecurity.

Some programmes become installed without the knowledge of the owner and they cause further damage to existing programmes. Malware is classified according to its behaviour.

The following types of malware are described below:

- *Adware*: It shows an advertisement on a system, it poses the most risk.
- *Spyware*: As it is named, this malware spies on the user's history and sends advertisements based on that history. This is how the outsider gets a way into the user's system.
- *Virus*: When files or programmes are shared between PCs, a bit of programming is installed without the permission of the client, making changes in other programmes and causing harm to the working system.
- *Worm*: A programme that copies itself and destroys data and records on the system.
- *Trojan*: It controls the system; its form is malicious code or software.
- *Rootkit*: A programme installed inside the system without permission and accesses its framework, causing harm.
- *Backdoor*: A method to bypass normal authentication and encryption.
- *Key loggers*: Keyboard action is monitored and the client is unaware. It depends on the keyboard's working style.
- *Ransomware*: It is malware software which disable the functionality of the computer's services and asking for ransom to restore the functionality of the system.
- *Browser hijacker*: A programme installed without permission of the client and changes the system's programme settings.

To detect malware, static and dynamic malware detection methods are used. In static malware detection, the malware binary code is analyzed and in dynamic malware detection, the programme is closely monitored. Different methods are used for these approaches. For static

analysis signature-based, permission-based, and filtering approaches
are used. In dynamic analysis behaviour-based, boot sequence, and
anomaly behaviour-monitoring methods are used.

5.5 Review of Federated Learning-Based Malware Detection Schemes

This section presents a review of the FL-based malware detection models proposed in the literature. Shukla et al. [4] proposed a
malware detection framework using FL. In this framework, it has
been assumed that at each node level, malware detection is divided
into two different phases: 1. HPC-based technique, a lightweight
approach. Feature extraction and feature reduction are carried out
based on principal component analysis. Then these features are given
to an ML model to generate predictions, but this approach is ineffi-
cient; and 2. Localized feature extraction, based on image processing.
For any given binary file, an image pattern is recognized and this
pattern sequence is given as input to the RNN-LSTM to predict the
malware class label. The label at node-level is given by comparing the
confidence of the two approaches. The authors have used four different models: CNN, HMM, DNN, and FL. Out of these, FL gives
highest accuracy of 91%. FL is used for backpropagation and complex
computation; a light approach is used to perform communications
with devices, which is expensive.

Alzaylaee et al. [5] has proposed a dynamic analysis for Android
malware detection using deep learning. Stateful and stateless input
results are compared. The dataset in this paper is taken from Intel
Security's McAfee Lab. It contains 31,125 Android samples out of
which 11,505 are malware samples and the remaining 19,620 are
benign samples. Pre-processing and feature extraction are performed
on the dataset. For the feature extraction phase, the applications are
installed on mobile devices and the features are extracted for stateful
and stateless scenarios using DynaLog. DynaLog is an open-source
tool to extract features, behaviours, API calls, actions, and events.
The entire features have binary content. These features are ranked
using information gain.

Using only dynamic features for detection, 97.6% accuracy is
obtained. When using dynamic as well as static features, a 99.6%
detection rate is achieved.

Hsu et al. [6] have proposed a privacy-preserving FL system to detect malware using static analysis and metadata analysis. The dataset is created by collecting APK files from a mobile store called Opera. Features are extracted using static and dynamic analysis. Data is preprocessed by latent Dirichlet allocation and non-English items such as numbers, website addresses, email addresses, and HTML tags are recognized. Data encoding is carried out as the features can be of different types. Before implementation, all features are converted to binary attributes. The architecture of the system reduces latency and preserves data privacy as it is based on edge computation. The proposed model consists of two types: Federated SVM and Secure Multi-Party Computation (SMPC).

- *Federated SVM*: The Stochastic Gradient Descent (SGD) model is applied on federated learning. The client exchanges their gradient with the server. The server receives the local gradient from all the clients and then the server uses a method called federated averaging to aggregate the local gradient to create a global model.
- *Secure Multi-Party Computation (SMPC)*: This allows the number of clients to merge their private data as input without seeing each other's data. This method has two components: Additive secret sharing and Smart Pastro Damgård Zakarias (SPDZ). For data confidentiality, it is assumed that data shared between client and server is secured. When N clients participate, one of them is chosen to generate a big prime Q; this value is known only to the client and is used in SMPC. The approach is as follows:
  - Train the local model using local data at the client side.
  - Additive sharing is used to share the local model parameter from client to server.
  - All the local models are aggregated using encryption on the model parameter using SMPC to generate a global model.
  - This global model is sent back to the clients. The clients decrypt the model and detect malware.

Ten-fold cross-validation is used to estimate the model as it has the ability to predict unknown datasets. This proposed approach reduces the computation time and also improves the accuracy as the number of users increases. For 15 and 30 clients, the accuracy rate is highest at 93.87%.

Lin et al. [7] have classified different categories of malware using a decentralized method. The dataset consists of 10 different categories of malware: PUA, ransom, Trojan, virus, backdoor, PWS, SoftwareBundler, Trojan downloader, VirTool, and worm. The dataset consists of 10,907 malware samples out of which 5907 samples are used for training the model and the remaining 5000 data samples are used for testing.

There are six features:

a. *1-Gram*: The malware sample is represented as a sequence of binary values described as an n-gram feature to get information about malware. N-gram is the continuous sequence of n items of a given sample.

b. *Entropy*: Measures the disorders and detects data that is difficult to understand in the malware file.

c. *Image*: Haralick features are detected using quantization, in which the grey-level in an image is reduced. To classify computer vision, a local binary pattern is used.

d. *Extract string length*: Frequency of different string length is counted.

e. *File size*: Based on bytes. It is a measure of how much storage is required for a computer file.

f. *Start address*: Some malwares have a special starting address, which is a portable executable entry point for files.

The author has used different models to train the dataset. Several models used are:

1. *SVM*: A supervised learning model used to analyse data for classification and regression.

2. *LSTM*: Features a recurrent neural network architecture. Three-layer LSTM is used, which has a feedback connection.

3. *LSTM with FL*: This decentralized network is used to avoid exchange of data samples.

4. *LSTM with two hidden layers with FL*: This method has sped up the training process and not reduced accuracy.

In this research, different combinations of algorithms are used and compared SVM and LSTM. The malware dataset from VirusTotal is used with accuracy of 91.67% using FL. Experimental results show that accuracy can be increased by malware sharing. Data privacy is achieved by using FL and also model complexity is reduced due to decentralized solution.

Mothukuri et al. [8] has proposed a federated-based anomaly detection for classification of attack on IOT network. The IoT is made of devices interacting and performing tasks. Due to FL, data privacy is added at the secure layer in the IoT, which has made devices more reliable. A Modbus-based network dataset is used. Modbus is the efficient way to communicate with the devices that have no built-in communication protocol. For a higher accuracy rate, gated recurrent units (GRUs) and long short-term memory networks (LSTMs) are used for initial training rounds. LSTMs and GRUs consist of different gates used to monitor information flow and control the learning process. Some compounds used in LSTMs and GRUs are:

- *Sigmoid function:* Used to decide if the data needs to be retained or discarded. Values range from 0 to 1; 0 means the information has to be forgotten and 1 indicates the information is to be kept for future use.
- *Tangent hyperbolic*: An activation function ranging from -1 to 1.
- *Cell state:* The information kept in the memory of LSTM.
- *Gates of LSTMs*: LSTM consists of three gates: the input gate, output gate, and forget gate. Gates are used to control information retention and deletion.
  - Forget gate: The information which is useless for the learning of LSTM is deleted from the cell.
  - Input gate: Helps decide if the information should be retained for the future use.
  - Output gate: Decides the end result of network.
- *Gate of GRUs*: Consists of two gates: the reset gate and update gate. It takes less time to train.
  - Reset gate: Similar to the forget gate of LSTM; it removes information if it has no future use.
  - Update gate: Decides if information needs to be retained for the future.

FL training is executed with the IoT instances. It is executed on each end-device using the following steps:

- Define the window size.
- Define virtual instance.
- Define GRU network for each window size.
- Share the GRU ML model parameter with each instance.
- The local model is trained on GRU parameters and shares the updates.
- Instances are aggregated at the central server and update the global model. For each window, the global model is obtained.
- Copy of the global model is sent to the end-devices.

Ensemble learning is used to combine the models and achieve the highest accuracy. Performance was compared with the non-FL version on the same dataset. The FL-based approach has greater accuracy as compared to the non-FL approach. The overall performance accuracy of the FL approach is 99.5%, while for non-FL is 86.134%

5.5.1 Semi-Supervised Federated Learning-Based Malware Detection

Semi-supervised learning (SSL) has both labelled and unlabelled data, which is used to train the model. Collecting label data can be expensive, but training the model becomes easy. In SSL, the main challenge is to learn information from unlabelled data. Users can label the features but they cannot be trusted. FL is successful when labelled data is used to train the model.

Gálvez et al. [9] has proposed a less-is-more, privacy-respecting malware detection framework using FL for a semi-supervised dataset. The local data at the device contains the missing label. To enhance accuracy, FL is combined with semi-supervised ensemble learning. The dataset is taken from AndroZoo and contains 25,000 benign apps and 25,000 malicious apps; this data is local to the client and shares the result for updating. FL accuracy is dependent on perfectly labelled data; the user cannot label the data properly, so in this study, the author trains the model on semi-supervised data. Label data is available at the cloud; when local data at the client is to be updated, an unlabelled sample is used to update the parameters of the semi-supervised model. Static and dynamic analyses are performed. The

API called graphs of the application and the characteristics behaviour that is examined during execution. The client can estimate their local SAFEW weights using classifiers and trained learners.

A federated malware classifier is setup with LiM and has a server with 200 clients and 50 iteration rounds. Due to the LiM, clients in FL can learn from each other. LiM uses different learners such as as K-Nearest Neighbour with 3 neighbours, logistic regression with regularization parameter as 3, Random Forest with different number of trees such as 50, 100, or 200, and linear SVM with regularization parameter as 1. All base learners are used in rotation. Random forest with 50 trees has performed best with a 73.7% F1 score and 200 features. During 50 rounds, LiM has F1 score of 70%.

5.5.2 Federated Learning-Based Malware Detection with Fog Computing

C. Zhou et al. [10] has proposed a privacy-preserving FL scheme in fog computing win which each fog node collects the data from the IoT devices and the learning task is completed. Fog computation deploys fog nodes, which are geographically distributed in the network. These fog nodes are used as a link between IoT devices and the cloud server; they provide high computation and storage. The scheme structure is divided into three: IoT devices, fog nodes, and cloud. IoT devices are the participants in FL. They have a different local dataset. The cloud is the aggregation server and parameter server, which are used for training, aggregating and updating models. This research has used an adversary model in which the model is semi-honest. The server and fog nodes are honest but curious. They have the following characteristics:

a. Protocol is executed honestly.
b. They will not interfere in the result calculations.
c. They are curious about input of other participants.

In this study, three types of different attackers are considered: data attackers that collect private information from IoT devices, model attackers that deduce information from training data, and collusive attackers that acquire model parameters of a fog node. In this research, it has been assumed that all the entities in the scheme do not trust each other. Consider there are n numbers of fog nodes, then (n-2) fog nodes can collude with the parameter server or malicious fog

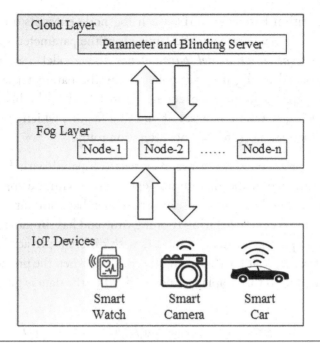

Figure 5.4 Privacy-preserving federated learning [10].

node. Figure 5.4 shows the block diagram of the privacy-preserving FL [10].

The scheme proposed has four phases:

1. *Initialization*: The cloud server contains the parameter server and blinding server. This cloud server needs initialization before training. The responsibility of the parameter server is to collect some local data in advance to train the initial model. The blinding server transmits the generated key pairs of Paillier homomorphic encryption and blinding factors to each fog node.

2. *Collection of IoT device data*: After initialization, the initial model is downloaded from the parameter server by every fog node. According to the amount of IoT devices, a privacy budget is assigned to them by each fog node. According to the privacy budget and sensitivity, Laplacian noise is added to dataset. This noisy dataset is added to the fog node.

3. *Fog node training*: Noisy data received by the fog node will get batches of data; the model is trained using a backpropagation

algorithm based on SGD. Each fog node encrypts and the blind model parameter then uploads to the parameter server.

4. *Aggregation of model parameters*: The model parameter uploaded by fog nodes is collected by the parameter server, is aggregated, and then updates global model. The blinding server generates a new set of blinding factors, which are sent to each fog node for the next iteration round.

When proposed scheme accuracy was compared with FL using SGD optimization and the training epoch as 18 with the appropriate number of samples, it was observed that they have similar accuracy. This scheme is effective during training time and has similar accuracy. While comparing accuracy of models with different privacy budgets, it was observed that model has higher accuracy when the privacy budget is smaller, so that Laplacian noise added to the data is greater.

5.5.3 Blockchain with Federated Learning for Malware Detection

Zhang et al. [11] has proposed a protected transmission method for data using edge computation, FL, and features of blockchain. This proposed transmission method is divided into three sections: edge equipment, edge server, and cloud server. Figure 5.5 shows the block diagram of blockchain-edge-based FL [11]. The model proposed in this research consists of two sections:

1. *Local data transmission*: The interaction between edge equipment and edge server.
2. *Remote data transmission*: The interaction between edge server and cloud servers.

The FL training process includes:

- *Task initialization*: Initial model parameters are sent from the cloud server to the edge server, and then the devices download the parameters.
- *Local model training and update*: Training is carried out in batches and after every batch, this original information goes through the first convolution veil and pooling veil; this manipulated information is then transmitted to the edge server. The updated value of parameters is calculated by the edge server

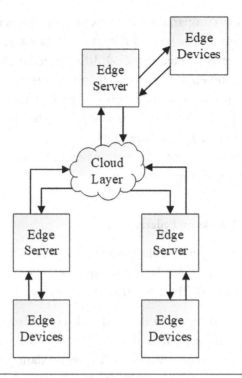

Figure 5.5   Blockchain-edge federated learning [11].

and sent to devices. Using this new parameter, the values local model is updated. Then this updated model is then sent to the edge server from devices. Aggregation models are transmitted to blockchain.

- *Global model aggregation and update*: The updated model is retrieved by the cloud from blockchain then all the local models are aggregated through a weighted average calculation to form a global model. Then, the cloud returns the parameters to the edge server.

The process of using blockchain in the proposed approach has three layers. Among these layers, blockchain is the top layer. Blockchain is the interconnected block structure. These blocks contain data and include two parts: block header and block body. These blocks of information are transferred from devices to servers to maintain the integrity of the data signature; a verification process–the elliptic curve digital signature algorithm (ECDSA)–is used by the author. ECDSA is a combination of ECC and DSA digital signature algorithms.

The author has compared the accuracy of the model in the training model and training loss with different samples sizes, i.e. batch and times the dataset is trained (epochs). It is observed that when batch size is constant and epochs increase, then training accuracy increases. When epochs are constant and batch size is smaller, training accuracy is higher. While in the case of training loss, batch size is directly proportional. When epochs are constant and batch size increases, training loss also increases. However, when batch size is constant and epochs increase, training loss decreases.

5.6 Poisoning Attacks on Federated Learning

Poisoning attacks occur while the model is still being developed or trained. In this attack, the data is manipulated from which the model is going to be trained. There are three kinds of poisoning attacks:

a. *Dataset poisoning*: It works on the idea of "poison the dataset, poison the model". It is the most simple and direct way to damage the dataset, which will directly damage the model and produce incorrect results. Incorrect data is added in dataset because the model becomes trained on the wrong data.

b. *Algorithm poisoning*: Logic becomes corrupted and the way the algorithm learns is changed. Through transfer learning, the attacker poisons the algorithm, which then transfers to other algorithms.

c. *Model poisoning*: In this attack, the model function is replaced with another poisoned function. In FL, this can happen in two ways: (1) The weights of the model, which are shared, are changed through model updates and (2) A regularization term is added to the objective function in the global shared model, which is injects poison into neurons [12, 13].

X. Zhou et al. [14] has presented a novel idea for a model poisoning attack in FL. In this research, the difficulties of effectiveness, persistence, and stealth due to the selection of a small amount of clients in each round are overcome. This paper has included two datasets, MNIST and CIFAR-10, to evaluate the model poisoning attack. These two datasets have 10 different classes. Features included are of different amounts and for both datasets, different CNN structures

Table 5.4 Comparative Summary of Research Papers

SR. NO.	AUTHORS	YEAR	FL TYPE	FL CLIENTS	FL AGGREGATOR	KEY CONTRIBUTIONS	LIMITATIONS	RESULT AND APPROACH
1.	Shukla et al. [4]	2019	VFL	IoT and computing devices	Cloud server	Malware detection based on HPC events and localized feature extraction using FL	Data security and privacy is not investigated	Accuracy: 91%
2.	Hsu et al. [6]	2020	HFL	Android mobile	Data centre	Privacy-preserving FL is used to detect android malware. Data is protected using SMPC.	Static analysis is not enough, dynamic analysis should be used	Accuracy: 93.87 (for 30 clients)
3.	Lin et al. [7]	2020	HFL	Edge devices	Data centre	A malware classification with decentralized data collection using FL and compared the results of SVM and LSTM.	-	Accuracy: 91.67%
4.	C. Zhou et al. [10]	2020	VFL	IoT devices	Cloud server	Proposed an approach for data security in IoT devices using Paillier homomorphic encryption. A privacy-preserving scheme for fog computing using FL is proposed.	Approach is inefficient and requires high computational overhead	Accuracy increases with an increase in privacy budget
5.	Gálvez et al. [9]	2021	HFL	Android mobile	Cloud server	Proposed an efficient way to combine FL with a semi-supervised ensemble method to detect malware	Malware families and categories are not classified by the given approach. Performance of LiM when the number of rounds are increased is not presented.	F1 score: 73.7%
6.	Zhang et al. [11]	2021	VFL	Edge equipment	Cloud server	Proposed a data transmission method using edge computation and FL with features of blockchain	Complexity of data transmission is not present	Accuracy: 98%
7.	Mothukuri et al. [8]	2021	HFL	IoT end-devices	Central server	Proposed an anomaly detection approach that uses GRUs to recognize intrusion in IoT devices using FL	Proposed approach is not tested on live data	Accuracy: 99.5%

are used. For MNIST the LetNet model is used and for CIFAR-10, ResNet is used. In FL, the global server's aim is to learn a model with the highest accuracy. A method used for aggregation in FL is weighted averaging. Injecting malicious data into the model regularization term in the objective function is used in a neural network. At the local dataset, the model is trained. The adversarial task is one in which adversarial features are embedded in a neural network to improve persistence.

For a large dataset such as CIFAR-10, the model proposed for the poisoning attack has a 90% success rate for adversarial tasks. Table 5.4 illustrates comparative analysis of the existing research papers related to malware detection.

5.7 Conclusions

In this chapter, we have presented an overview of FL. We have studied its different architecture, the few open-source platforms available for FL, and summarized their focus and supporting software. We have also discussed several malware detection schemes based on FL. Semi-supervised malware detection is introduced in [9, 15], which have achieved a 73.7% F1 score. We have summarized FL for malware detection using fog computing and blockchain. After a comparative study, we have found that using both dynamic and static features gives better results. In each paper, different methods are used to preserve the security and privacy of data such as a DSA, ECC, and PCA. We have also discussed poisoning attacks on FL.

References

1. Aledhari, Mohammed, Rehma Razzak, Reza M. Parizi, and Fahad Saeed. "Federated learning: A survey on enabling technologies, protocols, and applications." IEEE Access 8 (2020): 140699–140725.
2. Yang, Qiang, Yang Liu, Tianjian Chen, and Yongxin Tong. "Federated machine learning: Concept and applications." ACM Transactions on Intelligent Systems and Technology (TIST) 10, no. 2 (2019): 1–19.
3. Liu, Yang, Yan Kang, Chaoping Xing, Tianjian Chen, and Qiang Yang. "A secure federated transfer learning framework." IEEE Intelligent Systems 35, no. 4 (2020): 70–82.
4. Shukla, Sanket, Gaurav Kolhe, Houman Homayoun, Sai Manoj PD, and Setareh Rafatirad. Malware Detection using Federated Learning based on HPC Events and Localized Image features. 2019.

5. Alzaylaee, Mohammed K., Suleiman Y. Yerima, and Sakir Sezer. "DL-Droid: Deep learning based android malware detection using real devices." Computers & Security 89 (2020): 101663.

6. Hsu, Ruei-Hau, Yi-Cheng Wang, Chun-I. Fan, Bo Sun, Tao Ban, Takeshi Takahashi, Ting-Wei Wu, and Shang-Wei Kao. "A privacy-preserving federated learning system for android malware detection based on edge computing." In 2020 15th Asia joint conference on information security (AsiaJCIS), pp. 128–136. IEEE, 2020.

7. Lin, Kuang-Yao and Wei-Ren Huang. "Using federated learning on malware classification." In 2020 22nd international conference on advanced communication technology (ICACT), pp. 585–589. IEEE, 2020.

8. Mothukuri, Viraaji, Prachi Khare, Reza M. Parizi, Seyedamin Pouriyeh, Ali Dehghantanha, and Gautam Srivastava. "Federated learning-based anomaly detection for IoT security attacks." IEEE Internet of Things Journal (2021).

9. Gâlvez, Rafa, Veelasha Moonsamy, and Claudia Diaz. "Less is more: A privacy-respecting android malware classifier using federated learning." Arxiv Preprint (2020) https://doi.org/10.48550/arXiv.2007.08319.

10. Zhou, Chunyi, Anmin Fu, Shui Yu, Wei Yang, Huaqun Wang, and Yuqing Zhang. "Privacy-preserving federated learning in fog computing." IEEE Internet of Things Journal 7, no. 11 (2020): 10782–10793.

11. Zhang, Peiying, Yanrong Hong, Neeraj Kumar, Mamoun Alazab, Mohammad Dahman Alshehri, and Chunxiao Jiang. "BC-Edge FL: Defensive transmission model based on blockchain assisted reinforced federated learning in IIOT environment." IEEE Transactions on Industrial Informatics (2021).

12. Bhagoji, Arjun Nitin, Supriyo Chakraborty, Prateek Mittal, and Seraphin Calo. "Model poisoning attacks in federated learning." In Workshop on security in machine learning (SecML), collocated with the 32nd conference on neural information processing systems (NeurIPS'18), 2018.

13. Bhagoji, Arjun Nitin, Supriyo Chakraborty, Prateek Mittal, and Seraphin Calo. "Analyzing federated learning through an adversarial lens." In International conference on machine learning, pp. 634–643. PMLR, 2019.

14. Zhou, Xingchen, Ming Xu, Yiming Wu, and Ning Zheng. "Deep model poisoning attack on federated learning." Future Internet 13, no. 3 (2021): 73.

15. Payne, Joshua, and Ashish Kundu. "Towards deep federated defenses against malware in cloud ecosystems." In 2019 first IEEE international conference on trust, privacy and security in intelligent systems and applications (TPS-ISA), pp. 92–100. IEEE, 2019.

6

AN ENSEMBLE XGBOOST APPROACH FOR THE DETECTION OF CYBER-ATTACKS IN THE INDUSTRIAL IoT DOMAIN

R.K. PARERIYA, PRIYANKA VERMA, AND PATHAN SUHANA

Maulana Azad National Institute of Technology, Bhopal, Madhya Pradesh, India

Contents

6.1 Introduction

The Industrial Internet of Things (IIoT) is an addition to the standard Internet of Things (IoT), which has brought an incredible change in the industrial sector [1]. The IIoT is the utilization of intelligent sensors for production and industrial processes. It is also called Industry 4.0 or the industrial Internet. The concept quickly introduced innovative

DOI: 10.1201/9781003264545-6

ideas in logistics services, business idea development, industrial processes, and plenty of other strategic plans to grow national industries [2]. The driving idea behind IIoT is that smart machines are not simply better than people in continuously capturing and analyzing information, but they are also better at the communication of significant details that may be useful to drive business choices rapidly and accurately [3]. IIoT develops industry skills that offer efficiency and trustworthiness in its industrial operations. Recently, IIoT had been used by many industries including manufacturing, gas and oil, food processing, automotive, medical services, agriculture, and security monitoring. Real-time data from sensors and applications help the industrial and infrastructure devices in their decision-making by drawing closer with bits of knowledge and specific activities [4].

IIoT can be briefly represented as a four-layer structure. In the industrial field, construction contains the physical layer, network layer, middleware layer, and application layer. Sensors are utilized for detecting and collecting data from the environment [5]. They sense certain points or physical limitations to other intelligent devices in their environment. The network layer is duty-bound to link to smart devices, servers, and network devices. Its features are also used to transmit and process sensor data. The middleware layer connect the application layer and the network layer. It contains an app interface, Web services, and cloud storage. The application layer is the top of IIoT structure and helps many jobs and industries including smart industries, buildings, healthcare, smart cars, robots, etc.

However, IoT-enabled sensors and devices are considered devices with limited memory, power, and communication resources [6]. So, edge devices that consist of desks, small servers, routers, laptops, handheld devices, smartphones, and handheld devices are used as mediators between the cloud and sensor servers. The devices assemble the data from the sensors and after the required processing transmit the data to local servers. Because of the quick expansion in the numerous devices on the IoT side in the industry, numerous security and protection issues have emerged, which is a major challenge to the security and reliability of the IoT [7]. Compromised IoT gadgets can send malicious data to cloud workers or lead to unapproved admittance to significant industry achievements and marketable strategies. This can lead to economic loss and reputation. Ensuring cyber-security is a major challenge in today's industry. It also supplies edge-to-edge device protection against malware, unauthorized access, and physical privacy. Because of the vast amount of data, standard data-preparing strategies are not reasonable for IoT as well as for IIoT appliances. Hence, machine learning is viewed as one of the significant methods of calculation to give intelligence to IoT devices.

This chapter provides a simple XGBoost program based on the prediction of IIoT attacks. The proposed strategy detects IIoT attacks with great accuracy with less prediction time. The performance results are also compared to other machine learning classifiers.

6.1.1 Motivation and Contributions

The primary motivation of the research is to present a lightweight machine-learning-based attack-detection method for an IIoT network and give high accuracy and detection rates. The key contributions of the chapter are:

- An ensemble XGBoost machine learning classifier is presented for cyber-attack detection in the IIoT.
- The latest UNSW-NB15 dataset is used in this paper for cyber-attack detection. Various performance metrics such as accuracy, precision, F1 score, recall, log loss, and AUC ROC are utilized to analyze the performance or execution of the presented technique.
- The results of the proposed technique are also compared with other state-of-art algorithms.

6.2 Related Works

This section outlines some of the newest attack defence algorithms proposed by various researchers. Li et al. [8] suggested a combination of a flexible neural network for acquiring IoT findings. The NSLKDD database is used to test the introduced strategy. Their conclusion shows that the introduced scheme separated attacks well with good accuracy and less difficulty. Hassan and colleagues [9] proposed a weight dropped long short-term memory (WDLSTM) and a convolutional neural network (CNN). In their mechanism, CNN was used to retrieve the features from big IDS data and WDLSTM was used for attacks classification. Li et al. [10] also present an in-depth migration learning program. The authors executed the performance results of the model with the use of the KDD CUP 99 dataset.

Ugochukwu et al. [11] presented a comparative analysis of several machine learning algorithms such as J48, Bayes net, random forest, and random trees for the classification of cyber-attacks. The authors proved that random forest and random trees implementation was efficient in classifying the attack in comparison to other algorithms. Khammassi et al. [12] proposed the Genetic algorithm for feature extraction and logistic regression for the classification of attacks. The authors used the UNSW-NB15 dataset to execute the performance results of the model. Verma et al. [13] proposed a bio-inspired approach for the identification of attack requests. In the proposed approach, a Cuckoo search-based identification of requests is performed. de Souza et al. [14] presented a cyber-attack detection system, which works on a computerized layer of the IIoT network. The authors have introduced a binary classification technique containing K-Nearest Neighbours (KNN) and deep neural network (DNN).

Heikkonen and colleague [15] presented a cyber-attack detection mechanism based on a deep autoencoder. The authors used the KDD CUP 99 dataset for analysis of their presented scheme and achieved good attack-detection results. Vijayanand et al. [16] enhanced accuracy by introducing a support vector-based model. They performed the tests using the database ADFA-LD. Parra et al. [17] have developed an in-depth cloud-based learning framework for botnet and cyber-crime attacks. Huang et al. [18] proposed process-error detection of the IIoT network. The authors presented the DNN based on Gaussian-Bernoulli restricted Boltzmann machine (GBRBM) as their proposed system. Moustafa et al. [19] proposed a genetic algorithm accelerator (GAA) for feature selection and automatic dependent surveillance (ADS) for classification. The authors used the UNSW-NB15 dataset to execute the performance results of the model. Ravi et al. [20] introduced a scheme for distributed denial-of-service (DDoS) cyber-attack detection by using a non-paired learning algorithm. Investigators have succeeded in detecting a DDoS attack. Verma et al. [21] applied teacher-learner-based optimization (TLBO) for clustering the attack and benign requests. TLBO is used to find the optimal cluster centres.

The result shows that the proposed approach achieves high accuracy and false alarm rates. Kasongo et al. [22] used a feed-forward deep neural network (FFDNN) and wrapper-based technique for feature extraction using the UNSW-NB15 dataset. Alrashdi et al. [23] proposed anomaly detection of cyber-attacks using random forest. The authors used extra tree classifiers to retrieve the most prominent features and performed binary classification using random forest with high accuracy. Moustafa et al. [19] introduced distributed map matching (DMM) for feature extraction and ADS for the classification. The authors used the UNSW-NB15 dataset to execute the performance results of the model. They achieved good prediction results.

Many investigators have done an excellent job of introducing effective strategies for detecting IoT and IIOT platform attacks. But existing studies have some limitations such as: (i) Most authors have used the data from the old NSLKDD and the KDD CUP 99 datasets that have not been updated and are not suitable for modern industrial needs; (ii) Many researchers analyzed their proposed schemes with only some performance metrics, which did not provide a complete analysis; and (iii) Many previous programmes are complex and time-consuming and recommended for Dell Alienware or Raspberry Pi laptops.

6.3 Proposed Work

The proposed approach uses the XGBoost (eXtreme Gradient Boosting) binary classification technique for cyber-attack detection within IIoT systems. XGBoost is a further-developed version of decision tree-based gradient boosted algorithms. XGBoost was chosen for its speed and better performance. The block diagram of the proposed approach is shown in Figure 6.1 and consists of pre-processing involving data visualization, data cleaning, data normalization, and feature extraction and selection.

The data normalization technique is used to rescale the large values of the features. Normalizing is done with the use of the MinMax scaling method, which has a range of 0 to 1. Feature selection technique is performed by making the use of Extra Trees classifier. Extra Trees classifier is a kind of ensemble learning method that is implemented based on decision trees. Each tree will be given a random feature from

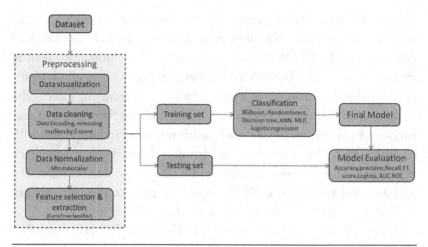

Figure 6.1 Block diagram of the proposed approach.

the set of features; every tree should choose the best or most important feature to split the data based upon mathematical criteria such as Gini or entropy (Gini is used here). Since the dataset is imbalanced, over-sampling and then under-sampling is performed, using the synthetic minority oversampling technique (SMOTE) and Tomek links technique. Based upon the Gini score, the most significant features of the dataset were selected. Finally, input data is ready to train on different machine learning algorithms. The XGBoost mathematical algorithm is given below [24]:

Algorithm 6.1:

Input: Dataset $\{(x_i, y_i)\}$ and hyperarameters
Where L(y,f) is the loss function.
Initialize $f_0(x)$;
for k = 1, 2, 3,....., N
Calculate $g_k = \dfrac{\partial L(y, f)}{\partial f}$;

Calculate $h_k = \dfrac{\partial^2 L(y, f)}{\partial f^2}$;

Determine the structure by choosing splits with maximum gain

$$A = \frac{1}{2}\left[\frac{G_L^2}{H_L} + \frac{G_R^2}{H_R} + \frac{G^2}{H}\right];$$

Determine the leaf weights $w^* = -\dfrac{G}{H}$

Determine the base model $\hat{b}(x) = \sum_{i=1}^{T} wI$;

Assemble the trees $f_k(x) = f_{k-1}(x) + \hat{b}(x)$;

Result: $f_k(x) = \sum_{k=0}^{N} f_k(x)$;

6.3.1 Working with XGBoost

XGBoost is an implementation of decision trees, which are trained cyclically. Weights will be assigned to all the independent features, which are given as input to the decision trees to predict the results. Training starts by calculating errors for each sample in the dataset. The weight of features predicted incorrectly by the tree is increased and is input into the second tree. The predictions are added to an ensemble of models. For every new prediction, all the predictions for previous models are added to calculate new errors and build a new model. This new model is added to the ensemble of all the previous models as shown in Figure 6.2. This cycle repeats and continues

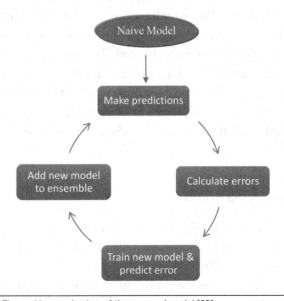

Figure 6.2 The working mechanism of the proposed model [25].

training and building a new model until it completes the specific number of trees. The number of tree or models to be formed are specified in input parameters. In Figure 6.2, the naive model was nothing but the first model or base model before starting the cycle. Even if its predictions are more inaccurate, the next additions will reduce those errors. Therefore, the algorithm is an ensemble of trees to get a strong model and better performance.

6.3.2 Dataset Used

The dataset used here is the UNSW-NB15 dataset. These are the most recent IIoT datasets that are broadly utilized for the efficient analysis of machine learning-dependent cyber-security applications. The dataset comprises an overall of 257,673 samples, of which 164,673 are attacked and the remaining 93,000 are normal. This dataset includes 45 features and 9 kinds of attacks. The type of attacks are fuzzers, analysis, backdoor, reconnaissance, exploit, generic, denial-of-service (DoS), shellcode, and worm attacks as mentioned in Table 6.1.

Dataset collection and data observation were the primary steps of this mechanism. Collection of the dataset and its evaluation is done in this step. In the following step, data pre-processing takes place, where data cleaning, data visualization, and data normalization, and feature selection are performed. After applying all these techniques, the selected data features are extracted. The dataset was divided into a training and test data set in a ratio of 72% and 28%, individually. The learning of the proposed ensemble XGBoost classifier is done using the training dataset. Subsequently, the ultimate model was analyzed with the use of a test dataset with several evaluation parameters.

6.4 Experiments and Results

The proposed approach is implemented on a Dell Inspiron 3576 model computer. The system is equipped with an Intel® Core™ i5-8250U CPU @ 1.60GHz, 1800 Mhz, 4 C processor, and 8 GB RAM. The program of the presented algorithm is written and executed in "Google Colab".

Table 6.1 Available Attacks Description Presented in the UNSW-NB15 Dataset [26]

ATTACKS	DESCRIPTION
Fuzzers	In Fuzzers, the attacker gives an unexpected or random amount of data as input, which leads to the crashing of any program, network, or operating system.
Backdoor	This is a kind of malware where, along with authorized users, unauthorized users also can gain access with normal security measures. Attackers use this malware to access to their financial and personal information.
Analysis	Analysis attacks target PC interruptions and malware events in which cyber-criminals gain access to a system or network by using the technical abilities of the users to misuse vulnerability.
Reconnaissance	Reconnaissance is where the attacker assembles the data of the computer vulnerabilities that can make use of the system control.
Exploit	An exploit attack is a program that takes advantage of security flaws and software vulnerabilities such as in the OS (Operating System), networks, or applications. In this, the attacker can gain illegal access.
Generic	Generic attacks work against all types of block-ciphers (with given key and block size) without considering the formation of the block-cipher.
DoS	In DoS, the attacker can shut down or suspend the machine or network resources by making them inaccessible to users. The attacker sends a large amount of ambiguous traffic to overload the network.
Shellcode	These are a few lines of code that execute instructions or commands in software for taking control of a machine.
Worm	These attacks exploit some of the dangerous and deepest security vulnerabilities in the host system and make copies of themselves.
Normal	If the attack is perfectly accurate, then it is called Normal.

6.4.1 Evaluation Matrices

Various evaluation parameters are determined to observe the performance of the proposed approach such as accuracy, precision, recall, F1 score, log loss, and AUC ROC.

1. *Accuracy*

   Accuracy is the most used metric for evaluating machine learning models. It is the relationship between well-predicted outcomes and all the predictions of a model.

   $$\text{Accuracy} = \frac{T_p + T_n}{\left(T_p + T_n + F_p + F_n\right)}$$

2. *Precision*

   It represents the fraction of true positive results among all the positives.

$$\text{Precision} = \frac{T_p}{\left(T_p + F_p\right)}$$

3. *Recall*

It represents the fraction of the truly positive results to the total results of each class.

$$\text{Recall} = \frac{T_p}{\left(T_p + F_n\right)}$$

4. *F1 Score*

It is considered a balanced average between recall and precision. It gives a result in the range of 0 to 1.

$$\text{F1 Score} = \frac{2 \times (recall \times precision)}{(recall + precision)}$$

5. *Log Loss*

It is the measure of performance or execution of the model with the use of probability of expected results. If the variation between the prediction probability and the actual value is high, then the log loss value will be high. A low score of log loss represents better performance.

$$-\sum_{i=1}^{N} y_{o,i} \ \log(p_{o,i})$$

6. **AUC ROC**

This is the curve plotting at different thresholds of a model. The graph uses the true positive rate (TPR) and false positive rate (FPR).

$$\text{TPR} = \frac{T_p}{\left(T_p + F_n\right)}$$

$$\text{FPR} = \frac{F_p}{\left(F_p + T_n\right)}$$

6.4.2 Performance Evaluation of Proposed Approach

The UNSW-NB15 [28] dataset was divided into training and testing datasets at a rate of 72% and 28%, individually. This work utilized 38

Table 6.2 Performance Analysis of the Presented Algorithm

PERFORMANCE METRICS	LEARNING RATES				
	0.050	0.075	0.100	0.500	0.750
Accuracy	**0.9688**	0.9671	0.9686	0.9652	0.9642
Precision	0.9764	0.9742	0.9746	0.9687	0.9673
Recall	0.9640	0.9604	0.9608	0.9604	0.9585
F1 Score	0.9688	0.9670	0.9671	0.9642	0.9633
Log loss	1.0760	1.1309	1.0802	1.2148	1.2568
AUC ROC	0.9688	0.9673	0.9686	0.9651	0.9641

of the most prominent features as an input. The n_estimators parameter was selected as 100, 300, 500, 800, and 1000. The XGBoost algorithm gives a better accuracy on 1000 n_estimators. The algorithms were executed on five different learning rates 0.050, 0.075, 0.100, 0.500, and 0.750. The algorithm gives high accuracy at low learning rates. A clear performance comparison is represented in Table 6.2. As per the results, the accuracy rates obtained on 0.075, 0.500, 0.750 are less than 96.7%. The best accuracy of the algorithm is achieved at a learning rate of 0.05 as mentioned in Table 6.1. The overall AUC ROC score is extremely high at 0.968, which shows the best detection results. However, the log loss is 1.076, which shows the best performance of the algorithm. So, the best learning rate is considered as 0.05. The best training accuracy and testing accuracy obtained with the proposed approach with the learning rate 0.05 are 99.4% and 96.88%, respectively.

6.4.3 Comparison of the Proposed Method with other State-of-Art Models

To show the effectiveness of the proposed approach, it is compared with eight other state-of-art algorithms including Support Vector Machine (SVM), LDA-based extreme learning machine (ELM), genetic algorithm-logistic regression (GA-LR), GAA-ADS, WFEU-FFDNN, DMM-ADS, LEDEM, and DAE. GA-LR achieves the testing accuracy of 82.42%, which is much less in comparison to the proposed technique. The testing accuracies for SVM, LDA, GAA-ADS, WFEU-FFDNN, DMM-ADS, LEDEM and DAE and are in the range of 94.50%, 92.35%, 91.80%, 87.48%, 94.30%, 96.28%, and 94.71%, respectively as shown in Table 6.3. To summarize the

Table 6.3   Performance Comparison with Other State-of-Art Algorithms

REFERENCE	MODEL	DATASET	ACCURACY
Vajayanand et al. [15]	SVM	ADFA-LD	94.50%
Zheng et al. [8]	LDA	NSL-KDD	92.35%
Khammassi et al. [12]	GA-LR	UNSW-NB15	82.42%
Moustafa et al. [19]	GAA-ADS	UNSW-NB15	91.80%
Kasongo et al. [22]	WFEU-FFDNN	UNSW-NB15	87.48%
Moustafa et al.[24]	DMM-ADS	UNSW-NB15	94.30%
Ravi et al.[18]	LEDEM	Own Synthetic	96.28%
Farahnakian et al.[13]	DAE	KDD CUP99	94.71%
Proposed model	**ETC-XGBoost**	**UNSW-NB15**	**96.88%**

comparison, the proposed extra tree classifier with XGBoost performs better than other algorithms.

6.4.4 Challenges and Future Research

The latest improvements in learning methods are very useful for the development of new machine learning and deep learning approaches to solve the security challenges in the IIoT and IoT networks. Many challenges should be solved to fulfil the complex needs of IIoT devices. Recently, the industry has seen a great demand for IoT and cloud computing devices. Due to this, many security and privacy problems have arisen [27]. To overcome all these challenges, some future research paths are presented here:

i. *Formation of new cyber-security related datasets*: In IIoT networks, the formation of the latest realistic high-quality dataset is a major challenge as things are changing rapidly day by day. The quality of the dataset is very important to the performance evaluation of deep learning and machine learning schemes and with new approaches. For this path, crowdsourcing can help to generate high-quality datasets for IoT and IIoT systems. Future datasets can further evaluate the XGBoost algorithm and any new schemes that will be proposed in the future.

ii. *Improvements in existing machine learning approaches for noisy data*: The IIoT and IoT network system consists of a large number of different devices. These devices have various distinct constraints such as power, money, and computing abilities, which affect the quality of data. So, improving the existing schemes and developing the new algorithms are needed to overcome noisy and low-quality data. For this path, researchers can develop effective machine learning and deep learning schemes to handle such kinds of data.

6.5 Conclusion

In this chapter, a simple and fast ensemble XGBoost-based approach was proposed for cyber-attack detection in IIoT systems. Compared to other state-of-art algorithms, the proposed XGBoost-based technique detects the attack with a high accuracy of 96.88% that is trained in a Dell Intel Core i5, low-power computing device. The best results of the XGBoost approach were obtained at a learning rate of 0.05. The accuracy of the presented XGBoost-based technique was greater than other state-of-art approaches. Additionally, various evaluation parameters such as F1 score, precision, recall, log loss, and AUC ROC are used to analyze the execution of the model. In the future, researchers can acquire better performance by other RNN-based algorithms, which need to be trained in high-power computing devices such as Raspberry Pi, Dell Alienware computer, etc.

References

1. Boyes, H., Hallaq, B., Cunningham, J., & Watson, T. (2018). The industrial internet of things (IIoT): An analysis framework. Computers in industry, 101, 1–12.
2. Sisinni, E., Saifullah, A., Han, S., Jennehag, U., & Gidlund, M. (2018). Industrial internet of things: Challenges, opportunities, and directions. IEEE transactions on industrial informatics, 14(11), 4724–4734.
3. Possey, B., Losencrance, L., & Shea, S. (2021). Internet of Things Agenda. Available online: https://internetofthingsagenda.techtarget.com/definition/Industrial-Internet-of-Things-IIoT.
4. Micro, T. (2021). Industrial internet of things (IIoT). Available on-line: https://www.trendmicro.com/vinfo/us/security/definition/industrial-internet-of-things-iiot.
5. Panchatcharam, P., & Vivekanandan, S. (2019). Internet of things (IoT) in healthcare–smart health and surveillance, architectures, security analysis, and data transfer: A review. International journal of software innovation (IJSI), 7(2), 21–40.

6. Huma, Z. E., Latif, S., Ahmad, J., Idrees, Z., Ibrar, A., Zou, Z., ... Baothman, F. (2021). A hybrid deep random neural network for cyber-attack detection in the industrial internet of things. IEEE access, 9, 55595–55605.

7. Da Costa, K. A., Papa, J. P., Lisboa, C. O., Munoz, R., & de Albuquerque, V. H. C. (2019). Internet of Things: A survey on machine learning-based intrusion detection approaches. Computer networks, 151, 147–157.

8. Li, Y., Xu, Y., Liu, Z., Hou, H., Zheng, Y., Xin, Y., ... Cui, L. (2020). Robust detection for network intrusion of industrial IoT based on multi-CNN fusion. Measurement, 154, 107450.

9. Huda, S., Yearwood, J., Hassan, M. M., & Almogren, A. (2018). Securing the operations in SCADA-IoT platform-based industrial control system using an ensemble of deep belief networks. Applied soft computing, 71, 66–77.

10. Li, D., Deng, L., Lee, M., & Wang, H. (2019). IoT data feature extraction and intrusion detection system for smart cities based on deep migration learning. International journal of information management, 49, 533–545.

11. Ugochukwu, C. J., Bennett, E. O., & Harcourt, P. (2019). An intrusion detection system using a machine learning algorithm. LAP LAMBERT Academic Publishing.

12. Khammassi, C, Krichen, S. (2017 Sep 1). A GA-LR wrapper approach for feature selection in network intrusion detection. Computers & security, 70, 255–77.

13. Verma, P., Tapaswi, S. J., & Godfrey, W. W. (2021). A request aware module using CS-IDR to reduce VM level collateral damages caused by DDoS attack in cloud environment. Cluster computing, 24(3), 1917–1933.

14. de Souza, C. A., Westphall, C. B., Machado, R. B., Sobral, J. B. M., & dos Santos Vieira, G. (2020). Hybrid approach to intrusion detection in fog-based IoT environments. Computer networks, 180, 107417.

15. Farahnakian, F., & Heikkonen, J. (2018, February). A deep auto-encoder-based approach for intrusion detection system. In 2018 20th International Conference on Advanced Communication Technology (ICACT) (pp. 178–183). IEEE.

16. Vijayanand, R., Devaraj, D., & Kannapiran, B. (2018). A novel intrusion detection system for wireless mesh network with hybrid feature selection technique based on GA and MI. Journal of intelligent & fuzzy systems, 34(3), 1243–1250.

17. Parra, G. D. L. T., Rad, P., Choo, K. K. R., & Beebe, N. (2020). Detecting internet of things attacks using distributed deep learning. Journal of network and computer applications, 163, 102662.

18. Huang, H., Ding, S., Zhao, L., Huang, H., Chen, L., Gao, H., & Ahmed, S. H. (2019). Real-time fault detection for IIoT facilities using GBRBM-based DNN. IEEE internet of things journal, 7(7), 5713–5722.

19. Moustafa, N., Slay, J., & Creech, G. (2017 Jun 14). Novel geometric area analysis technique for anomaly detection using trapezoidal area estimation on large-scale networks. IEEE transactions on big data, 5(4), 481–94.

20. Ravi, N., & Shalinie, S. M. (2020). Learning-driven detection and mitigation of DDoS attack in IoT via SDN-cloud architecture. IEEE internet of things journal, 7(4), 3559–3570.

21. Verma, P., Tapaswi, S., & Godfrey, W. W. (2021). An impact analysis and detection of HTTP flooding attack in cloud using bio-inspired clustering approach. International journal of swarm intelligence research (IJSIR), 12(1), 29–49.

22. Kasongo, S. M., & Sun, Y. (2020 May 1). A deep learning method with wrapper-based feature extraction for wireless intrusion detection system. Computers & security, 92, 101752.

23. Alrashdi, I., Alqazzaz, A., Aloufi, E., Alharthi, R., Zohdy, M., & Ming, H. (2019, January). Ad-IoT: Anomaly detection of IoT cyberattacks in smart city using machine learning. In 2019 IEEE 9th Annual Computing and Communication Workshop and Conference (CCWC) (pp. 0305–0310). IEEE.

24. Deok-Kee, Choi. Data-driven materials modeling with XGBoost algorithm and statistical inference analysis for prediction of fatigue strength of steels.

25. Dansbecker. How to build and optimize models with the powerful xgboost library. Available on-line: https://www.kaggle.com/dansbecker/xgboost.

26. UNSW-NB15 dataset available online: https://research.unsw.edu.au/projects/unsw-nb15-dataset

27. Latif, S., Zou, Z., Idrees, Z., & Ahmad, J. (2020). A novel attack detection scheme for the industrial internet of things using a lightweight random neural network. IEEE access, 8(1), 89337–89350.

7

A REVIEW ON IoT FOR THE APPLICATION OF ENERGY, ENVIRONMENT, AND WASTE MANAGEMENT

System Architecture and Future Directions

C. RAKESH, T. VIVEK, AND K. BALAJI

School of Mechanical Engineering, Vellore Institute of Technology (VIT) University, Vellore, Tamil Nadu, India

Contents

DOI: 10.1201/9781003264545-7

7.1 Introduction

The devices, tools, machines, etc. connected to the Internet that can communicate with the network are commonly termed the Internet of Things (IoT). Zillions of devices are connected to the Internet at present, soon to extend beyond 50 billion things. IoT unites various technologies such as "Big Data", "cloud computing", and "machine learning". With the breakthrough of wireless technologies, the present-day Internet is not just about connecting individuals it is about connecting things [1]. The users become secondary in receiving and generating various types of data, instead an enormous amount of data is transmitted from the devices/things, which leads to complex IoT. The definition of IoT is "the network of physical objects that contain embedded technology to communicate and sense or interact with their internal states or the external environment" (Gartner Research). Specifically, IoT is described as "any-time, any-place, and any-one connected". Its inference is based on innovation that can make individuals and things closer.

The physical objects or things are personal devices such as phones, watches, tabs, and digital cameras, etc. Daily-use technology like vehicles, home appliances, security cameras, and office laptops connected through a common gateway are also termed as "things" [2]. Each individual provides an enormous amount of data that which has to be analyzed, captured, and stored, with the phrase "volume, variety, and velocity" (Big Data) making the devices smarter. Adding intelligence to these things is termed the Internet of Intelligent Things (IoIT). When the device is smarter, or intelligent, it can make its own decisions without any human intervention and can manage and improve functionality. The flexibility of multiple devices, their ability

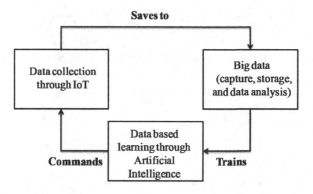

Figure 7.1   Simplified relationship of IoT, Big Data, and artificial intelligence.

to adapt, the enhanced level of security, and autonomous home operations that are remotely controlled, in turn, increases the efficiency.

Figure 7.1 represents the relationship between IoT, Big Data, and artificial intelligence (AI). IoT involves physical devices, data collection, and networking. As multiple devices are connected, the IoT will uncover insights from various types of data (unstructured, structured, contextual, real-time, images, dark data) based on the application [3]. Big Data will effectively capture, store, and extract value from a continuous stream of sensor data and filter the unnecessary data. AI will lead to cutting-edge technologies for real-time decisions for data analytics via deep learning techniques. IoT technology includes an embedded system that supports the sensing of the test environment, whereas Big Data focuses on storing an enormous amount of information and artificial intelligence is for logical decision making.

Figure 7.2 represents the major emerging application of AI and IoT included in healthcare sectors, agriculture drones, livestock monitoring, home security, assets tracking, defence, smart city, smart grids, smart farming, smart water management, precision farming energy conservation, commercial energy, environmental monitoring, waste management, traffic signal sensors, vehicle tracking, unmanned aerial vehicles, and AI/IoT law enforcement [4].

7.1.1 Healthcare Sector

The number of chronic diseases on the rise, problems in patient monitoring and documentation of patient history and medication, adverse drug reactions and side effects, children's health information systems,

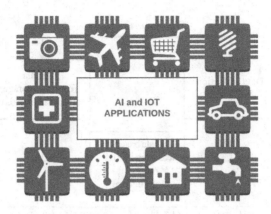

Figure 7.2   Integration of AI into IoT applications.

rehabilitation management, body temperature management, the consumer experience, data and analytics, and interoperability data access are all current issues in the healthcare sector [5].

7.1.1.1 Components of IoT Healthcare

- *Sensing layer*: All types of sensors, Bluetooth, radio frequency identification (RFID), and wireless sensor networks.
- *Aggregated layer*: Multiple types of aggregators based on the sensing layer.
- *Processing layer*: Servers for processing information flow from the previous layer.
- *Cloud platform*: Data processes are uploaded here and users can access these services.

Figure 7.3 represents the components of the IoT healthcare system interacting in the closed-loop with optimum feedback system and processing.

7.1.1.2 IoT and AI Solutions

- *IoT and AI healthcare real-time monitoring*: Sensors collect comprehensive physiological medical information from the patients through a smartphone app, where the data are stored in the cloud via the gateway [6]. Wirelessly the filtered analytics data are communicated to the physician and caretaker.

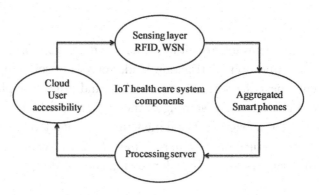

Figure 7.3   Components of the IoT healthcare system.

- *IoT and AI healthcare remote monitoring*: Patients are remotely monitored wherever they are instead of visiting the health-care centre. Patient medical data are collected and analyzed through IoT-based sensors wirelessly and the data are shared with the physician for further recommendations.
- *End-to-end connectivity between the machines*: Enables machine-to-machine communication; the data flow takes place effectively [7], thus, increasing the delivery efficiency of the medical sectors.
- *Data analysis and filtering*: IoT devices collect, filter, record, and analyze the data in real-time, which eliminates the storage of data.
- *Tracking and alerts*: Notification through apps via mobile/ linked devices when a patient's vitals leads to emergency alerts for the caretakers.
- *Mobility solutions*: Instantly check and report.

With the advancement of sensor technology, an IoT device collect patient data over time enables preventive care, understand the effects of therapy on a patient, ability to collect the data on their own, and includes automation which reduces the risk of error, increases efficiency and reduces the cost. Physicians can obtain data anytime and anywhere by the use of technology [8]. AI technology helps in data-driven insights, improves allocation and planning, utilization of better-quality resources, scheduled visits. IoT helps in detailed healthcare analysis of the patients, which maximizes the decision-making of the healthcare professionals.

7.1.2 *Agriculture Drones*

The major problems in agriculture which are to be monitored is as follows the identification of irrigation land, analysis of soil, crop health assessment, the difference between healthy and unhealthy plants are complex to identify, early warning of the forest fire, fisheries monitoring and disaster management, soil moisture and water level monitoring [9], monitoring irrigation system, recycling of organic waste and vermicomposting, autonomous vehicle for sowing and weeding system.

7.1.2.1 *Components of IoT Agriculture Drones*

- *Sensing layer*: Data collection from the UAV setup includes image acquisition, video streaming, etc
- *Processing layer*: Communication between aerial and ground by the use of airborne drones. Flexible UAV and ground-based data processing and analysis are performed [10] via the image processing Technique.
- *Application layer*: Management, strategies, decision making, and recommendations are notified

Figure 7.4 represents the major components involved in agriculture drones from sensing layer to application.

7.1.2.2 *IoT and AI Solutions*

- *Field management*: High-definition images from the drones help during the cultivation period by identifying the requirement of fertilizer or pesticides, the requirement of water to the crops, mapping field layout, etc. This helps in resource management and inventory.
- *Crops health monitoring*: Remote monitoring techniques with the aid of laser scanning and spectral imaging techniques help in crop metrics for the acres of land. Farmland can be monitored

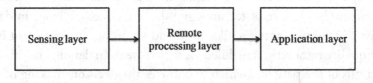

Figure 7.4   Major components of IoT agriculture drones.

using drone approach techniques by the farmers, saving time. Crop yield can be reported by this approach [11] as well.

- *Planting*: Drones can spread seeds and nutrients into the soil.
- *Spraying*: To spray pesticides, a drone sprinkling system automatically navigates to the identified infected areas with the aid of GPS through a self-learning technique. These technologies reduce the waste of chemicals and are faster than the conventional method.
- *Farmland monitoring*: Maintenance of the extensive fields and protection of the crops are the major concerns associated with the traditional method. Drones can enhance the protection of crops and farmland by scheduling sequential monitoring techniques based on deep learning methods, spraying pesticides and insecticides, and creating barricades for the birds and animals. In case of any emergency, an alarm notification is communicated to the farmer.

Drones or unmanned aerial vehicles benefit crop health monitoring, planting, and spraying, which results in flexibility, reliability, time savings, and enhances potential to maximize yield. Mapping, strategic planning, and real-time monitoring are the key aspects of cutting-edge drone technology [12]. Drone data includes the breadth and depth of the plant life cycle and prediction of yields, plant height, and nutrients in plants and can also record nitrogen content in crops, chlorophyll presence, pressure mapping of weeds, and mapping of field water and drainage.

7.1.3 Livestock Monitoring

Monitoring related to the reproduction, health, feeding, environment, growth, quality, inventory, and transport of livestock is a crucial task for the farmer. The behaviour of herds [13], critical illness, and monitoring of the animal reproductive cycle are uncertain and involve a tedious process, making them significant issues in monitoring livestock.

7.1.3.1 IoT and AI Solutions

- *Health monitoring*: IoT and AI solutions prevent loss for the farmer by closely monitoring and diagnosing the disease of their livestock. To accomplish these tasks, the livestock is fitted with smart devices, which analyze the heart rate, blood pressure, respiratory rate, temperature, and other critical health parameters. The data are communicated via a gateway to the cloud, with the intent that farmers can take preliminary precautions.

- *Monitoring fertility cycles*: With the assistance of the IoT apparatus, an alert system is provided to detect when the animal is going into oestrus. This data permits the farmers to take precautionary measures for reducing the calving intervals, which impacts farmers' profits and productivity.

- *Location tracking*: Animal location can be tracked with the aid of IoT devices,. These smart wearable trackers help farmers when the animals spread over the vast fields. "Location monitoring can be extremely useful to farmers raising free-range or pastured livestock as it allows them to better account for the livestock" [14]. Location tracking and monitoring help to identify and locate unhealthy animals to be isolated and diagnosed.

- *Improvised feeding*: Motion sensors are used to understand the activity of the herds. The data relating to feeding frequency rate, socializing, sleep time intervals, and chewing rate can be studied and analyzed with the IoT and deep learning techniques, which helps the farmers understand the requirements of the feed rate and the particular behaviour of the herds.

IoT sensors such as motion, pressure, RFID, GPS trackers, and biometric help to monitor and track the location of livestock. Data related to the fertility rate, health, activity, and location can help farmers increase their productivity and profitability [15]. The real-time data help the farmers to understand the herd patterns such as the birth rate or if they are prone to any diseases. These preliminary-stage data are helpful for precautionary measures.

7.2 IoT Architecture and Applications

IoT devices are equipped with essential building blocks, such as sensors, which sense the physical phenomena around them, connect to a network via the cloud, and, based on the detected data from the

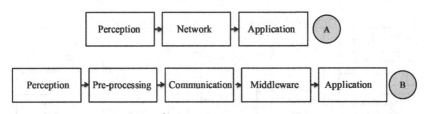

Figure 7.5   Three-layer (A) and five-layer (B) IoT architecture representation.

sensors, use actuators to accomplish dynamic actions on the physical conditions. A detailed description through the layers of architecture follows [16]. Figure 7.5 depicts the early and latest stages of IoT architecture.

- a. *Perception layer*: Consists of sensors that detect or measure a physical property and record and indicates or otherwise responds to the external parameters of the ambient conditions.
- b. *Network layer*: Processes and transmits sensed information; it acts as a bridge between the various embedded systems to communicate information.
- c. *Application layer*: Liable for conveying application-explicit administrations to clients, such as smart homes, smart grid, smart energy management, etc., in which IoT can be deployed. These three layers are not sufficient to understand the in-depth analysis [17] of the technology; the first two layers are the same and the third layer that is the network layer that is split into pre-processing, communication, and the middleware, which is indicated in five-layer architecture.
- d. *Pre-processing layer*: Fundamentally channels and sums up information before forwarding it on the system. These units conventionally have a little measure of short storage, a processing unit, and reduced security functionalities.
- e. *Communication layer*: Uses assorted arrangements of protocols and standards based on security, scalability, energy efficiency, bandwidth management, interfacing, interoperability, and low data-rate monitoring. The communication layer has to be designed.
- f. *Middleware*: Creates a barricade for the developer with the end goal of the hardware equipment being kept confidential [18]. This upgrades the interoperability of smart things and in turn, aids to enhance the services.

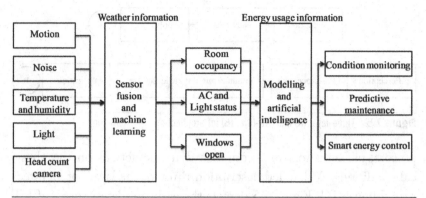

Figure 7.6   IoT and machine learning approaches for building.

This chapter primarily focuses on the integration of artificial intelligence in IoT architecture to its application in smart building automation, waste management, and environmental monitoring.

7.2.1 Smart Building

Smart building automation includes lighting systems, control systems, and heating and cooling systems to reduce power consumption and to improve building energy management systems [19]. Figure 7.6 represents the IoT and artificial intelligence approach for buildings.

The IoT platform uses different types of sensors and systems such as lighting, heating, ventilation, air-conditioning, and security devices connected to a common protocol. "IoT is a fast expanding digital ecosystem connected to devices" [20]. The aim of the IoT in retrofitting the existing building is energy-saving potential in heating and cooling systems, predictive maintenance using machine learning techniques to determine when service should be performed, and condition monitoring [21].

7.2.1.1 IoT-Based Architecture for Smart Building   Figure 7.7 represents the proposed architecture chain for IoT-based smart building.

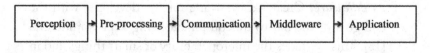

Figure 7.7   IoT-based architecture for smart building.

1. *Perception layer*: Manages information and data collection from the physical world and is typically constituted by detecting and activation [22]. The perception layer is generally bolstered by the accompanying technologies:
   a. **Sensor networks** comprise of various types of sensors that can quantify the physical world conditions, for example, position, inhabitants, motion, activities, movement, and temperature. This adaptable and dynamic design permits remote checking through sensor hub communication.
   b. **Smart cameras** determine the energy used by the occupants and their activity.
   c. **Radio frequency identification:** RFID involves electromagnetic fields, which help identify the object through labels. RFID can identify and track objects or individuals and communicates the data suitable for smart-built environment applications.

   The perception layer involves sensors such as temperature, humidity, indoor air environment sensors, cameras, RFID, and smart meters. The main challenges involved are feasibility, privacy, power consumption, security, storage requirements, sensing range limitations, cost, and complex data and their stability [23].

2. *Pre-processing layer*: Liable for preparing and transmitting the raw information acquired from the first layer. In addition, this layer deals with capacities, for example, figuring and information the executive's form. To transmit information among systems, wired and remote communications principles are involved [24]. Remote innovation has more advantages and uses over a wired connection and the subsequent IoT will be extended to the overall scale. The following are some of the primary remote advances/media:
   a. **Wi-Fi** is a correspondence innovation that utilizes radio waves for the local area among devices dependent on the Institute of Electrical and Electronics Engineers (IEEE) standard "IEEE 802.11".
   b. **Bluetooth** is another remote correspondence innovation for the trade of information between devices over short distances.

c. **Zigbee** is an "IEEE 802.15.4-based specification" intended for momentary correspondence, which involves low-vitality and power utilization. Other mainstream advances in the system layer incorporate "Z-Wave, RFID, WAVE, IrDA, and USB (wired)" [25].

3. *Communication layer*: The transmission of information in the system layer must communicate with correspondence conventions on the side of the IoT framework. These conventions or measures are defined and proposed by different standards, for example, IETF, IEEE, ETSI [26], and so on, and are officially acknowledged in the business for the unified executives.

   a. **IPV6 (6LoWPAN)**: 6LoWPAN is structured by integrating "low-power wireless personal area networks (LoWPAN)" and "IPv6". The focal points incorporate high network and similarity with low-power utilization.

   b. **Message Queue Telemetry Transport (MQTT)**: A message convention for associating remote implanted sensors and middleware. It is one of the application layer conventions

   c. **Constrained Application Protocol (CoAP)**: CoAP is a messaging convention that depends on "REST" services on top of "HTTP" functionalities. CoAP empowers minimal devices with reduced power, energy, computation, and capabilities to use in "RESTful interactions".

4. *Middleware layer*: Middleware acts as an intermediate software layer between the hardware and application that makes use of the data generated by the underlying technology. It helps to hide the involved heterogeneity and simplifies the development of applications [26].

   a. **HYDRA:** Renamed as a link smart project in 2014, is a middleware for an intelligent arranged embedded system that involves a service-oriented type of architecture. HYDRA can be applied for designing applications in the smart home, healthcare, and agriculture domains.

   b. **Awesome:** A Web service middleware designed for ambient intelligence environments. It is developed as a part of a smart IHU project for smart-university deployment.

   c. **CASAS:** "Smart Home in a Box" is a project initiated by the CASAS research group. The project aims to provide large-scale smart environment data and tool infrastructures. It is a lightweight event-based middleware providing an easy-to-install smart-home environment.

d. **Context-aware middleware for ubiquitous computing systems (CAMUS):** A tuple-based middleware rendering support for the development of smart-home applications.

e. **Smart home service middleware (SHSM):** Utilized to execute administration reconciliation and insightful assistance in-job. SHSM depends on the incorporated programming sending model. SHSM executes a gadget administration specialist for coordinating heterogeneous administrations inside the home space.

5. *Application layer*: The application layer accommodates the working modules of the IoT framework. The application layer fills in as the front-end interface to give dynamic analytic outcomes for clients in associated business with augmented knowledge, which is identified with the scientific apparatuses that enhance the ability to depict, anticipate, and use relativeness with different phenomena. It is a type of conceptualization of deep learning, an enlarged insight emphasizing upgrading human knowledge as opposed to supplanting it.

a. **Predictive analytics:** A technique to design a complicated algorithm and model that initiates the devices to predict like humans. In industries, it is called a prescient investigation.

b. **Cloud computing:** The reality of "Big Data" relating to processing capacity is important to help information stockpiling and analysis. Distributed computing is a type of Web-based figuring technique that gives shared PC assets to different devices on request. Since normal sensors don't generally have adequate figuring ability, distributed computing will assume the significant job of information handling for the next generation.

7.2.2 Smart Waste Management System

Management of waste addresses activities required to oversee waste from its origin to its last removal. This includes the "assortment,

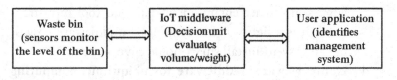

Figure 7.8   IoT-based smart waste management system.

transportation, treatment, and removal of waste together" with checking the guideline. Squander assortment strategies shift broadly among various nations [27]. Urban communities with raising populations experience depleted waste assortment administrations, a lack of oversight, and uncontrolled dumpsites, with the issue only getting worse. Waste assortment techniques in developing countries are facing numerous challenges and the administrational guidelines are transient due to rapid urbanization.

The technologically-based solution to these problems is addressed by IoT-based methodology that disposed of waste from a smart receptacle continuously checked by sensors that indicate how full each compartment is [28]. This information is carried out and handled in an IoT middleware, giving data for assortment enhanced courses and producing significant measurable information for observing waste collection precisely as far as an asset the board and the gave services to the network.

Figure 7.8 represents an IoT-based approach for smart waste management. Sensors are located in the physical bin and the raw data are communicated to the middleware where the decision units are placed. The decision units evaluate the data in terms of volume or weight and forwards the notification to the user, reporting the percentage of the vacant portion available in the bin. The smart waste administration framework can proficiently change the way individuals manage their trash and advance monetary and material assets.

7.2.2.1 IoT-Based Architecture for Waste Management System   Figure 7.9 represents the proposed architecture chain for IoT-based waste management systems.

1. ***Identification*:** For IoT, service classification and integration to meet demand is the major priority, therefore, various identification methods are supported by IoT, "such as the electronic

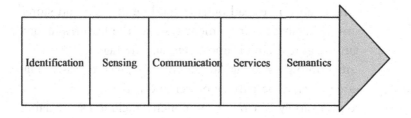

Figure 7.9 Schematic architecture chain for waste management systems.

product code (EPC) and ubiquitous codes (u code) and GPS location tracking". To distinguish a specific item inside the telecommunication organization, an identification and IP address are given. The identification alludes to the address of the item, e.g., "P1" for a particular temperature sensor and its location alludes to a number that recognizes that gadget inside the system. The techniques for object-settling inside an IoT system may incorporate IP form 4 (IPv4) and variant IPv6 [29]. IPv6 on low-force individual systems (6LoWPAN) gives a temperature component. As a strategy for distinguishing objects inside a system, an open IP address aids for the significant information from objects on a system and forwards them to the cloud for analysis.

2. *Sensors:* Defined as smart actuators or versatile devices. Numerous IoT arrangement sensors with single-board computers integrated with devices (for instance, the Arduino Yun, Raspberry Pi, and BeagleBone Black) interface with application programming in a focal administration to record data for the customer's requirement.

3. *Communication:* To integrate different objects and provide specific services within an IoT environment, it is necessary to apply communication technologies such as Wi-Fi, IEEE 802.15.4, Lora, wave Z, GSM/GPRS, broadband code division multiple access (WCDMA), long-term evolution (LTE) and advanced LTE (LTE-An), near field communication (NFC), ultra-wideband (UWB) and 6LoWPAN, and the IoT nodes must operate with the reduced power consumption.
   - RFID data are encoded digitally via tags, the encoded data can be read by the readers, which are similar to barcodes.

The data can be read outside the line of sight and stored in the database management system. The features involve an integrated circuit and antenna. The tags may be classified into passive tags and active tags, where passive tags are powered via battery power and active tags have their power supply. The main components include a smart label, an RFID reader, and an antenna; the application includes smart labels, assets tracker, inventory management, personal tracking, and ID badging [29].

- UWB, otherwise called "802.15.3", is a correspondences innovation structured by the IEEE to work inside regions of low inclusion and transfer speed prerequisites. Wi-Fi utilizes radio waves for correspondence inside 100 meters and permits devices to connect through an impromptu configuration, i.e., without the utilization of a switch.
- Bluetooth is a correspondence innovation broadly utilized for communication between devices at a short distance. It utilizes essential radio waves with short frequencies to ensure spared battery use.
- 802.15.4, created by the IEEE, gives specifications on low-force remote systems for both the physical layer and the medium air conditioning access control layer by advancing solid and adaptable correspondence.
- LTE is a remote correspondence standard that enables rapid data movement between cell phones dependent on GSM/UMTS to arrange advances and incorporate devices moving at high speeds, giving multicast-based administrations and communication. LTE-An is an improved rendition LTE and incorporates broadband, spatial multiplexing, more noteworthy inclusion, and better execution with lower latencies. Also called the fourth era of versatile correspondence is a development of "WCDMA (3G) and GSM/GPSR (2G)".

4. *Computation:* This layer communicates to the computational limit of IoT because of programming and applications. There is an enormous scope of hardware improvement stages for IoT application activity; a few models are: "Arduino, UDOO, Friendly ARM, Intel Galileo, Raspberry Pi, Gadgeteer,

BeagleBone, Cubie board, Z1, Wi Sense, Mulle, and T-Mote Sky". Working frameworks are viewed as crucial because they run through the whole framework execution period. "TinyOS, LiteOS, and RIoTOS" offer a lightweight working framework, and it is conceivable to refer to the "Contiki RTOS", which is broadly utilized in IoT situations for IoT environments.

Clouds are another significant part of an IoT subset. These stages give the capacity to accept information from smart articles to be handled in the future; clients can benefit from the information on the separated information. The information analysis stage inside the IoT is critical due to the specific qualities of this kind of arrangement, given its heterogeneous information and frameworks mix [12].

IoT-based solid waste management works with ongoing information that requires relationships and sharing. To meet these prerequisites in a framework with a large volume of associated gadgets producing information by different flows, it is increasingly important to receive distributed computing where capacity, preparation, and association limit are required by the developing interest for information investigation.

5. *Services*: Service-based IoT administrations can be classified into four groups: Services identified with the character that communicates to the most basic to different service ;a pplications that initiated to take the object from this present reality to the virtual must first distinguish them; data conglomeration administrations responsible for summing up the raw data that should be prepared and presented to the applications; community-oriented mindful administrations following up on total administration dynamics; and universal administrations, bolstering administrations.

6. *Semantics:* Alludes to the capacity to separate information shrewdly, yet through different prospects and to the extent where administration is required [30]. This extraction of information covers the disclosure and utilization of demonstrating assets and data and incorporates the acknowledgment and examination of the information with the goal that it settles on sense for the correct choice by providing the specific service. Semantics is like the cerebrum of IoT, forwarding

requests to the specific asset. Such prerequisites are upheld by semantic Web advances, for example, "RDF, OWL (Web ontology language), and efficient XML interchange (EXI)".

7.2.3 Environmental Monitoring

With an expanding populace, urbanization, vitality, transportation, and rural developments, pollution is degrading the earth's environment at an ever-expanding pace. The degradation of the earth because of pollution can influence the nature of human life by affecting well-being issues. To maintain a strategic distance from well-being dangers due to the degraded environment, it is fundamental to monitor its state [30].

Research on the condition of environmental data is the need of the hour. It is necessary to build up a framework that can proficiently gather and investigate information on the earth's environment to avoid any likely dangers [31]. The Internet is one of the vital devices that can be utilized to build up a framework equipped for screening and sharing data on ecological contamination.

The study proposes the use of the Internet of Things (IoT) in an environmental monitoring system as shown in Figure 7.10. The

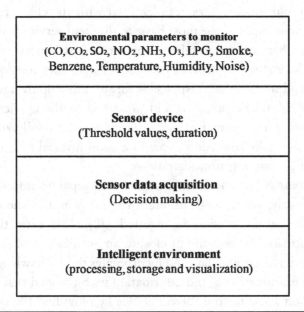

Environmental parameters to monitor
$(CO, CO_2, SO_2, NO_2, NH_3, O_3, LPG, Smoke,$
Benzene, Temperature, Humidity, Noise)

Sensor device
(Threshold values, duration)

Sensor data acquisition
(Decision making)

Intelligent environment
(processing, storage and visualization)

Figure 7.10   IoT-based environment monitoring system.

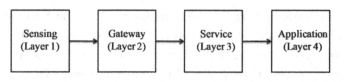

Figure 7.11   The architecture of the smart environment system.

proposed framework meets the district's explicit condition for monitoring the harmful gases in the environment, air quality in terms of parts-per-million, and contamination, while likewise encouraging secure information transmission over the system, solves security issues in the IoT framework.

7.2.3.1 Functional Layer of the System   The proposed framework is the solution to record the harmful gases and decibels of noise with the aid of remote- and wireless communication-based IoT [32]. The proposed framework is progressively versatile and distributive. The strategy of the proposed framework involves four practical layers as shown in Figure 7.11.

1. ***Sensing layer***: Comprises sensor hubs for recording environmental data. The different sensors for gathering information are on gas fixation, temperature, and moistness and decibel levels are executed here. All sensor hubs are validated utilizing hash capacities.
2. ***Gateway layer***: This is a local gateway device that has been executed at this layer, which is for the validation of sensor hubs and transmission of encoded information. At this layer, the information being transmitted over the Web is secured utilizing encryption strategies. This layer consists of network parts and gives Web availability to the framework.
3. ***Service layer***: Comprises a cloud server and storage of data. Information is permanently stored in this layer. This layer has the rationale for processing the information produced by sensor hubs. It additionally produces triggers and cautions according to the characterized rules. The information at this layer is secured through confirmation, approval, and encryption techniques [33].

4. *Application layer*: Provides the interface to the framework. Clients can monitor and control the framework with the user interface. The client is ensured through confirmation. The applications are created for PCs and cell phones [34].

The proposed smart environmental framework depends on the following factors: a) Sensor junctions are examined before the data are forwarded to the server, b) the gateway layer checks for the validation of the data received from the sensors, and c) after the authentication, the data are transferred to the cloud server with the aid of the Internet [35]. In the end, the IoT cloud server analyzes the filtered secured data for suitable authorization and authentication. The authorized data are securely stored in the cloud-based database system. The IoT cloud server is additionally responsible for approving the sensor hub to ensure that the right information is being distributed at the right "message queuing telemetry transport (MQTT)" [36] point. The cloud server at that point forms the information for the application layer with the goal that significant data are feasibly produced.

The cloud server represented in IoT confirms the client of the framework, gateway hub, etc. The correspondence between the gateway layer, handling layer, and application layer are protected utilizing encryption. The application framework shows continuous data about the environment to the client. This layer likewise permits advantaged clients to remotely set the edge esteems manually [37]. The proposed framework is exceptionally secure as it controls the progression of information in the framework by legitimate authentication, approval, information encryption, and job-based security [38].

7.3 Challenges and Recommendations

7.3.1 Challenges in IoT Integration and Implementation

The major challenge involved in the integration of insightful procedures for IoT-based applications is represented in Figure 7.12.

The major concern is about hardware limitations [39], which include, improper camera positioning, lack of random access of memory, the manual adjustment that requires necessary extensive examination for finding the achievable arrangement and controller issues,

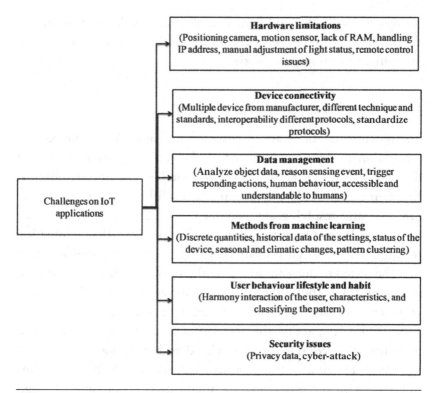

Figure 7.12 Challenges in IoT applications.

and concern about the device connectivity issues leads to different techniques and standards being adopted by device manufacturers, leading to the communication problems associated with various protocol and its standardization

Concern identified with the executive's information being separated from different sensors is in the raw structure, which has higher reflection and is mind-boggling to comprehend for people or interpretable by machines and information the board framework stays indistinct. Concerns about machine learning include conflicts between many rules and uncertainty [40], as limited information could lead to serious information loss. The patterns collected should have high quality for evaluation.

It is critical and complex to analyze user behaviour, lifestyle, and habits, due to their dynamics and that they involves multiple parameters that are not controlled. Security issues such as cyber-attacks and privacy play a vital role, as hackers can remotely collect the MAC address of the device and launch a cyber-attack, leading to privacy data leaks and various penalties and reputational damage as they do not mitigate legal responsibilities.

7.3.2 Recommendations in IoT Implementation

The recommendations are represented in Figure 7.13. The recommendation to developers related to the filtering and analyzing of the data indicates that data collection method should take place at the source and should extract only the useful information from the raw data and resolving any conflict rules that have occurred. The recommendation for performance verification states that automation testing must be given priority and that prototype implementation must be tested in due care so that real-world implementation will be hassle-free [41]. The recommendation in consideration of all parameters is that consumer behaviour in energy usage needs be studied in detail and its impact on the performance on each application must be mapped. Recommendations related to benefiting users include the enhancement of security protections, security protocols to communicate with smart devices, and managing functionalities through mobile [42].

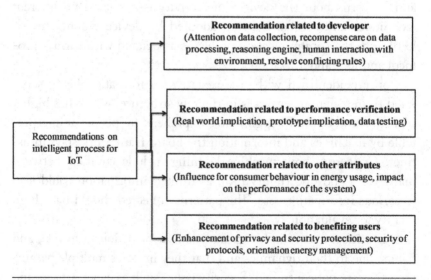

Figure 7.13   Recommendations for IoT applications.

7.4 Industrial Standardization of IoT and AI Analysis

Today, we are surrounded by IoT devices. It isn't exceptional to see lights that can turn on naturally when they identify individuals, or heating and cooling frameworks that can turn on if the temperature drops or surpasses marginal limits [43]. Also, items that are commercially available like smart pots can be initiated remotely with the aid of a smartphone, and smart thermo-controllers can turn air-conditioners on or off based on the home's inhabitant activity. Moreover, voice-enacted products with virtual and augmented reality are developing in prominence. Such devices incorporate exact voice examination, empowering the network supporters to help the client in everyday tasks. Equivalently, our urban areas are additionally smart. For instance, IoT tools and devices are currently being used for various phenomena such as environmental monitoring, monitoring and managing parking, digital twin pumps, asset management, monitoring traffic, and tracking residents, which empowers the investigation-changing propensities for the urban populace. In business ventures, novel sensors are being utilized to gauge and monitor office conditions, including temperature inside clinical storerooms or clinical vehicles and tracking important products.

Similarly, IoT devices with auto-determination abilities are being utilized in automobiles to impart continuous caution signs to crisis administrations, and even to accidents. IoT has had a sizeable effect in current economies and helps residents, such as the computerized economy. Despite these gains, the quick development of IoT is additionally a reason for significant concern. As discussed, normalization across the industry has been able to stay current with the quick integration of IoT by the business, retail, and private segments. Powerless verification, encryption, and attack avoidance instruments have made the IoT business an ideal target of bad actors. Furthermore, these vulnerabilities have prompted issues, such as diminished end-client security. Countless insufficiently secured IoT devices create the danger of enormous scope cyber-attacks, which might incorporate state-supported assaults. The dangers referenced previously can be mitigated through guidelines and enactment for the IoT business.

It is foreseen that long after the guidelines are presented, the probability of outright consistency in the business will take time. This inconsistency can be connected to numerous reasons. Primarily, because there are no incentives for the product owners to actualize the changes since manufacturers are commonly not the victims of assaults, along these, they do not possess intimate at the financial expense of digital assaults. Furthermore, the financial expense of consistency has expanded the both need for technology and the deficiency of ability for businesses, which could create a significant disincentive for manufacturers. It is recommended to boost consistency, that public sectors need to present consistent incentives. Compliance with principles would improve buyer certainty and the flexibility of IoT devices against digital assaults.

7.4.1 Intervention in Industries

The shortfall of the guidelines in IoT business needs instantaneous action. From the point of administration, normalization in the IoT business is a mind-boggling and testing task [40]. The prerequisite for precision in the production of the most noteworthy arrangement of determinations for an expansive range of "microcontrollers, modules, sensors, actuators, availability, and programming stages" is a demanding assignment that requires cooperation among numerous worldwide associations. At a national level, a few activities recently have been attempted by the businesses.

7.4.2 Internet Industrial Consortium (IIC)

The Internet Industrial Consortium (IIC) is an association formed in 2014 to hasten the development of interconnected devices. The association intends to build a union of global companies, public sectors, and the educational institutions to team up on the improvement of testbeds for ongoing applications. The association has effectively partaken in pushing the requirements for principles in the IoT business.

7.4.3 Industrial Internet Task Force (IETF)

The Industrial Internet Task Force (IETF) is one of the associations centred around the advancement of rules for Internet-associated devices [44]. Established in 1986, the IETF has mostly focused on

IoT and urges designers and makers to receive their rules intentionally. Their present work incorporates a meaning of multiple conventions to help IPv6 from the reduced controlled 6LoWPAN and advancements.

7.4.4 IoT Security Foundation (IoTSF)

The IoT Security Foundation (IoTSF) is a non-profit association with the goal, "Build Secure, Buy Secure, Be Secure", has been associated with the IoT business since 2015. Through courses, training, and inside created IoT security rules, the IoTSF has recognized issues and is endeavouring to overcome them through a cooperative activity with firms that negotiate in IoT. This coordinated effort expects to work through sharing information, aptitude, trading best practices, and consultancy [44]. The IoTSF additionally offers an IoT system as a registration. They urge the IoT producers to actualize and self-guarantee, to show consistency with their IoTSF systems.

7.5 Significance of Big Data Analytics in IoT

An IoT framework contains billions of devices, sensors, and actuators that liaise with one another. Besides broad development and extension about IoT platforms, the number of multiple sensors, devices, tools, and equipment is expanding swiftly. The devices interface with one another and transfer enormous amounts information over the Internet. This tremendous flow of information is termed "Big Data" and is consistent in the development of IoT-dependent systems, offering to tackle complex issues such as the management of information, storage processing, investigation, and analysis. For example, IoT integrated with a Big Data framework is helpful to manage a few of the issues of smart buildings such as indoor temperature control, monitoring of toxic gases, oxygen, and carbon dioxide levels, and lightning and heating systems [45]. Such a system can gather the information from the sensors integrated into the buildings to perform data investigation in a dynamic model. Modern industrial products can be updated by utilizing an IoT-based digital-physical framework that is integrated with data investigation and information securing procedures [46].

Traffic is a significant issue within smart urban communities. Constant traffic data can be gathered via IoT devices and sensors implemented in the peak hours of gridlock, and this data can be further analyzed in an IoT-based traffic executive's framework. In a healthcare investigation, the IoT sensors create a great deal of continuous data about the well-being of patients [47]. This enormous measure of data should be incorporated into one database and must be handled quickly to make brisk decisions with high precision; Big Data innovation is the optimal solution for this activity [48].

7.6 Conclusion

The IoT plays a vital role in our day-to-day applications, from communicating on a virtual level to live connections. IoT has given a new dimension to the Internet by effectively understanding the needs of the people and their products, to produce a smarter insightful environment. This has led to the vision of "anytime, anywhere, anyway, anything" communication. IoT is termed as the centerpiece of the conventional Internet for the next-generation digital ecosystem, which ought to have an exceptionally drastic change in the field of a healthcare centre, educational sector, industries, etc. One such example, the integration of AI into the Internet of things, has led to an innovative technique of detecting chronic viruses through voice recognition.

Thus, the architecture concept for different applications is studied and discussed in detail for smart building automation, smart waste management, and environmental monitoring. IoT architecture involves five major layers that indicate innovation and research at every stage, making it smarter with a unique identity and communication with humans at each level of the layers. The modern IoT, which is mostly concentrated on machine-to-machine communications, is trending getting reduced depending on several factors. Advanced mathematical formulations are being researched for the optimization of devices and techno-economic analysis. The challenges and recommendations suggested in the study can be further researched in terms of theoretical and experimental validations for numerous IoT applications. The modern IoT has initiated the people to focus and research on vertical silos of architecture, this commercial type of architecture available in major applications deals with publish/subscribe model but lacks concentration on flexibility, scalability, security, interoperability, and addressability issues. Crowdsourcing might be fused into the structural brevity.

Futuristic IoT will rely upon flexibility in adapting advanced technological devices, manufacturing reliable, sophisticated, and energy-efficient devices, collecting data from heterogeneous sources, and reducing expenses with maximum efficiency. The eventual goal of IoT is to be "consistent, unified, and unavoidable". Large-scale deployment of the products should be well within the guidelines of the standards specified. In this manner, the advancements of IoT as a smart framework can be met with interoperability, vitality supportability, protection, and security.

IoT engineers and scientists are working to expand the scope of this technology for the benefit of society to the most noteworthy level. Upgrades are conceivable if boundaries are considered on the different issues and inadequacies in the current specialized methodologies are resolved. In this chapter, the investigation introduced a few issues and difficulties that IoT engineers must consider to build up an efficient product. Significant challenges of IoT are additionally discussed that hamper the efforts of IoT designers and scientists. The IoT can offer many types of assistance, but also creates an immense amount of information. Subsequently, the significance of Big Data analytics is additionally examined, which can offer solutions that could be used to build an improved IoT framework.

Acknowledgment

The authors thank the Vellore Institute of Technology (VIT), Vellore for providing technical and financial support.

References

[1] Hung, M., 2017. Leading the IoT, Gartner insights on how to lead in a connected world. *Gartner Research*, pp. 1–29.

[2] Wang, P., Valerdi, R., Zhou, S., and Li, L., 2015. Introduction: Advances in IoT research and applications. *Information Systems Frontiers, 17*(2), pp. 239–241.

[3] Ghosh, A., Chakraborty, D., and Law, A., 2018. Artificial intelligence in the Internet of Things. *CAAI Transactions on Intelligence Technology, 3*(4), pp. 208–218.

[4] Rabah, K., 2018. The convergence of AI, IoT, Big Data, and blockchain: A review. *The Lake Institute Journal*, *1*(1), pp. 1–18.

[5] Tyagi, S., Agarwal, A., and Maheshwari, P., 2016, January. A conceptual framework for IoT-based healthcare system using cloud computing. In *2016 6th International Conference-Cloud System and Big Data Engineering (Confluence)* (pp. 503–507). IEEE.

[6] Chowdhary, C.L., Das, T.K., Gurani, V., and Ranjan, A., 2018. An improved tumour identification with Gabor wavelet segmentation. *Research Journal of Pharmacy and Technology*, *11*(8), pp. 3451–3456.

[7] Gope, P., and Hwang, T., 2015. BSN-Care: A secure IoT-based modern healthcare system using a body sensor network. *IEEE Sensors Journal*, *16*(5), pp. 1368–1376.

[8] Ahmadi, H., Arji, G., Shahmoradi, L., Safdari, R., Nilashi, M., and Ali, M., 2019. The application of the Internet of Things in healthcare: A systematic literature review and classification. *Universal Access in the Information Society*, pp. 1–33.

[9] Alsamhi, S.H., Ma, O., Ansari, M.S., and Almalki, F.A., 2019. Survey on collaborative smart drones and the Internet of Things for improving the smartness of smart cities. *IEEE Access*, *7*, pp. 128125–128152.

[10] Saha, A.K., Saha, J., Ray, R., Sircar, S., Dutta, S., Chattopadhyay, S.P., and Saha, H.N., 2018, January. IoT-based drone for improvement of crop quality in the agricultural field. In *2018 IEEE 8th Annual Computing and Communication Workshop and Conference (CCWC)* (pp. 612–615). IEEE.

[11] Kamilaris, A., Gao, F., Prenafeta-Boldu, F.X., and Ali, M.I., 2016, December. Agri-IoT: A semantic framework for Internet of Things-enabled smart farming applications. In 2016 IEEE 3rd World Forum on the Internet of Things (WF-IoT) (pp. 442–447). IEEE.

[12] Pardini, K., Rodrigues, J.J., Kozlov, S.A., Kumar, N., and Furtado, V., 2019. IoT-based solid waste management solutions: A survey. *Journal of Sensor and Actuator Networks*, *8*(1), p. 5.

[13] Pedersen, S.M., Pedersen, M.F., Ørum, J.E., Fountas, S., van Evert, F.K., van Egmond, F., Kernecker, M., and Mouazen, A.M., 2020. Economic, environmental and social impacts. In Agricultural Internet of Things and Decision Support for Precision Smart Farming (pp. 279–330). Academic Press.

[14] Saravanan, K., and Saraniya, S., 2018. Cloud IoT-based novel livestock monitoring and identification system using UID. *Sensor Review*, 38(1).

[15] Alonso, R.S., Sittón-Candanedo, I., García, Ó., Prieto, J., and Rodríguez-González, S., 2020. An intelligent Edge-IoT platform for monitoring livestock and crops in a dairy farming scenario. *Ad Hoc Networks*, *98*, p. 102047.

[16] Zhang, J., Kong, F., Zhai, Z., Han, S., Wu, J., and Zhu, M., 2016. Design and development of IoT monitoring equipment for an open livestock environment. *International. Journal. Simulation: Systems Science & Technology*, *17*(26), pp. 2–7.

[17] Lee, I., 2019. The Internet of Things for enterprises: An ecosystem, architecture, and IoT service business model. *Internet of Things*, 7, p. 100078.

[18] Navani, D., Jain, S., and Nehra, M.S., 2017, December. The Internet of Things (IoT): A study of architectural elements. In *2017 13th International Conference on Signal-Image Technology & Internet-Based Systems (SITIS)* (pp. 473–478). IEEE.

[19] Soni, A., Upadhyay, R., and Jain, A., 2017. Internet of Things and wireless physical layer security: A survey. In Computer Communication, Networking, and Internet Security (pp. 115–123). Springer, Singapore.

[20] Verma, A., Prakash, S., Srivastava, V., Kumar, A., and Mukhopadhyay, S.C., 2019. Sensing, controlling, and IoT infrastructure in the smart building: A review. *IEEE Sensors Journal*, *19*(20), pp. 9036–9046.

[21] Shah, A.S., Nasir, H., Fayaz, M., Lajis, A., and Shah, A., 2019. A review of energy consumption optimization techniques in IoT-based smart building environments. *Information*, *10*(3), p. 108.

[22] Zaidan, A.A., and Zaidan, B.B., 2020. A review of the intelligent process for smart home applications based on IoT: Coherent taxonomy, motivation, open challenges, and recommendations. *Artificial Intelligence Review*, *53*(1), pp. 141–165.

[23] Noura, M., Atiquzzaman, M., and Gaedke, M., 2019. Interoperability in the Internet of Things: Taxonomies and open challenges. *Mobile Networks and Applications*, *24*(3), pp. 796–809.

[24] Jia, M., Komeily, A., Wang, Y., and Srinivasan, R.S., 2019. Adopting Internet of Things for the development of smart buildings: A review of enabling technologies and applications. *Automation in Construction*, *101*, pp. 111–126.

[25] Wang, X., Tao, Y., and Xu, X., 2015. SHSM: A service middleware for smart home. In *2015 IEEE International Conference on Mobile Services* (pp. 475–479). IEEE.

[26] Henricksen, K., and Robinson, R., 2006, November. A survey of middleware for sensor networks: State-of-the-art and future directions. In *Proceedings of the International Workshop on Middleware for Sensor Networks* (pp. 60–65).

[27] Chowdhury, B., and Chowdhury, M.U., 2007, December. RFID-based real-time smart waste management system. In *2007 Australasian Telecommunication Networks and Applications Conference* (pp. 175–180). IEEE.

[28] Folianto, F., Low, Y.S., and Yeow, W.L., 2015, April. Smart bin: Smart waste management system. In *2015 IEEE Tenth International Conference on Intelligent Sensors, Sensor Networks, and Information (ISSNIP)* (pp. 1–2). IEEE.

[29] Zeb, A, Ali, Q., Saleem, M.Q., Awan, K.M., Alowayr, A.S., Uddin, J., Iqbal, S., and Bashir, F., 2019. A proposed IoT-enabled smart waste bin management system and efficient route selection. *Journal of Computer Networks and Communications*, *2019*(3), pp. 1–9.

[30] H IoT and E Sustainability, 2020. How IoT and AI can enable Using IoT and AI for reducing e-waste Applying IoT and AI for agricultural sustainability Leveraging IoT and AI for species protection Using IoT and AI for cleaner air, pp. 9–12.

[31] Tellez, M., El-Tawab, S., and Heydari, H.M., 2016, April. Improving the security of wireless sensor networks in an IoT environmental monitoring system. In *2016 IEEE Systems and Information Engineering Design Symposium (SIEDS)* (pp. 72–77). IEEE.

[32] Mois, G., Folea, S., and Sanislav, T., 2017. Analysis of three IoT-based wireless sensors for environmental monitoring. *IEEE Transactions on Instrumentation and Measurement, 66*(8), pp. 2056–2064.

[33] Ibrahim, H., Mostafa, N., Halawa, H., Elsalamouny, M., Daoud, R., Amer, H., Adel, Y., Shaarawi, A., Khattab, A., and ElSayed, H., 2019. A layered IoT architecture for greenhouse monitoring and remote control. *SN Applied Sciences, 1*(3), pp. 1–12.

[34] Xu, K., Kong, L., Wu, F., Chen, Q., and Chen, G., 2019, December. Mobile sampling strategy for environment information reconstruction from view of cloud. In *2019 IEEE International Conference on Smart Cloud (SmartCloud)* (pp. 25–30). IEEE.

[35] Marche, T., Maheshwary, P., and Kumar, R., 2019. Environmental monitoring system for smart city based on secure Internet of Things (IoT) architecture. *Wireless Personal. Communications, 107*, pp. 2143–2172,.

[36] Madakam, S., Ramaswamy, R., and Tripathi, S., 2015. Internet of Things (IoT): A literature review. *Journal of Computer and Communications, 3*(5), pp. 164–173.

[37] Gomez, C., Chessa, S., Fleury, A., Roussos, G., and Preuveneers, D., 2019. Internet of Things for enabling smart environments: A technology-centric perspective. *Journal of Ambient Intelligence and Smart Environments, 11*, pp. 23–43.

[38] Thantharate, A., Beard, C., and Kankariya, P., 2019. CoAP and MQTT based models to deliver software and security updates to IoT devices over the air. In *The 2019 International Conference on Internet of Things (iThings) and IEEE Green Computing and Communications (GreenCom) and IEEE Cyber, Physical and Social Computing (CPSCom) and IEEE Smart Data (SmartData)* (pp. 1065–1070). IEEE.

[39] Sayed, E., Ahmed, A., and Yousef, M.E., 2019, July. Internet of Things in smart environment : Concept, applications, challenges, and future directions. *World Scientific News, 134*(1), pp. 1–51.

[40] Saleem, J., Hammoudeh, M., Raza, U., Adebisi, B., and Ande, R., 2018. IoT standardization: Challenges, perspectives, and solution. In *Proceedings of the 2nd International Conference on Future Networks and Distributed Systems* (pp. 1–9).

[41] Khan, R., 2012. Applications and key challenges future internet: The Internet of Things architecture, possible applications, and key challenges. pp. 257–260.

[42] Samaila, M.G., Neto, M., Fernandes, D.A., Freire, M.M., and Inácio, P.R., 2017. Security challenges of the Internet of Things. In Beyond the Internet of Things (pp. 53–82). Springer, Cham.

[43] Radanliev, P., De Roure, D., Nurse, J., Montalvo, R.M., and Burnap, P., 2019. Standardization of cyber risk impact assessment for the Internet of Things (IoT). arXiv Preprint arXiv:1903.04428.

[44] Pereira, C., Pinto, A., Aguiar, A., Rocha, P., Santiago, F., and Sousa, J., 2016, June. IoT interoperability for actuating applications through standardized M2M communications. In *2016 IEEE 17th International Symposium on A World of Wireless, Mobile and Multimedia Networks (WoWMoM)* (pp. 1–6). IEEE.

[45] Cai, H., Xu, B., Jiang, L., and Vasilakos, A.V., 2016. IoT-based big data storage systems in cloud computing: Perspectives and challenges. *IEEE Internet of Things Journal*, 4(1), pp. 75–87.

[46] Liu, C., Yang, C., Zhang, X., and Chen, J., 2015. External integrity verification for outsourced big data in cloud and IoT: A big picture. *Future Generation Computer Systems*, 49, pp. 58–67.

[47] Colony, B., Al-Fuqaha, A., Gupta, A., Benhaddou, D., Alwajidi, S., Qadir, J., and Fong, A.C., 2019. Leveraging machine learning and big data for smart buildings: A comprehensive survey. *IEEE Access*, 7, pp. 90316–90356.

[48] BP Forum, D Bpf, and O Report, 2019. IGF 2019 Best Practices Forum on Internet of Things Big Data Artificial Intelligence Draft BPF Output Report, no. November.

8

ANALYSIS OF FEATURE SELECTION METHODS FOR ANDROID MALWARE DETECTION USING MACHINE LEARNING TECHNIQUES

SANTOSH K. SMMARWAR, GOVIND P. GUPTA, AND SANJAY KUMAR

Department of Information Technology, National Institute of Technology, Raipur, Chhattisgarh, India

Contents

DOI: 10.1201/9781003264545-8

8.1 Introduction

The tremendous growth of Android-based smartphones has made a big impact on the daily routine work of a user's life. The use of mobile phones has reached almost every field such as academic work, online shopping, social networking, online transactions and banking, messaging, etc. Therefore, Android devices are undoubtedly the leading operating system used worldwide. The Android phone's functionality depends on permission-based models that are utilized in the Android stage to shield the gadgets from malicious applications. The advancement and more sophisticated features of these devices have made them more popular. This increasing popularity and dependency on Android phones have made the users victims of cyber-attacks or malware attacks [1]. Android application stores, for example, outside business sectors and the official Google Play store have become a hub for malware application distribution [2]. Even though Google attempts to remove malware-contaminated applications from its market, the Google Play store at times has dangerous applications available. With the installation of these applications, malware can compromise a user's privacy, data integrity, and security, and destroy sensitive documents with system files, etc. Due to the availability of various antivirus software that can detect malware easily, attackers have changed malware into a new variant, making it impossible to easily identify malware applications in the Android environment. Subsequently, machine learning calculations offer a new stage in malware detection [3, 4]. Machine learning puts together arrangements concerning removing highlights from applications for training [5]. A number of different feature selection algorithms select a subset of features from the original feature set, which can be used to train learning models to achieve a better detection rate. A growing number of Android malware detection models implemented different feature subset selection algorithms and achieved better detection rates [6]. This chapter deals with binary and multiclass malware classification methods. Binary class malware comprising portmap and multiclass has SMSMALWARE_BIIGE, SMSMALWARE_BEANBOT, and SCAREWARE subclasses of malware.

8.2 Literature Review

In the paper [7] author presented the deep learning-based malware classification approach that used feature engineering to create a new feature subset from ASM and Byte file datasets. This method creates the hybrid dataset of extracted opcode features using a wrapper feature selection. However, this proposed approach is not able to detect new variants of malware. In [8], author used two types of features for Android malware categorization by using the different combinations of bio-inspired optimization techniques in static analysis. However, the accuracy achieved by this proposed method could be further increased by other techniques. The work [9] discusses the loss of meaningful features, which is helpful in the identification of malware classification used directly in machine learning without properly examining the structure of code. To resolve these issues, the authors proposed graph-based feature generation to detect Android malware. However, this approach is applicable for binary classification not for malware sub-family classification. Another problem associated with malware detection in [10] discusses the interdependency check among static as well as dynamic features creates more misclassification by classifiers. Therefore, the authors proposed the tree-augmented Naïve Bayes hybrid model to check the malicious nature of applications. However, this approach takes more time to recognize malicious apps. The other work [11] proposed a lightweight malware detection system by using the latent semantic indexing and generates the new feature space vector of opcode features for Android malware detection. However, this method works for static malware features analysis and has lower scalability. The author [12] presented a framework for the Internet of Medical Things (IoMT) to prevent the cyber-threat of malware attacks. This framework is based on a hybrid approach by using deep learning techniques to detect malware efficiently and early. The author in [13] addressed the limitations of medical devices and healthcare frameworks that continuously face the risk of cyber-attacks. To tackle these issues, the authors proposed an ensemble learning and fog-cloud-based framework for the IoMT environment. This framework has 96.35% accuracy and a lower false-alarm rate. However, the performance of this framework can be improved by using different feature optimization techniques.

8.3 Methodology

Figure 8.1 shows the process of the automatic classification system for Android malware detection: (1) Sample dataset pre-processing (which involves feature extraction), (2) feature subset selection, and (3) the classification of application as benign or malicious [14].

The number and quality of features used to train models to identify Android apps as benign or malware (malicious) with reasonable accuracy are critical. Until training the models, feature selection is used to remove obsolete, redundant, constant, duplicated, and associated features from the raw features. In Android malware detection systems, several methods for selecting the best features have been commonly used. Brief descriptions of the different feature selection algorithms are explained in the following sections.

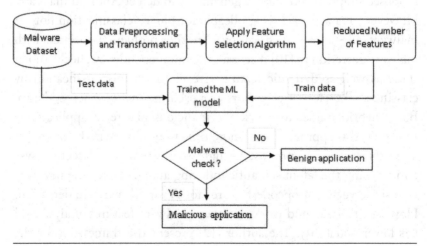

Figure 8.1   General diagram of the malware detection process.

8.3.1 Analysis of Variance (ANOVA)

This is the statistical method used to find the variance of means among groups. Analysis of Variance (ANOVA) determines the similarity of relevant features, reduces their dimensionality, and extracts the best feature of the most importance to enhance the result [4]. The calculated value in this test is called the F-score or F-statistics and is computed as the ratio of within-group variance and between-group variance as follows:

$$F - statistics = \frac{Variation\ between\ sample\ means}{Variation\ within\ sample\ means}$$

8.3.2 Linear Regression

Linear regression is the process of finding the relationship between independent and dependent variables. In the line plot, the best-fit line among the different data points is predicted for a given input. It is supervised machine learning with a continuous and constant slope expected performance. Rather than attempting to classify values, it is used to estimate values within a continuous range (e.g. revenue, price). There are two types of regression, simple regression and multivariate regression.

8.3.3 Logistic Regression

Logistic regression is the extended form of linear regression, also known as regularization. This strategy is used to overcome overfitting and feature selection to build a less complex model when we have a large number of features in our dataset. It has two forms, L1 regularization and L2 regularization.

8.3.4 Random Forest

This is widely used in feature selection to remove unwanted features using tree forms and it improves the purity of features. It is effective because they it has strong predictive efficiency, low overfitting, and is simple to interpret in general. Random forest feature selection falls under the category of embedded methods.

Filter and wrapper methods are combined in embedded methods. Algorithms with built-in feature selection methods are used to implement them [4].

8.3.5 Recursive Feature Elimination (RFE)

Recursive Feature Elimination (RFE) is based on the wrapping approach used to eliminate meaningless features until the best feature is selected. This means that in the centre of the process, a different machine-learning algorithm is provided and used, which is wrapped by RFE and used to help select the best features. RFE is a wrapper-style feature selection algorithm that internally employs filter-based feature selection and rates each feature and picks the features with the highest (or lowest) score. [4].

8.3.6 Gradient-Boosted Decision Trees

This is the performance enhancement method used to tackle the prediction of the model for classification as well as regression purpose of the samples. This concept improves learning ability by easing the objective and lowering the number of iterations to obtain the optimal result. The attribute in your data collection is an individual measurable property or trait of a phenomenon. Various estimates, patterns, peak analysis, autocorrelations and cross-correlations, and other features may be included. Once the features have been extracted from the data, they are fed into the gradient-boosted decision trees (GBDT) as input. However, since the GBDT is prone to overfitting, it's necessary to reduce the number of features, leaving only those that aid the classifier, particularly for small datasets [13].

8.3.7 Linear Discriminant Analysis

Linear discriminant analysis (LDA) is a feature reduction method used in machine learning and pattern classification applications as a pre-processing phase. The main aim of feature-reduction techniques is to minimize dimensions by eliminating redundant and dependent features and transforming them from a higher-dimensional vector space to a lower-dimensional vector space [4].

8.3.8 Principal Component Analysis

This is an unsupervised algorithm for generating linear combinations of the original features. The new characteristics are orthogonal, meaning they are unrelated. They're also rated according to how much "explained variation" they have. The first principal component (PC1) in your dataset describes the most variation, followed by PC2, PC3, and so on.

8.3.9 Constant Quasi-Constant and Duplicate Feature Removal

Constant features are those that have a single value for all of the outputs in the dataset. Constant features have no details that can be used to classify the current record. As a result, all constant features should be removed from the dataset [4].

8.4 Classification Algorithms

There are six supervised-learning algorithms, namely Naïve Bayes, K-Nearest Neighbour, random forest, AdaBoost, gradient boosting, and decision tree are used in this chapter [15].

8.4.1 Naïve Bayes

Since Naïve Bayes integrates a simple model for simplifying the data, learning data, and predicting groups, it is an attribute probabilistic classifier algorithm used in multiclass classification problems. Taking all features that are independent and visible within the given features, Naïve Bayes defines a special class without having any relations to the other features. The goal is to accurately predict the class of malware [16].

8.4.2 Gradient Boosting

Gradient boosting is a generalized machine learning technique that works for regression and classification task problems that generate a prediction capability model from an ensemble of weak prediction groups, usually decision trees. The derived algorithm is called a gradient-boosted tree when a decision tree is a weak learner, and it normally outperforms random forest. It forms the model in the same stage-by-stage manner as other boosting approaches, but it broadens the scope by allowing optimization of any differentiable loss function [16].

8.4.3 Decision Tree

A decision tree is a model of supervised learning that is widely used to solve different types of classification and regression-based problems, but it is most often used to solve classification issues. It is composed of internal nodes that represent dataset attributes, branches that represent decision laws, and leaf vertexes that each indicates the outcome in this tree-form classifier. The decision vertex and the leaf vertex are the two vertexes in a decision tree. The leaf vertex is the product of such decisions and does not have any extra branches, while decision vertex is used to make any decision and has several outgoing branches [15].

8.4.4 K-Nearest Neighbour

The K-Nearest Neighbour (k-NN) is a manageable classification procedure that tries to interpret the finite set of output, continuous value as a number and predict the accuracy of the model and work for a small size dataset. It has been used in a variety of applications, including health departments, finance sectors, raw text data, face detection, and fraud and malware analysis [13]. Further data distributions, as well as no prior knowledge, are used less in k-NN. The number of nearby neighbours of a test input point is represented by the constant "K" in the k-NN algorithm [20].

8.4.5 AdaBoost

One of the ensemble boosting classifiers is AdaBoost or adaptive boosting. It incorporates several distinct classifiers to enhance accuracy. AdaBoost is a tool for creating iterative ensembles and combines many low-performing classifiers, resulting in an improved high-accuracy classifier. AdaBoost sets a payload of classifiers and trains the input data in repetition, so that accurate predictions of unusual detection can be made. Any classification-learning algorithm that obtains payloads on the training data can be used as a base classifier [15].

8.4.6 Random Forest

Random forest is a collection of decision trees that work on ensemble learning concepts and learn to make strong predictions for the weak learner using training data. It has important properties that make it the most popular classifier such as defining rule sets that can be easily understood, being capable of managing high-dimensional data, supporting non-linear numeric and categorical predictors, calculating variable importance for the classifier, and selecting the most useful attribute for prediction [13].

8.5 Performance Metrics

The following performance indicators are used to evaluate the performance of the classifier [17–21].

- $Accuracy = \dfrac{Correctly\ classified\ instances}{Total\ number\ of\ instances}$

- $Precision = \dfrac{True\ Positive(TP)}{True\ Positive(TP) + False\ Positive(FP)}$

- $Recall = \dfrac{TP}{TP + FN}$

- $F - score = 2 \times \dfrac{Precision \times Recall}{Precision + Recall}$

8.6 Dataset Description

8.6.1 Multiclass Classification

The malware dataset consists of a total of 73,178 files including legitimate files (66,525) and various malware files (6653). Malware files include SMSMALWARE_BEANBOT (2878), SCAREWARE (1108), and SMSMALWARE_BIIGE (2667). There are various features (80) to define each file with the major one being flow duration, the total length of packets, etc.

Source of the dataset – CICMalAnal2017 Android malware dataset available at:

http://205.174.165.80/CICDataset/CICMalAnal2017/Dataset/CSVS/

8.6.2 Binary Classification

The malware dataset consists of a total of 191,694 files including legitimate files (6050) and various malware files (185,644). Malware files are all portmaps. There are various features (82) to define each file with the major one being flow duration, the total length of packets, etc.

Source of the dataset – AAGM dataset, http://www.unb.ca/cic/datasets/android-adware.html

8.7 Results and Discussion

Exhaustive implementation was done when two different datasets were applied with 10 feature selection methods and 6 different algorithms. Results appeared to be highly varied across all the entities. Starting with a dataset, there were a lot of scopes to apply and the varied imbalance ratio was to be set to achieve considerable accuracy. Starting with binary classification, the natural dataset was giving accuracy as high as 100%, so there was no need to change the imbalance ratio, which was fixed at 0.03. In multiclass classification, to achieve better outputs, the right imbalance ratio was to be set. After various experiments, it was fixed at 10. Different feature selection techniques are used with each selecting a different number of features ranging from 60 in constant quasi-constant duplicate removal to 1 in LDA. For binary classification, a dominating feature selection was not found, as 100% accuracy was shown by many. Fascinatingly, without feature selection, good results were also shown with 100% accuracy, which points to the skewed nature of the dataset. In multiclass, logistic L1 Lasso dominated all the feature selections with the highest accuracy. Without feature selection, acceptably showed one of the least performances. With six algorithms applied, varied results were analyzed. For binary, gradient-boosting dominated other algorithms and also showed 100% accuracy in much of the feature selections. For multiclass, random forest dominated with maximum feature selection in the maximum accuracy bracket, but lost to gradient boosting in the highest score. Naïve Bayes appeared to be the worst algorithm in both binary and multiclass cases. Four performance metrics were also used to have a comparative study. The precision score appeared the maximum in the binary case and also gave 100% accuracy.

The accuracy score tends to have a lower score comparatively. In multiclass, the accuracy score is a clear winner with the maximum number of feature selection with high accuracy, but the highest accuracy was given with precision score. Recall showed the least accuracy in most cases. Next are the tabular and graphical representations of all the feature selections with each algorithm in every performance matrix of multiclass and binary class classification.

8.7.1 Multiclass Classification

Table 8.1 illustrates the outcome by different classifiers of machine learning tested on the multiclass dataset without using any feature selection technique. In this experiment, we have 80 features. From Table 8.1, it is observed that all algorithms have scored approximately coequally and the best classifier is a random forest with 50 estimators, giving a 91.99% accuracy score.

Table 8.2 illustrates the performance of different machine learning classifiers applied on the multiclass dataset after removing the constant quasi-constant and duplicate features. In this experiment, 60 out of 80 features were selected. From Table 8.2, it is observed that all algorithms have scored approximately on similar lines except for Naïve Bayes. The best classifier is random forest with 50 estimators, giving 92.16% accuracy score.

Table 8.3 illustrates the outcome by different classifiers of machine learning tested on the multiclass dataset after doing an ANOVA F-test as feature selection. In this experiment, 49 out of 80 features were selected. From Table 8.3, it is observed that all algorithms have

Table 8.1 Performance Comparison of Different Machine Learning Classification Models, without Feature Selection

FEATURE SELECTED – 80	WITHOUT FEATURE SELECTION		
CLASSIFIER	ACCURACY (%)	PRECISION (%)	RECALL (%)	F1 SCORE (%)
Random forest	91.99	72.62	42.84	89.93
Naïve Bayes	74.75	27.47	31.16	78.86
Gradient boosting	91.18	86.12	29.74	86.89
Decision tree	90.84	35.75	28.01	86.89
k-NN	90.95	58.87	35.64	88.45
AdaBoost	90.76	31.22	27.41	86.73

Table 8.2 Performance Comparison of Different Machine Learning Classification Models, with Feature selection

FEATURE SELECTED – 60	AFTER CONSTANT QUASI-CONSTANT DUPLICATE REMOVAL			
CLASSIFIER	ACCURACY (%)	PRECISION (%)	RECALL (%)	F1 SCORE (%)
Random forest	92.16	75.13	43.84	90.10
Naïve Bayes	76.26	27.66	30.53	79.61
Gradient boosting	91.15	67.11	29.39	87.30
Decision tree	90.84	35.80	28.90	86.98
k-NN	90.95	66.96	42.67	88.94
AdaBoost	90.76	37.90	40.21	86.73

scored consistently except for Naïve Bayes and the best classifier is the random forest with 50 estimators, giving a 92.19% accuracy score.

Table 8.4 illustrates the outcome by different classifiers of machine learning tested on the multiclass dataset with features selected by linear regression. In this experiment, 3 out of 80 features are selected. From Table 8.4, it is observed that all algorithms have scored approximately 86%, this feature selection has the most equal scores across all classifiers and the best classifier is the decision tree classifier with a maximum depth of 4 and an accuracy score of 90.90%.

Table 8.5 illustrates the outcome by different classifiers of machine learning tested on the multiclass dataset with features selected by logistics L1 regularization (Lasso). In this experiment, 35 out of 80 features are selected. From Table 8.5, it is observed that all algorithms scored very well, but Naïve Bayes had the worst scores. Random forest was the best classifier with 100 estimators, giving a 92.55% accuracy score.

Table 8.3 Performance Comparison of Different Machine Learning Classification Models

FEATURE SELECTED – 49	ANOVA TEST			
CLASSIFIER	ACCURACY (%)	PRECISION (%)	RECALL (%)	F1 SCORE (%)
Random forest	92.19	76.52	45.75	90.04
Naïve Bayes	76.99	27.80	33.55	80.98
Gradient boosting	91.17	89.47	28.01	86.89
Decision tree	90.94	35.80	28.70	86.89
k-NN	90.97	59.12	35.85	88.94
AdaBoost	90.78	31.88	27.52	86.75

Table 8.4 Performance Comparison of Different Machine Learning Classification Models

FEATURE SELECTED – 03	LINEAR REGRESSION			
CLASSIFIER	ACCURACY (%)	PRECISION (%)	RECALL (%)	F1 SCORE (%)
Random forest	87.27	39.58	35.71	86.33
Naïve Bayes	89.85	24.75	26.49	87.20
Gradient boosting	90.86	30.23	25.67	86.63
Decision tree	90.90	35.23	25.57	90.32
k-NN	90.68	53.23	30.94	87.53
AdaBoost	90.83	31.50	26.54	86.70

Table 8.6 illustrates the outcome by different classifiers of machine learning tested on the multiclass dataset with features selected by logistics L2 regularization (Ridge). In this experiment, 8 out of 80 features are selected. From Table 8.6, it is observed that all algorithms have scored very well and the best classifier is random forest with 100 estimators, giving a 92.38% accuracy score. We also observed that Naïve Bayes accuracy improved and is on par with other classifiers.

Table 8.7 illustrates the outcome by different classifiers of machine learning tested on the multiclass dataset using random forest for feature selection. In this experiment, 18 out of 80 features are selected by random forest. From Table 8.7, it is observed that all algorithms have scored approximately coequal except the Naïve Bayes classifier, and the best classifier is random forest with 100 estimators, giving a 92.12% accuracy score.

Table 8.8 illustrates the outcome by different classifiers of machine learning tested on the multiclass dataset using recursive feature elimination (RFE) for feature selection. In this experiment, 15 out of 80 features were selected by RFE. From Table 8.8, it is observed that

Table 8.5 Performance Comparison of Different Machine Learning Classification Models

FEATURE SELECTED – 35	LOGISTIC L1 LASSO			
CLASSIFIER	ACCURACY (%)	PRECISION (%)	RECALL (%)	F1 SCORE (%)
Random forest	92.55	78.93	45.19	90.69
Naïve Bayes	23.95	26.24	31.34	35.52
Gradient boosting	91.08	94.20	27.49	87.01
Decision tree	90.97	45.50	26.13	86.01
k-NN	91.94	66.14	41.95	86.73
AdaBoost	90.92	36.63	26.12	86.71

Table 8.6 Performance Comparison of Different Machine Learning Classification Models

FEATURE SELECTED – 08	LOGISTIC L2 RIDGE			
CLASSIFIER	ACCURACY (%)	PRECISION (%)	RECALL (%)	F1 SCORE (%)
Random forest	92.38	82.38	41.65	90.20
Naïve Bayes	87.52	28.71	26.88	85.28
Gradient boosting	91.01	61.66	26.70	86.89
Decision tree	90.99	60.11	27.50	86.82
k-NN	90.91	59.88	33.25	88.09
AdaBoost	90.93	38.02	26.23	86.72

Table 8.7 Performance Comparison of Different Machine Learning Classification Models

FEATURE SELECTED – 18	RANDOM FOREST			
CLASSIFIER	ACCURACY (%)	PRECISION (%)	RECALL (%)	F1 SCORE (%)
Random forest	92.12	76.04	42.91	89.97
Naïve Bayes	78.11	27.54	30.43	80.61
Gradient boosting	91.12	78.94	28.97	87.20
Decision tree	91.01	41.99	27.25	86.87
k-NN	91.08	61.62	35.33	88.49
AdaBoost	90.89	34.51	26.78	89.72

Table 8.8 Performance Comparison of Different Machine Learning Classification Models

FEATURE SELECTED – 15	RECURSIVE FEATURE ELIMINATION			
CLASSIFIER	ACCURACY (%)	PRECISION (%)	RECALL (%)	F1 SCORE (%)
Random forest	91.99	74.73	41.82	89.74
Naïve Bayes	79.10	27.40	29.57	81.07
Gradient boosting	91.02	75.52	28.38	87.04
Decision tree	90.97	45.47	26.13	86.73
k-NN	91.02	59.94	35.24	88.45
AdaBoost	90.79	32.01	27.97	86.79

all algorithms have scored consistently and Naïve Bayes is trying to compete with other classifiers. The best classifier is random forest with 100 estimators, giving a 91.99% accuracy score.

Table 8.9 illustrates the outcome by different classifiers of machine learning tested on the multiclass dataset using gradient boost for selecting features. In this experiment, 4 out of 80 features are selected. From Table 8.9, it is observed that all algorithms have scored on par with each other and are perfectly alike. The best classifier is random forest with 100 estimators, giving a 92.29% accuracy score.

Table 8.9 Performance Comparison of Different Machine Learning Classification Models

FEATURE SELECTED – 04	GRADIENT BOOST TREE			
CLASSIFIER	ACCURACY (%)	PRECISION (%)	RECALL (%)	F1 SCORE (%)
Random forest	92.29	78.69	42.75	90.24
Naïve Bayes	88.75	26.90	26.62	85.81
Gradient boosting	90.97	90.97	26.47	86.85
Decision tree	90.93	40.05	26.01	86.70
k-NN	90.86	58.82	31.34	87.74
AdaBoost	91.86	31.43	25.88	86.65

Table 8.10 Performance Comparison of Different Machine Learning Classification Models

FEATURE SELECTED – 01	LINEAR DISCRIMINANT ANALYSIS			
CLASSIFIER	ACCURACY (%)	PRECISION (%)	RECALL (%)	F1 SCORE (%)
Random forest	84.12	29.38	29.42	83.93
Naïve Bayes	90.50	26.21	26.34	87.52
Gradient boosting	90.95	38.75	26.79	86.79
Decision tree	90.94	42.18	25.79	86.68
k-NN	90.94	42.64	26.81	88.73
AdaBoost	90.93	40.59	25.56	86.65

Table 8.11 Performance Comparison of Different Machine Learning Classification Models

FEATURE SELECTED – 02	PRINCIPAL COMPONENT ANALYSIS			
CLASSIFIER	ACCURACY (%)	PRECISION (%)	RECALL (%)	F1 SCORE (%)
Random forest	88.77	44.13	36.42	87.30
Naïve Bayes	88.36	25.01	25.62	85.57
Gradient boosting	90.89	45.95	25.37	86.62
Decision tree	90.92	31.07	25.14	86.64
k-NN	90.66	53.25	32.55	87.79
AdaBoost	90.91	22.73	25.30	86.58

Table 8.10 illustrates the outcome by different classifiers of machine learning tested on the multiclass dataset using LDA for feature extraction. In this experiment, 1 out of 80 features is selected by using LDA. From Table 8.10, it is observed that random forest surprisingly performed the worst among the classifiers and the best classifier is the gradient boost classifier, giving a 90.95% accuracy score.

Table 8.11 illustrates the outcome by different classifiers of machine learning tested on the Multiclass Dataset using principal component analysis (PCA) for feature extraction. In this experiment, 2 out of 80 features are selected by using PCA. From Table 8.11, it is observed that random forest again performed relatively low among the classifiers and the best classifier is a decision tree with max depth of 4, giving a 90.92% accuracy score.

8.7.2 Binary Classification

Table 8.12 illustrates the outcome by different classifiers of machine learning tested on the binary dataset without using any feature selection technique. We have 82 features in this experiment. From Table 8.12, it is observed that all algorithms have scored approximately 100%, except the Naïve Bayes classifier. The best classifier is gradient boosting with 50 estimators, giving a 100% F1 score.

Table 8.13 illustrates the outcome by different classifiers of machine learning tested on the binary dataset after removing the constant quasi-constant and duplicate features. In this experiment, 57 out of 82 features are selected. From Table 8.13, it is observed that all algorithms have scored approximately 100%, except the Naïve Bayes classifier. The best classifier is gradient boosting with 50 estimators, giving a 99.99% F1 score.

Table 8.14 illustrates the outcome by different classifiers of machine learning tested on the binary dataset after doing the ANOVA F test as feature selection. In this experiment, 56 out of 82 features are selected. From Table 8.14, it is observed that all algorithms have scored approximately 100%, except the Naïve Bayes classifier and the best classifier is gradient boosting with 50 estimators, giving a 99.99% F1 score.

Table 8.12 Performance Comparison of Different Machine Learning Classification Models

FEATURE SELECTED – 82	WITHOUT FEATURE SELECTION		
CLASSIFIER	ACCURACY (%)	PRECISION (%)	RECALL (%)	F1 SCORE (%)
Random forest	99.99	100	99.99	99.99
Naïve Bayes	98.02	98.13	99.87	98.99
Gradient boosting	100	100	100	100
Decision tree	99.92	99.97	99.95	99.96
k-NN	99.93	99.97	99.95	99.96
AdaBoost	99.98	99.99	99.99	99.99

Table 8.13 Performance Comparison of Different Machine Learning Classification Models

FEATURE SELECTED – 57	AFTER CONSTANT QUASI-CONSTANT DUPLICATE REMOVAL			
CLASSIFIER	ACCURACY (%)	PRECISION (%)	RECALL (%)	F1 SCORE (%)
Random forest	99.99	100	99.99	100
Naïve Bayes	98.08	98.12	99.95	99.02
Gradient boosting	100	100	100	100
Decision tree	99.92	99.87	99.95	99.96
k-NN	99.93	99.97	99.95	99.96
AdaBoost	99.98	99.98	99.94	99.99

Table 8.14 Performance Comparison of Different Machine Learning Classification Models

FEATURE SELECTED – 56	ANOVA F TEST			
CLASSIFIER	ACCURACY (%)	PRECISION (%)	RECALL (%)	F1 SCORE (%)
Random forest	99.99	100	99.99	99.99
Naïve Bayes	98.07	98.11	99.94	99.02
Gradient boosting	100	100	100	100
Decision tree	99.92	99.97	99.95	99.96
k-NN	99.93	99.97	99.95	99.96
AdaBoost	99.98	99.99	99.99	99.99

Table 8.15 Performance Comparison of Different Machine Learning Classification Models

FEATURE SELECTED – 03	LINEAR REGRESSION			
CLASSIFIER	ACCURACY (%)	PRECISION (%)	RECALL (%)	F1 SCORE (%)
Random forest	99.57	99.61	99.94	99.78
Naïve Bayes	97.63	97.77	99.85	98.80
Gradient boosting	99.53	99.59	99.93	99.76
Decision tree	99.50	99.61	99.87	99.74
k-NN	99.58	99.62	99.95	99.79
AdaBoost	99.38	99.54	99.82	99.68

Table 8.15 illustrates the outcome by different classifiers of machine learning tested on the binary dataset (AAGM) with features selected by linear regression. In this experiment, 3 out of 82 features are selected. From Table 8.15, it is observed that all algorithms have scored approximately 98%, except the Naïve Bayes classifier and the best classifier is k-Nearest Neighbour classifier with 5 neighbours and an F1 score of 99.78%.

Table 8.16 Performance Comparison of Different Machine Learning Classification Models

FEATURE SELECTED – 29	LOGISTIC L1 LAASO			
CLASSIFIER	ACCURACY (%)	PRECISION (%)	RECALL (%)	F1 SCORE (%)
Random forest	99.99	100	99.99	99.99
Naïve Bayes	99.61	100	99.60	99.80
Gradient boosting	99.99	100	99.99	100
Decision tree	99.94	99.97	99.98	99.97
k-NN	99.93	99.98	99.95	99.97
AdaBoost	99.99	99.99	99.99	99.99

Table 8.16 illustrates the outcome by different classifiers of machine learning tested on the binary dataset (AAGM) with features selected by logistics L1 regularization (Lasso). In this experiment, 29 out of 82 features are selected. From Table 8.16, it is observed that all algorithms have scored approximately 100% and the best classifier is gradient boosting with 50 estimators, giving a 99.996% F1 score. We also observed an improvement in the score of the Naïve Bayes classifier.

Table 8.17 illustrates the outcome by different classifiers of machine learning tested on the binary dataset (AAGM) with features selected by logistics L2 regularization (Ridge). In this experiment, 14 out of 82 features are selected. From Table 8.17, it is observed that all algorithms have scored approximately 99% and the best classifier is random forest with 100 estimators, giving a 100% F1 score

Table 8.18 illustrates the outcome by different classifiers of machine learning tested on the binary dataset (AAGM) using random forest with 100 estimators for feature selection. In this experiment, 14 out of 82 features are selected by random forest. From Table 8.18, it is observed that all algorithms have scored approximately 100%, except

Table 8.17 Performance Comparison of Different Machine Learning Classification Models

FEATURE SELECTED – 14	LOGISTIC L2 RIDGE			
CLASSIFIER	ACCURACY (%)	PRECISION (%)	RECALL (%)	F1 SCORE (%)
Random forest	100	100	100	100
Naïve Bayes	99.27	99.46	99.80	99.63
Gradient boosting	99.99	100	99.99	99.99
Decision tree	99.87	99.97	99.98	99.96
k-NN	99.93	99.98	99.95	99.97
AdaBoost	99.98	99.99	99.98	99.99

Table 8.18   Performance Comparison of Different Machine Learning Classification Models

FEATURE SELECTED – 14	RANDOM FOREST			
CLASSIFIER	ACCURACY (%)	PRECISION (%)	RECALL (%)	F1 SCORE (%)
Random forest	99.98	100	99.98	99.99
Naïve Bayes	98.23	98.38	99.82	99.10
Gradient boosting	99.95	99.97	99.99	99.97
Decision tree	99.91	99.97	99.94	99.93
k-NN	99.86	99.94	99.91	99.97
AdaBoost	99.95	99.94	99.91	99.97

the Naïve Bayes classifier and the best classifier is gradient boosting with 50 estimators, giving a 99.97% F1 score.

Table 8.19 illustrates the outcome by different classifiers of machine learning tested on the binary dataset (AAGM) using RFE with 100 estimators for feature selection. In this experiment, 15 out of 82 features are selected by RFE. From Table 8.19, it is observed that all algorithms have scored approximately 99% and the best classifier is gradient boosting with 50 estimators, giving a 100% F1 score.

Table 8.20 illustrates the outcome by different classifiers of machine learning tested on the binary dataset (AAGM) using gradient boost with 100 estimators for selecting features. In this experiment, 12 out of 82 features are selected by random forest. From Table 8.20, it is observed that all algorithms have scored approximately 100% and the best classifier is gradient boosting with 50 estimators, giving a 100% F1 score.

Table 8.21 illustrates the outcome by different classifiers of machine learning tested on the binary dataset (AAGM) using LDA for feature extraction. In this experiment, 1 out of 82 features is selected using

Table 8.19   Performance Comparison of Different Machine Learning Classification Models

FEATURE SELECTED – 15	RECURSIVE FEATURE ELIMINATION			
CLASSIFIER	ACCURACY (%)	PRECISION (%)	RECALL (%)	F1 SCORE (%)
Random forest	99.99	100	99.98	100
Naïve Bayes	99.16	99.62	99.52	99.57
Gradient boosting	100	100	100	99.99
Decision tree	99.95	99.99	99.97	99.98
k-NN	99.91	99.97	99.95	99.96
AdaBoost	99.99	99.99	100	100

Table 8.20 Performance Comparison of Different Machine Learning Classification Models

FEATURE SELECTED – 12	GRADIENT BOOST TREE			
CLASSIFIER	ACCURACY (%)	PRECISION (%)	RECALL (%)	F1 SCORE (%)
Random forest	100	100	100	100
Naïve Bayes	99.65	100	99.64	99.82
Gradient boosting	100	100	100	100
Decision tree	99.91	99.97	99.98	99.99
k-NN	99.89	99.93	99.95	99.94
AdaBoost	99.99	99.99	100	100

Table 8.21 Performance Comparison of Different Machine Learning Classification Models

FEATURE SELECTED – 01	LINEAR DISCRIMINANT ANALYSIS			
CLASSIFIER	ACCURACY (%)	PRECISION (%)	RECALL (%)	F1 SCORE (%)
Random forest	99.90	99.96	99.94	99.95
Naïve Bayes	99.52	100	99.51	99.75
Gradient boosting	99.92	99.98	99.99	99.96
Decision tree	99.93	99.98	99.94	99.96
k-NN	99.92	99.98	99.97	99.95
AdaBoost	99.91	99.97	99.94	99.95

Table 8.22 Performance Comparison of Different Machine Learning Classification Models

FEATURE SELECTED – 02	PRINCIPAL COMPONENT ANALYSIS			
CLASSIFIER	ACCURACY (%)	PRECISION (%)	RECALL (%)	F1 SCORE (%)
Random forest	99.85	99.91	99.93	99.92
Naïve Bayes	83.94	100	82.58	90.46
Gradient boosting	99.74	99.85	99.88	99.87
Decision tree	99.56	99.66	99.89	99.77
k-NN	99.84	99.95	99.88	99.92
AdaBoost	99.63	99.85	99.76	99.81

LDA. From Table 8.21, it is observed that all algorithms have scored approximately 100% and the best classifier is the decision tree classifier with a 99.95% F1 score.

Table 8.22 illustrates the outcome by different classifiers of machine learning tested on the binary dataset (AAGM) using PCA for feature extraction. In this experiment, 2 out of 82 features are selected using PCA. From Table 8.22, it is observed that all algorithms have scored approximately 100%, but in this case, Naïve Bayes surprisingly showed a very low score comparatively. The best classifier is random forest with 100 estimators, giving a 99.92% F1 score.

8.8 Comparison of Results

Tables 8.23 and 8.24 show the summary of the highest accuracy obtained by machine learning classifiers using different feature selection methods on multiclass and binary class datasets.

8.9 Conclusion and Future Work

After a rigorous analysis of the accuracy of various algorithms on varying feature selection techniques and performance metrics, we concluded the performance of various algorithms. For multiclass classification, various features were selected using 10 feature-selection techniques. From the experiment, random forest was found to be the best algorithm most of the time and its accuracy showed the best score in most cases. The maximum score of 92.55% accuracy was achieved by using random forest feature selection in the logistic L2 Ridge classifier. For binary classification, a different number of features were selected by 10 feature-selection techniques. Among the results,

Table 8.23 Multiclass Classification Performance Comparison of Different Classifiers

SR. NO	FEATURE SELECTION METHOD	NUMBER OF FEATURES SELECTED	MACHINE LEARNING ALGORITHM	ACCURACY (%)
1	Without feature selection	80	Random forest	91.99
2	Constant quasi-constant duplicate removal	60	Random forest	92.16
3	ANOVA test	49	Random forest	92.19
4	Linear regression	3	Decision tree	90.90
5	Logistic L1 Lasso	35	Random forest	92.55
6	Logistic L2 Ridge	8	Random forest	92.38
7	Random forest	18	Random forest	92.12
8	Recursive feature elimination	15	Random forest	91.99
9	Gradient boost tree	4	Random forest	92.29
10	LDA	1	Gradient boosting	90.95
11	PCA	2	Decision tree	90.92

Table 8.24 Performance Comparison of the Different Classifiers on Binary Classification

SR. NO	FEATURE SELECTION METHOD	NUMBER OF FEATURES SELECTED	MACHINE LEARNING ALGORITHM	ACCURACY (%)
1	Without feature selection	82	Gradient boosting	100
2	Constant quasi-constant duplicate removal	57	Gradient boosting	100
3	ANOVA test	56	Random forest	100
4	Linear regression	3	K-Nearest Neighbour	99.58
5	Logistic L1 Lasso	29	AdaBoost	99.99
6	Logistic L2 Ridge	14	Random forest	100
7	Random forest	14	Random forest	99.98
8	Recursive feature elimination	15	Gradient boosting	100
9	Gradient boost tree	12	Random forest	100
10	LDA	1	Decision tree	99.93
11	PCA	2	Random forest	99.85

gradient boosting appeared to be the best algorithm most of the time. The maximum score of 100% accuracy was achieved in three cases with gradient boosting as an algorithm. The future scope of this study is to design and develop an efficient malware-filtering model using different machine learning or deep learning algorithms for IoT devices.

References

1. Sharmeen, S., Huda, S., Abawajy, J. H., Ismail, W. N., & Hassan, M. M. (2018). Malware threats and detection for industrial mobile-IoT networks. *IEEE Access*, 6, 15941–15957.
2. Feng, R., Chen, S., Xie, X., Meng, G., Lin, S. W., & Liu, Y. (2020). A performance-sensitive malware detection system using deep learning on mobile devices. *IEEE Transactions on Information Forensics and Security*, 16, 1563–1578.
3. Wang, X., Wang, W., He, Y., Liu, J., Han, Z., & Zhang, X. (2017). Characterizing Android apps' behavior for effective detection of malapps at large scale. *Future Generation Computer Systems*, 75, 30–45.
4. Alazab, M. (2020). Automated malware detection in mobile app stores based on robust feature generation. *Electronics*, 9(3), 435.
5. Abawajy, J. H., Chowdhury, M., & Kelarev, A. (2015). Hybrid consensus pruning of ensemble classifiers for big data malware detection. *IEEE Transactions on Cloud Computing*, 8(2), 398–407.

6. Wu, W. C., & Hung, S. H. (2014, October). DroidDolphin: A dynamic Android malware detection framework using big data and machine learning. In *Proceedings of the 2014 Conference on Research in Adaptive and Convergent Systems* (pp. 247–252).

7. Rafique, M. F., Ali, M., Qureshi, A. S., Khan, A., & Mirza, A. M. (2019). Malware classification using deep learning based feature extraction and wrapper based feature selection technique. Arxiv Preprint Arxiv:1910.10958.

8. Pye, J., Issac, B., Aslam, N., & Rafiq, H. (2020, October). Android malware classification using machine learning and bio-inspired optimisation algorithms. In *2020 IEEE 19th International Conference on Trust, Security and Privacy in Computing and Communications (TrustCom)* (pp. 1777–1782). IEEE.

9. Liu, X., Lei, Q., & Liu, K. (2020). A graph-based feature generation approach in Android malware detection with machine learning techniques. *Mathematical Problems in Engineering, 2020*, 1–15.

10. Surendran, R., Thomas, T., & Emmanuel, S. (2020). A TAN based hybrid model for android malware detection. *Journal of Information Security and Applications, 54*, 102483.

11. Singh, A. K., Wadhwa, G., Ahuja, M., Soni, K., & Sharma, K. (2020). Android malware detection using LSI-based reduced opcode feature vector. *Procedia Computer Science, 173*, 291–298.

12. Khan, S., & Akhunzada, A. (2021). A hybrid DL-driven intelligent SDN-enabled malware detection framework for Internet of Medical Things (IoMT). *Computer Communications, 170*, 209–216.

13. Kumar, P., Gupta, G. P., & Tripathi, R. (2021). An ensemble learning and fog-cloud architecture-driven cyber-attack detection framework for IoMT networks. *Computer Communications, 166*, 110–124.

14. Lashkari, A. H., Kadir, A. F. A., Taheri, L., & Ghorbani, A. A. (2018, October). Toward developing a systematic approach to generate benchmark android malware datasets and classification. In *2018 International Carnahan Conference on Security Technology (ICCST)* (pp. 1–7). IEEE.

15. Lopez, C. C. U., & Cadavid, A. N. (2016, April). Machine learning classifiers for android malware analysis. In *2016 IEEE Colombian Conference on Communications and Computing (COLCOM)* (pp. 1–6). IEEE.

16. Chebbi, C. (2018). *Mastering Machine Learning for Penetration Testing: Develop an Extensive Skill Set to Break Self-learning Systems Using Python.* Packt Publishing Ltd.

17. Smmarwar, S. K., Gupta, G. P., & Kumar, S. (2021, April). Design of a fused triple convolutional neural network for malware detection: A visual classification approach. In *International Conference on Advances in Computing and Data Sciences* (pp. 279–289). Springer, Cham.

18. Smmarwar, S. K., Gupta, G. P., & Kumar, S. (2022). A study on data sharing using blockchain system and its challenges and applications. In *Advances in Malware and Data-Driven Network Security* (pp. 199–218). IGI Global, UK.

19. Smmarwar, S. K., Gupta, G. P., & Kumar, S. (2022). Research trends for malware and intrusion detection on network systems: A topic modelling approach. In *Advances in Malware and Data-Driven Network Security* (pp. 19–40). IGI Global, UK.

20. Kumar, P., Gupta, G. P., & Tripathi, R. (2021). Toward design of an intelligent cyber attack detection system using hybrid feature reduced approach for IoT Networks. *Arabian Journal for Science and Engineering*, *46*(4), 3749–3778.

21. Kumar, P., Gupta, G. P., & Tripathi, R. (2021). A distributed ensemble design based intrusion detection system using fog computing to protect the internet of things networks. *Journal of Ambient Intelligence and Humanized Computing*, *12*(10), 9555–9572.

9

AN EFFICIENT OPTIMIZING ENERGY CONSUMPTION USING MODIFIED BEE COLONY OPTIMIZATION IN FOG AND IoT NETWORKS

POTU NARAYANA[1], CHANDRASHEKAR JATOTH[2], PREMCHAND PARAVATANENI[1], AND G. REKHA[3]

[1]*Department of Computer Science and Engineering, Osmania University Hyderabad, Hyderabad, Telangana, India*

[2]*Department of Information Technology, National Institute of Technology Raipur, Chhattisgarh, India*

[3]*Department of Computer Science and Engineering, Koneru Lakshmaiah Education Foundation, Vijayawada, Andhra Pradesh, India*

Contents

9.1 Introduction

A large number of objects or "things" are interconnected due to the applications of the Internet of Things (IoT) in a spatially distributed network. Seamless services are, thus, provided to the end-users

DOI: 10.1201/9781003264545-9

without any intervention, which is the major aim of the IoT applications. In a one-hop manner, the real-time applications of the neighbouring devices are processed by increasing the potentiality of the IoT resources. However, the fog devices have limitations in their storage and computation capabilities to process those applications [1]. Thus, both the cloud computing (CC) and fog computing have their respective inherent limitations in addressing the issues related to performance and energy consumption (EC) as the paradigms pit one at the cost of the other. Hence, it is required to combine both the paradigms for developing an IoT infrastructure with high resource utilization for smart IoT applications [2–4]. In the cloud-fog environment, the challenging problem is to allocate the IoT applications efficiently to the appropriate devices, which include cloud data centres as well as fog nodes. For instance, the delay may be minimized by running various tasks on fog nodes, but the energy consumption of those fog nodes will increase greatly. In the cloud, the transportation of tasks can save the fog node's energy, however it increases the delay time of the tasks [5, 6]. Hence, a trade-off strategy between energy consumption and delay must be proposed to minimize the consumption of energy and delay in fog computing. In this research study, a cloud-fog cooperation scheduling algorithm called modified honey bee search algorithm based on Gaussian probability threshold value is designed to reduce the EC and increase resource utilization. The honey bee algorithm is robust when compared to other heuristic algorithms, as a stochastic global optimization procedure is used in the proposed method. The delay is sought to be reduced by introducing the Gaussian probability in the optimization algorithm, where the tasks are allocated to overloaded or underloaded servers. The simulation is conducted by using the iFogSim simulator to verify the effectiveness of proposed modified honey bee algorithm.

The remaining chapter is organized as follows: Section 9.2 discusses the studies of various existing techniques in fog computing. The detailed explanation of optimization problem is illustrated in Section 9.3. The problem is addressed by the proposed methodology is described in Section 9.4. The validation of the proposed method with existing techniques to reduce energy and delay is represented in Section 9.5. Finally, the conclusion of the research study with future work is discussed in Section 9.6.

9.2 Literature Survey

Today, researchers are focused on fog computing architecture to minimize EC by developing various techniques. In this section, a detailed discussion of traditional techniques is provided with their key benefits and drawbacks in ensuring the quality of service (QoS) parameters.

A. Toor, *et al.* [7] implemented the blockchain model for effectively adding the security layer as well as authentication layer to the sensitive data, which was used to secure the centralized ledger of those used data. In addition, the fog-IoT environment developed an energy-aware and adaptive performance scheme for the concept of green renewable energy with dynamic frequency scaling. The simulations were carried out in the iFogSim simulator and the results proved that the developed study provided better performance on the basis of QoS parameters in both power save and conservative modes. Each time the system was subjected to CPU speed alterations, the workload value was updated manually, which leads poor CPU configurations.

M. Adhikari and H. Gianey [8] developed a sustainable infrastructure to process the intensive delay and resource applications with an optimal task offloading strategy. The main aim of the developed firefly algorithm was to reduce the average consumption time and minimize the overall EC with less delay for processing the IoT applications. The experiments were conducted on two real-time datasets to test the efficiency of the developed method in terms of EC, emission of carbondioxide, computational time, and temperature emission. Some of the IoT applications might be executed only if the micro-services of the IoT devices met the resource requirements; otherwise, the tasks were offloaded to the cloud data centre, which reduced the overall accuracy.

H. Sun, *et al.* [9] developed a generic architecture initially, and the energy-time cost minimization problem was solved by implementing the energy and time efficient computation offloading and resource allocation (ETCORA) algorithm. The simulations were presented to evaluate the performance of the ETCORA algorithm in terms of computation time, EC, task completion deadline, and energy efficient cost. When compared with existing techniques, the ETCORA method highly reduced the EC and completion time of the requests. However, when evaluating the continuous tasks per second, the corresponding computing resources on the fog layers were not fully used.

B. M. Nguyen, *et al.* [10] concentrated on the problem of task scheduling to process a large-scale Bag-of-Tasks application in the fog environment. According to genetic algorithm, a Time-Cost aware Scheduling (TCaS) was proposed to solve the above-mentioned issue. A good trade-off between execution time and operation costs was achieved, because the algorithm was flexibly adapted with the different user's requirements. The performance of TCaS was compared with the existing techniques, namely modified MPSO as extra gradient PDS (EPSO), Round Robin (RR), and Bee Life Algorithm (BLA). However, the TCaS algorithm was sensitive to the initialization of population, because the optimal solution was found in the local optimum of convergence.

A. Mukherjee, *et al.* [11] implemented a femtolet-based fog network on a fifth-generation (5G) wireless network device to minimize the EC and delay time. The sensors were used to provide the data for this architecture for processing and the data were maintained inside the fog and edge devices. If the femtolet was incapable to process, then either the local or the remote cloud servers process the sensor data. The simulation was carried out on the Qualnet 7 on the basis of average delay, power consumption, average jitter, unicast received throughput, and EC. However, femtolet was an indoor base station with data storage and processing ability, therefore, the response to the user request in this environment was very slow.

X. Li, *et al.* [12] proposed a non-orthogonal multiple access (NOMA) in IoT-fog environment for supporting the vast amount of device connections with limited resources and low latency. According to the QoS requirements, the allocation of resource blocks was optimized and the power was transmitted to multiple IoT devices. The system EC and optimization problem were minimized by introducing an improved genetic algorithm (IGA). The experimental results proved that the NOMA achieved better performance by means of outage probability, throughput, EC, and delay. However, the NOMA failed to investigate the computation offloading problem and multiple optimization issues that led to minimize the overall network performance.

From the analysis of existing techniques, it can be noted that the researchers didn't concentrate on CPU configurations to reduce the delay and energy. This research study implements a Gaussian probability threshold value in the honey bee algorithm to deal with this issue. The explanation of the proposed method is briefly discussed in the next section.

9.3 Optimization Problem

In this section, the research study describes the optimization problem, which is also considered as the minimization of EC and delay. The total delay of the system can be identified by combining the values of delay time of mobile nodes, cloud nodes, and fog nodes. The total EC can be identified by combining the values of energy of mobile nodes, fog nodes, and cloud nodes. The problem is identified as an optimization problem, aiming at an optimal solution using the proposed modified honey bee search algorithm.

9.3.1 Makespan

The total time required to complete all tasks is defined as makespan. Equation 9.1 shows the formula for calculating makespan.

$$MinMakespan = \frac{\sum_{i \leq k \leq n} length \ (T_k)}{\sum_{i \leq i \leq n} CPUrate \ (N_i)} \tag{9.1}$$

9.3.2 Total Cost

If a task is performed, then a certain cost should be paid for the bandwidth, memory usage, and processing. This cost is estimated as the node N_i processes task T_k, and is expressed in Equation 9.2.

$$Cost(T_i^k) = c_p(T_i^k) + c_m(T_i^k) + c_b(T_i^k) \tag{9.2}$$

$$TotalCost = \sum_{T_k^i \in NodeTasks} Cost(T_k^i) \tag{9.3}$$

At mobile terminal device as i, the tasks are processed for the EC as E_{mt}^i, where the mathematical Equation 9.4 shows the energy for mobile nodes.

$$E_{mt}^i = T_{mt} \times P_{mt} = \frac{X_{mt}^i}{\mu - \lambda} \times P_{mt} \tag{9.4}$$

Where, power of the mobile terminal device is represented as P_{mt}, working time is illustrated as T_{mt}, tasks at service rate is described as μ, tasks at arrival rate is presented as λ, and, finally, workload assigned to the mobile device is depicted as X_{mt}. The research study considered only the computing delay for the mobile device, because it has only a small communication delay. Therefore, delay can be expressed as in Equation 9.5 as:

$$D^i_{mt} = \frac{\lambda}{\mu(\mu - \lambda)} \tag{9.5}$$

Huge numbers of computation functions are used to model the EC of a fog node, where the computation function is a strictly convex and monotonic increasing function. There are two alternatives present in the fog nodes, namely a quadratic function and a piecewise linear function. The proposed method chose the quadratic function for its simplicity without generality loss. According to the workload of fog nodes as X^j_{fog}, the EC of fog node as E^j_{fog} is mathematically defined in Equation 9.6:

$$E^j_{fog} = aX^{j2}_{fog} + bX^j_{fog} + e \tag{9.6}$$

Mathematical Equation 9.7 denoted the total EC of the system as:

$$E_{Total} = \sum_{i \in N} E^i_{mt} + \sum_{j \in M} E^j_{fog} \tag{9.7}$$

Where, $0 < k \leq K$, $0 < i \leq N$, $0 < j \leq M$. Equation 9.8 illustrates the total delay of the system, which is stated as:

$$D_{Total} = \sum_{i \in N} D^i_{mt} + \sum_{j \in M} D^j_{fog} \tag{9.8}$$

Therefore, it will minimize the delay, but the EC is increased when the tasks are on fog nodes. On the other hand, the energy of the fog nodes are minimized by offloading the tasks to the cloud server, however, the transmission delay is increased.

9.4 Proposed Methodology

The sensitive tasks with latency are immediately responded in the IoT environment scenarios. When there is no extension in the workload, the allocated layers executed the tasks. If the workloads of layers are exceeded, then tasks are not executed directly. Hence, it is important to implement the modified bee search scheduling algorithm for high utilization of the resources and minimization of the EC. The Bees Algorithm is a search procedure inspired by the way honey bees forage for food. The algorithm, with its basic version, performs a kind of neighborhood search combined with random search and can be used for both combinatorial optimization and functional optimization. In addition, the Bees Algorithm is an optimization algorithm inspired by the natural foraging behaviour of honey bees to find the optimal solution.

Algorithm: Modified Honey Bee Algorithm based on Gaussian probability threshold value.

Input: A set of tasks randomly assigned, the number of VMs and the capacity of the VMs.

Output: A capacity and loads of all VMs and a set of balanced VMs.

Initialize the Bees (Based on food source positions, xi, i = 1,..., sn/2), No. of iterations, No. of VMs;

Evaluate the capacity and loads of all VMs

Evaluate the fitness value for Bees

If $\sigma \leq Ts$:

System is balanced.

Exit

End If

Take load balancing decision based on load. If *load > max.capacity* then exit.

Group the VMs according to the Loads as Loaded VM (LVM), Balanced VM (BVM) and Overloaded VM (OVM)

Performing Load Balance:

Supplying each VM in Underloaded VM (UVM) is

$$\text{Supply of } LVM = Max\_capacity - (load/Capacity)$$

Demand of each VM in OVM is

Demand of $OVM = load/Capacity - Max\_capacity$

Do computing the bee's fitness value according to the formula;
Do computing the each best of bee's value according to the formula;
Do If fitness value is greater than each best;
Then using the fitness value to instead the each best;
End If
  Do computing the global best according to the formula;
Do If fitness value is greater than global best;
  Then using the global fitness values as fitness value;
End If
Sort VMs in OVM by descending order
Sort VMs in UVM by descending order
  If there are more than one VM in UVM

    If *cpuvalue* < *Gaussian _ probabilityvalue*

      Add VM to LVM

    Else If *cpuvalue* == *Gaussian _ probabilityvalue*

      Add VM to BVM
    Else:
      Add VM to OVM
    Update the number of tasks assigned to VM.
    Update sets OVM, LVM, BVM
    Sort VMs in OVM by descending order
    Sort VMs in LVM by descending order
  End Load Balance.

9.5 Results and Discussion

In this section, the validation of the developed method with existing optimization techniques is conducted and the results are stated on the basis of makespan, total cost, delay time, and EC. Initially, the experimental setup and parameter evaluation are discussed.

The performance of proposed bee algorithm based on Gaussian probability threshold value is compared with standard PSO, EPSO, TCaS [13], and standard honey bee algorithm. The proposed method works based on the velocity of the bees, hence it considered the PSO

Table 9.1 Comparative Analysis of Proposed Method by Means of Makespan

NO. OF TASKS	PSO	TCaS	HONEY BEE	MPSO	PROPOSED MBCO
200	1243.02	633.28	298.32	303.23	256.52
250	1510.65	816.59	301.05	305.45	261.23
300	2068.33	1052.92	306.15	308.59	272.08
350	2167.55	1241.28	311.62	315.26	275.12
400	2428.48	1486.92	316.66	317.86	283.17
450	2813.32	1754.18	337.50	337.50	292.68
500	3126.68	1994.21	342.53	342.53	309.15

heuristic algorithm for comparing the makespan results. The standard PSO and honey bee are implemented in this research work on the various numbers of tasks. The simulated values are tabulated in Table 9.1, where the graphical representation is shown in Figure 9.1.

Table 9.1 and Figure 9.1 prove that the proposed modified honey bee algorithm achieved better makespan than other heuristic techniques. When the number of tasks increases, the makespan of proposed method also increases. For instance, the proposed modified honey bee achieved 272.08s for the 300th tasks, where the same method achieved 309.15s makespan for the tasks 500. While comparing with the standard honey bee algorithm, the proposed method reduced nearly 37–40% of makespan for every task, as the Gaussian probability threshold value will allocate the balanced, overloaded, and underloaded VMs according to the conditions. When comparing with TCaS and standard PSO, the proposed modified honey bee algorithm achieved better performance for all the tasks. For instance, the PSO and TCaS achieved makespan of 2167.55s and 1241.28s,

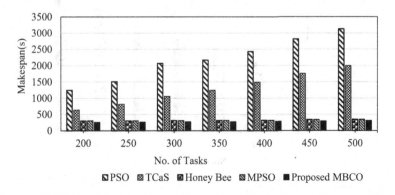

Figure 9.1 Makespan comparison of the proposed honey bee algorithm.

Table 9.2   Total Cost of Proposed Modified Honey Bee Algorithm

NO. OF TASKS	PSO	TCaS	HBO	EPSO	PROPOSED MBCO
200	4268.53	4403.63	1368.21	1380.33	1246.18
250	5112.23	5485.85	1375.53	1383.59	1255.33
300	5986.11	6740.36	1384.95	1385.49	1271.53
350	6800.09	7666.27	1385.68	1385.54	1288.16
400	7865.35	8877.14	1388.04	1389.54	1291.13
450	8993.16	10,124.56	1390.81	1391.58	1303.58
500	10,020.26	11,299.53	1396.75	1397.25	1324.63

where the proposed modified honey bee algorithm achieved only 275.12s makespan for the 350th tasks. In Table 9.2, the total cost of the proposed method with existing techniques is explained and Figure 9.2 shows the graphical illustration of total cost.

In Table 9.2, the proposed algorithm shows the superiority of scheduling length on every dataset. While comparing with the other traditional heuristic algorithms, the total cost is highly reduced with the proposed modified honey bee algorithm. Among the existing techniques, TCaS provided poor performance in terms of total cost, for instance, standard PSO achieved 5112.23G$, but the TCaS achieved 5485.85G$ for the 250th tasks. The standard honey bee and MPSO achieved better performance than TCaS and standard PSO for all the tasks length. By using the Gaussian probability threshold value, the proposed method reduced the total cost for all the tasks nearly 2–5% than standard honey bee algorithm and MPSO. For instance,

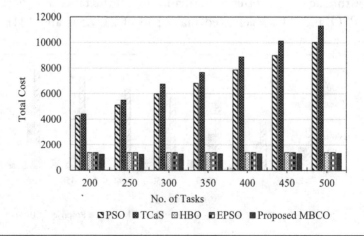

Figure 9.2   Analysis of total cost for the proposed modified honey bee algorithm.

the proposed method achieved 1288.16G\$ cost, where the standard honey bee and MPSO achieved 1385.60G\$ for the 350th tasks.

In general, response time is an important factor to ensure the QoS as it directly affects a user's experience. Therefore, end users would be willing to spend a little more to experience higher performance services. According to the analysis of makespan and total cost scenarios, the proposed modified honey bee method reached better tradeoff than other traditional algorithms to prove the superiority of time optimization. Standard PSO with a simple mechanism provided poor performance on makespan, where TCaS gave poor results on total cost.

The performance of the proposed method is validated with existing techniques, namely standard PSO, MPSO, Honey Bee and femtolet-based IoT [14] in terms of delay time and EC. In this research study, the data transmission from 100 to 400 in MB is considered for the validation process. Initially, delay time of the proposed method is stated in the Table 9.3 and the Figure 9.3 shows the graphical representation of delay time with various existing techniques.

While transmitting the data, the process may get delayed due to various reasons, for example the cloud server may be overloaded or processing other tasks. This delay time must be calculated to provide better QoS to the end users. In the proposed modified honey bee algorithm, 100 MB of the data was processed with minimum delay time compared to traditional techniques. For instance, while the standard PSO and honey bee delayed the tasks for 6 seconds, our proposed modified honey bee algorithm delayed those tasks only for 5 seconds. This is because, the CPU must be verified whether it is overloaded or underloaded for processing the tasks by using the Gaussian probability

Table 9.3 Validation of Proposed Method with Existing Techniques by Means of Delay Time

AMOUNT OF DATA TRANSMISSION (MB)	DELAY TIME (SEC)				
	PSO	MPSO	FBI	HONEY BEE	PROPOSED MBCO
100	6	5	5	6	5
150	9	8	7	8	7
200	15	13	11	11	8
250	18	16	15	16	10
300	21	15	14	18	12
350	24	18	16	21	14
400	26	18	18	23	18

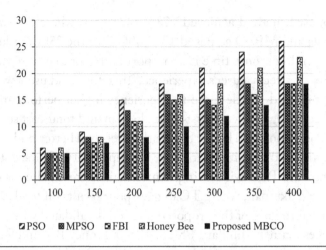

Figure 9.3 Comparative analysis of the proposed method in terms of delay time.

threshold value. When the data sizes are increased, the delay time of the proposed method is also increased, for example, the delay time of 250 MB of data is 10 seconds, whereas the delay time for 400 MB of data is 18 seconds in the proposed modified honey bee algorithm. When compared with other techniques, standard PSO provided poor performance for processing the various sizes of tasks due to its simple mechanisms. Table 9.4 shows the EC of the proposed method for the same size of the tasks; the graphical illustration is given in Figure 9.4.

From Table 9.4 and Figure 9.4, it is clearly evident that the proposed modified honey bee algorithm achieved less EC for various data sizes than other heuristic traditional algorithms. When compared with standard PSO, the proposed modified honey bee algorithm reduced nearly 15–25% of energy for all the data sizes. However, there is only

Table 9.4 Consumption of Energy for the Proposed Method with Existing Techniques

AMOUNT OF DATA TRANSMISSION (MB)	ENERGY CONSUMPTION (KWH)				
	PSO	MPSO	FBI	HBO	PROPOSED MBCO
100	0.25	0.12	0.12	0.15	0.08
150	0.38	0.16	0.19	0.22	0.11
200	0.46	0.29	0.30	0.38	0.26
250	0.67	0.33	0.42	0.46	0.37
300	1.02	0.49	0.58	0.63	0.51
350	1.35	0.61	0.72	0.81	0.68
400	1.72	0.73	0.90	1.02	0.76

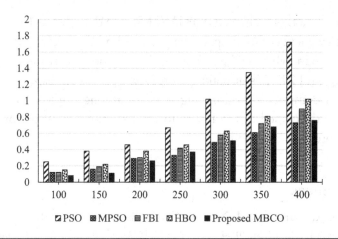

Figure 9.4   Energy consumption in the proposed method with traditional techniques.

a slight difference between existing femtolet-based IoT and the proposed honey bee algorithm for minimizing the EC. For instance, the existing technique achieved 0.30 kWH, where the proposed method achieved only 0.26 kWH for the 200 MB of data. From the experimental analysis, the results show that the proposed method reduced the delay time and EC for processing the tasks more than the other heuristic algorithms.

9.6 Conclusion

The IoT applications encouraged the cooperation between CC and fog computing, because the processing and storage resources are effectively provided to the end users. Even though fog computing supports the context/location awareness and mobility support, it increases the delay time and EC of the tasks. This chapter proposed the modified honey bee algorithm as an approach to deal with this problem to optimize the EC and reduce the delay. In the proposed method, tasks are assigned to the underloaded or overloaded servers based on the value of Gaussian probability threshold. Therefore, the energy of the nodes as well as delay time are reduced once the server is balanced. The simulated experiments are conducted to validate the performance of the proposed method in terms of EC, makespan, total cost, and delay time. While the existing techniques of the standard PSO and honey bee algorithm achieved 0.25 kWH and 0.15 kWH, our proposed method achieved 0.08 kWH for the data size of 100 MB. In the experiments of makespan, the proposed method achieved 256.52s of makespan, whereas the MPSO and honey bee algorithms achieved 303.23s and 298.32s of makespan for the 200th task, respectively. An efficient computation offloading strategy among multiple fog nodes must be developed in the future to improve the overall performance of the proposed method.

References

1. D. Rahbari, and M. Nickray, "Task offloading in mobile fog computing by classification and regression tree". *Peer-to-Peer Networking and Applications*, vol. 13, no. 1, pp. 104–122, 2020.
2. J. Luo, L. Yin, J. Hu, C. Wang, X. Liu, X. Fan, and H. Luo, "Container-based fog computing architecture and energy-balancing scheduling algorithm for energy IoT". *Future Generation Computer Systems*, vol. 97, pp. 50–60, 2019.
3. E. M. Borujeni, D. Rahbari, and M. Nickray, "Fog-based energy-efficient routing protocol for wireless sensor networks". *The Journal of Supercomputing*, vol. 74, no. 12, pp. 6831–6858, 2018.
4. L. Liu, Z. Chang, X. Guo, S. Mao, and T. Ristaniemi, "Multiobjective optimization for computation offloading in fog computing". *IEEE Internet of Things Journal*, vol. 5, no. 1, pp. 283–294, 2017.
5. J. Wu, M. Dong, K. Ota, J. Li, W. Yang, and M. Wang, "Fog-computing-enabled cognitive network function virtualization for an information-centric future Internet". *IEEE Communications Magazine*, vol. 57, no. 7, pp. 48–54, 2019.
6. G. Li, J. Yan, L. Chen, J. Wu, Q. Lin, and Y. Zhang, "Energy consumption optimization with a delay threshold in cloud-fog cooperation computing". *IEEE Access*, vol. 7, pp. 159688–159697, 2019.
7. M. Mishra, S. K. Roy, A. Mukherjee, D. De, S. K. Ghosh, and R. Buyya, "An energy-aware multi-sensor geo-fog paradigm for mission critical applications". *Journal of Ambient Intelligence and Humanized Computing*, pp. 1–19, 2019.
8. G. Zhang, F. Shen, Z. Liu, Y. Yang, K. Wang, and M. T. Zhou, "FEMTO: Fair and energy-minimized task offloading for fog-enabled IoT networks". *IEEE Internet of Things Journal*, vol. 6, no. 3, pp. 4388–4400, 2018.
9. P. G. V. Naranjo, E. Baccarelli, and M. Scarpiniti, "Design and energy-efficient resource management of virtualized networked Fog architectures for the real-time support of IoT applications". *The Journal of Supercomputing*, vol. 74, no. 6, pp. 2470–2507, 2018.
10. D. Wang, Z. Liu, X. Wang, and Y. Lan, "Mobility-aware task offloading and migration schemes in fog computing networks". *IEEE Access*, vol. 7, pp. 43356–43368, 2019.

11. Z. Guan, Y. Zhang, L. Zhu, L. Wu, and S. Yu, "EFFECT: An efficient flexible privacy-preserving data aggregation scheme with authentication in smart grid". *Science China Information Sciences*, vol. 62, no. 3, p. 32103, 2019.
12. A. Zanella, N. Bui, A. Castellani, L. Vangelista, and M. Zorzi, "Internet of Things for smart cities". *IEEE Internet of Things journal*, vol. 1, no. 1, pp. 22–32, 2014.
13. M. Adhikari, and H. Gianey, "Energy efficient offloading strategy in fog-cloud environment for IoT applications". *Internet of Things*, vol. 6, p. 100053, 2019.
14. A. Mukherjee, P. Deb, D. De, and R. Buyya, "IoT-F2N: An energy-efficient architectural model for IoT using femtolet-based fog network". *The Journal of Supercomputing*, pp. 1–22, 2019.

Index

Printed in the United States
by Baker & Taylor Publisher Services